ATLA BIBLIOGRAPHY SERIES
edited by Dr. Kenneth E. Rowe

1. *A Guide to the Study of the Holiness Movement,* by Charles Edwin Jones. 1974.
2. *Thomas Merton: A Bibliography,* by Marquita E. Breit. 1974.
3. *The Sermon on the Mount: A History of Interpretation and Bibliography,* by Warren S. Kissinger. 1975.
4. *The Parables of Jesus: A History of Interpretation and Bibliography,* by Warren S. Kissinger. 1979.
5. *Homosexuality and the Judeo-Christian Tradition: An Annotated Bibliography,* by Tom Horner. 1981.
6. *A Guide to the Study of the Pentecostal Movement,* by Charles Edwin Jones. 1983.
7. *The Genesis of Modern Process Thought: A Historical Outline with Bibliography,* by George R. Lucas, Jr. 1983.

THE GENESIS OF MODERN PROCESS THOUGHT: a historical outline with bibliography

by

George R. Lucas, Jr.

ATLA Bibliography Series, No. 7

The Scarecrow Press, Inc. and The American Theological Library Association

METUCHEN, N.J., & LONDON 1983

Library of Congress Cataloging in Publication Data

Lucas, George R.
   The genesis of modern process thought.

   (ATLA bibliography series ; no. 7)
   Bibliography: p.
   Includes index.
   1. Process philosophy--History--Bibliography.
2. Philosophy, Modern--Bibligoraphy. I. Title.
II. Series.
Z7128.P88L8 1983   016.146   82-16798
[BD372]
ISBN 0-8108-1589-3

For two process philosophers,

LEWIS S. FORD

and

GEORGE L. KLINE,

with my enduring gratitude.

CONTENTS

EDITOR'S FOREWORD

The American Theological Library Association Bibliography Series is designed to stimulate and encourage the preparation of reliable bibliographies and guides to the literature of religious studies in all of its scope and variety. Compilers are free to define their field, make their own selections and work out internal organization as the unique demands of the subject indicate. We are pleased to publish this guide to the literature of process thought as number seven in our series. The work was originally commissioned by Garrett-Evangelical Theological Seminary in Evanston, Illinois for the Garrett-Evangelical Bibliographical Lecture series.

Professor Lucas has earned degrees with honors from the College of William and Mary, Garrett Theological Seminary, and Northwestern University, where he took the doctorate in Philosophy. He has taught at Randolph-Macon College and currently serves as Assistant Professor of Philosophy in the University of Santa Clara, Santa Clara, California. Professor Lucas is author of two previous works: Two Views of Freedom in Process Thought: A Study of Hegel and Whitehead (1979) and Lifeboat Ethics: The Moral Dilemmas of World Hunger (1976). In addition to being the author of several important articles and essays, Professor Lucas also serves as review editor for the journal Process Studies.

Kenneth E. Rowe
Drew University Library
Madison, New Jersey

PREFACE AND ACKNOWLEDGMENTS

The perspective from which this work is written is primarily that of a historian of philosophy in the analytic tradition, rather than that of an ardent disciple of process thought. I treat as normative in this regard the definition and task of historical analysis outlined by R. F. Atkinson: to gain a knowledge of historical data not so much by arranging them in a chronological narrative, but by bringing them under general classifications in a manner analogous to "the more descriptive reaches of natural science."* In keeping with such objectives, then, this work is neither an apologia for, nor is it a polemic against, process philosophy as such.

I mention this at the outset because I am particularly eager that certain intellectual or scholastic stereotypes not be allowed to intrude a priori on the evaluation of the data here analyzed. Unfortunately, it is the case that such stereotypes regarding philosophical orthodoxy all too frequently do intrude. It is a symbol of such times, perhaps, that this research has been sponsored primarily by organizations whose theological orientation is not always treated kindly in portions of this study--and especially in its conclusions. Nonetheless, the support of such organizations has been generous, and their tolerance of adverse views is akin to that associated once upon a time with the discipline of philosophy.

It is the case in philosophy that a certain iconoclasm regarding both "orthodox" subject matter and methodology continues to dominate the intellectual horizon in a manner which strikes me (as it struck the later Wittgenstein) as arbitrary, capricious, and unreflective. As a topic of investigation, process philosophy now seldom falls within the established canons of philosophical orthodoxy. Process philosophy now

---

*R. F. Atkinson, Knowledge and Explanation in History: An Introduction to the Philosophy of History (Ithaca, N.Y.: Cornell University Press, 1978), p. 21f.

is primarily of interest to philosophers of religion and philosophical theologians in any of several religious traditions. Especially (but not exclusively) in its Teilhardian formulation, process philosophy has proven a useful vehicle as well in East-West, "Christian-Marxist" dialogues over the last two decades. And finally, process philosophy continues to exercise a lively interest among many whose pursuits include cosmology, formal philosophy of science, or the more speculative pursuit of a philosophy of nature.

Whatever else it entails, this catalogue of its interested audience suggests that process philosophy--far from being dead, or simply representing a historical anachronism--continues, rather, as a growing and influential philosophical tradition. As process philosophy has its modern historical origins in philosophical movements over two hundred years old, I argue that the endurance of the tradition warrants a careful study of the history it has. Only by examining their history can process philosophers be fully appraised of the difficult critical questions facing their enterprise. Likewise, only by a more careful attention to the history of process philosophy can the adherents of other traditions and movements--including those critical of process thought--appraise for themselves the challenging questions process philosophy continues to pose for them.

The present work is intended to initiate that considerable historical task. I do so by endeavoring to supplement present knowledge of principal figures and primary-text arguments with a comprehensive catalogue of lesser-known secondary scholarship, focusing on critical and historical analysis and comparison of varieties of process philosophers and process "schools."

Principal research for this project was carried out at the Widener Library at Harvard University, and at the libraries of Northwestern University, the University of Massachusetts-Amherst, the University of Virginia, and Boston University. I wish to express my gratitude to the many staff members of these institutions who courteously and efficiently assisted with this work.

This project began during my tenure as a graduate student at Northwestern University, under the auspices of a generous bibliographical fellowship from Garrett Theological Seminary (now Garrett-Evangelical Seminary). The introductory chapter is a revision of a bibliographical lecture given at Garrett in April of 1978. I am particularly grateful to

John Batsel and Alva Caldwell, under whose direction the initial research was undertaken.

My tenure as a bibliographical fellow of the American Theological Library Association permitted major additions to and revisions of this project at Harvard and the University of Massachusetts-Amherst, without which the project could not have been satisfactorily completed. The manuscript itself was revised and prepared for publication during my tenure in 1982 as a fellow of the American Council of Learned Societies.

Throughout the several years since its inception, I have received useful advice from Tyler Thompson, Walter G. Muelder, Lewis S. Ford, and most recently, Julian N. Hartt. While I am deeply indebted to each, none should be held responsible for the results. I am especially grateful to Prof. Thompson for a meticulous reading and correction of an initial draft of this work. One of my students in philosophy, Mr. Robert Lewis, prepared the author index and researched certain aspects of the influence of evolution on American pragmatism as a project for my seminar on the history of evolutionary cosmologies. Our philosophy department assistant, Mrs. Brigid Mullins, provided invaluable assistance in preparing the final version of the manuscript for publication.

My wife, Carolyn, helped to proofread and type portions of the manuscript, and often presented a refreshingly unbiased (and often unimpressed) perspective on this research over the last five years. All of us, in our research, need to be reminded on occasion not to take our private interests too seriously.

George R. Lucas, Jr.
Santa Clara, Calif.
October 1982

THE GENESIS OF MODERN
PROCESS THOUGHT

INTRODUCTION

A distinguished teacher and historian of philosophy in 1967
observed:

> Historians often group such disparate thinkers as
> Descartes and Spinoza and Leibniz together as lead-
> ers in the School of Rationalism, and Locke and
> Berkeley and Hume together as leaders in the School
> of Empiricism. One would not be any more arbi-
> trary if one grouped Bergson and James and White-
> head and Dewey together as leaders in a school of
> philosophy in whose thought the fact of change is
> made a central feature of any just interpretation of
> the world. These distinguished writers, of course,
> do not agree with one another on many points. But
> in and through their many differences, there is, I
> believe, a kinship which future historians of philos-
> ophy will indicate in their chapter headings and their
> arrangements of the details of their narratives. [1]

This view was perhaps less prophetic than merely reflective
of the congenial and occasionally uncritical eclecticism with
which contemporary adherents of process philosophy appropriate their own historical antecedents. Thus, while Lamprecht's prediction already has come to pass in the designation of numerous chapter headings and the organization of
many narratives, one wonders on occasion whether his implied concern regarding a certain arbitrariness and lack of
discrimination--resulting in a high degree of incoherence in
the historical self-understanding of process philosophy--has
not likewise been realized.

What, after all, is "process philosophy?" One might
be tempted to pursue this question according to the dictates
of convention and ordinary language, by replying that "process
philosophy" is what its adherents say it is. The obvious dilemma, however, is that while disciples of this tradition con-

cur in designating broad (and occasionally ambiguous) criteria
of identification--such as an "emphasis on time" and "change"
--there is wide diversity and often substantial divergence both
in what they say about the movement, and in whom they include within it.

The term "process philosophy" has come to designate
the system of philosophy developed by Alfred North Whitehead,
and further elaborated by Whitehead's principal disciple,
Charles Hartshorne. This customary identification, however,
is highly problematic. Whitehead, for example, continually
misconstrues the historical antecedents of his own thought.
He expresses frequent indebtedness to John Locke,[2] one of
the principal authors in the seventeenth century of a "substance metaphysics," whose work--apart from a stated
realist perspective--bears little resemblance to Whitehead's
own. Whitehead permits himself to criticize Hegel on several
occasions, following the trend of his time in the English-
speaking world in evident unawareness of the numerous strong
similarities between his own work and Hegel's.[3] Whitehead
describes philosophy as "a series of footnotes to Plato,"[4]
when in fact his own thought also represents a series of footnotes to Aristotle, including his compromise formulation of
universals as deficiently actual "eternal objects," having real
instantiation only in finite, concrete occasions of experience.
Since Whitehead apparently never read Aristotle's Metaphysics,
he was evidently unaware of these similarities, as R. G. Collingwood notes, until a friend pointed them out to him.[5]

Charles Hartshorne's encounter with Whitehead's thought
represented an adaptation by Hartshorne of Whitehead's more-
developed philosophical system, which Hartshorne found entirely compatible with his own, earlier interests. Those interests had been shaped independently on the basis of Hartshorne's prior study of the logic and evolutionary cosmology
of C. S. Peirce.[6] Peirce--together with William James,
John Fiske and others--was a principal founding member of
the "Metaphysical Club" in Cambridge, Massachusetts in the
1870's, the major nucleus from which American pragmatism
emerged. Whitehead himself acknowledges an indebtedness to
William James, quoting the latter with approval in several of
his writings.[7] In turn Whitehead's contemporary, John Dewey,
accepted with criticism certain elements of Whitehead's
thought. Several studies have been made comparing these
two philosophers.[8] What precisely are the similarities which
permit this frequent (though perhaps too casual) grouping of
Whitehead and some pragmatists as "process philosophers"?

Do these similarities indicate an exact correspondence of metaphysical principles, or (as I indicate briefly elsewhere[9]) is pragmatism deficient in certain of the metaphysical concepts integral to process philosophy? Such questions cannot be adjudicated properly apart from a full historical and conceptual understanding of the process tradition in its entirety.

Whitehead likewise cites with approval the work of Henri Bergson, Samuel Alexander, and especially F. H. Bradley.[10] The first of this trio is a vitalist or "emergent evolution" cosmologist. The last named is one of the most famous and influential of the English Hegelians. Alexander renounced his earlier participation in the Hegelian movement in order to deal more intimately with themes such as nature, time and contingency--all of which he felt to be neglected in the English interpretation of Hegel.[11] In what sense, if at all, can the cosmologies of idealism or emergent evolutionism be identified as "process" cosmologies?

Lastly, some would cite by way of definition the "patron saint" of the process tradition, Heraclitus.[12] This suggestion likewise is problematic, largely due to a lingering uncertainty regarding Heraclitus' precise views.[13] While a belief in the fundamental character of change and process does seem to characterize his philosophy, Heraclitus is also credited with the suggestion that there is an unchanging principle of all change, a structure or order exhibited in all process. That is, Heraclitus is credited with the earliest formulation of the classic Greek doctrine of the Logos--the rational, intelligible principle of order exhibited in all the forms of becoming which together comprise reality. If Heraclitus indeed can be portrayed, in some legendary sense at least, as the "founder" of process philosophy, does this not suggest that process philosophy also is characterized by a stress on the principle of order--the organizing structure or pattern exhibited in all change and in some sense governing or guiding such creative process toward an ultimate issue in novel determinateness?

Such queries concerning anomalies in definition, influence, and historical development often are answered by adherents of the process tradition with the suggestion that process philosophy is distinguished from other movements by its stress on the primacy of change, becoming, and the event-character of reality, in opposition to what Whitehead termed the static or "vacuous" actualities of traditional substance metaphysics. Yet it is clear that this understanding alone is seriously

deficient. [14]   While Bertrand Russell differed from his teacher
and colleague on many other issues, he, too, despite many
alternations in his views, consistently eschewed a "substance"
interpretation of materialism and realism in favor of what
might best be described as an "event metaphysics."[15]   Likewise, existentialism is not understood as a "process" philoso-
phy--and yet Heidegger and Sartre attain perhaps their greatest clarity and precision in their respective discussions of
the importance of an adequate metaphysical concept of time:
the conditioning of the present by the "facticity" of the past,
without attendant limitations on freedom (Heidegger); and the
influence of the future on the present as the realm of open,
alternative possibilities necessitating decision as a response
(Sartre).   Such themes are integral to process philosophy as
well.   If these figures are not process philosophers, why are
they not?

         If this were not sufficiently confusing, there has de-
veloped during the past twenty-five years a considerable interest in the apparent similarities of Whitehead's views with
those of the "Blessed One" of Buddhism--similarities suggested by such otherwise divergent thinkers as H. H. Price and
Charles Hartshorne. [16]   It is surely the case that there are
certain parallel emphases in Buddhist and Whiteheadian metaphysics, although this is likely to portend greater ecumenical
than philosophical significance.   But (to ring a change on
Lamprecht) one would be no less arbitrary in classifying the
Buddha as a quasi-mythological symbol for contemporary philosophical analysis, in that cosmology and speculative metaphysics are eschewed as so much irrelevant nonsense, as distinguished from the "empirical observables" stressed in the
"Four Noble Truths. "[17]

         Thus, the testimony of process philosophers themselves
leaves us more confused than ever concerning both the definition and history of the tradition.   While it is clear that Whitehead, Hartshorne, Bergson, Teilhard de Chardin, William
James and John Dewey must be considered, [18] others might
argue for the expansion of the list to include Hegel.   But if
Hegel, why not Marx?   Or what of the more conservative and
rationalistic traditions of idealism represented by Royce or
Bradley?   Indeed, what of Spinoza, Leibniz, Augustine, Plato,
Aristotle--indeed, what of Heraclitus or the Buddha?   The
fear of indiscriminate incoherence seems to be borne out in
such classifications.

         This sort of descriptive and historical chaos is ripe

for philosophical and historical analysis, whose primary function is to clarify and elucidate. The legitimate question that the process tradition poses is this: On what grounds are persons or movements included or excluded as "process" philosophies? Are such classifications merely a function of common language, custom, convention, habit, personal preference or acquaintance, ad hominem polemics; or, as one might hope, do such classifications both presuppose, and in some imperfect sense illustrate, a consistent set of criteria? If the last is the case, how may these criteria best be identified and exhibited?

To date, there have been two sorts of answers given to this problem, which we might label the "a priori" and the "conventional" approaches. The a priori approach is illustrated by Charles Hartshorne and Andrew Reck, both of whom delineate a set of categories specifying process thought, and subsequently attempt to group individual philosophers and philosophical theologians according to their manifestation of such categories in their work.[19] The irony of this approach taken in isolation is that it ignores altogether the historical genesis and development of the very categories of process themselves. In point of fact, the lists that are produced are themselves a result of a process of historical development. One could hardly expect philosophers of different epochs to entertain precisely the concerns that would lead to the exemplification of some a priori list.

This is to suggest that process philosophy itself has a developmental history that a priori logical classification cannot exhibit. It is not surprising, then, to discover that such specific lists, utilized in isolation from the relevant historical data, tend to produce identifications and classifications that appear, in some cases, arbitrary and suspect.

The "conventional" approach, by contrast, classifies according to historical identification and the personal confessions of individual thinkers.[20] The difficulties with this approach taken in isolation already have been cited: "convention" itself frequently is arbitrary, incomplete, and often erroneous since one lacks in this approach a clear statement of the criteria by which persons are excluded or included in the tradition. Since it obviously will not suffice to utilize such criteria a priori, we can remedy the problems in accurate classification only by fusing these two traditional approaches under the auspices of a historical recovery of origins, influence, and development.

The present work intends to initiate this much-needed

historical research. In particular, I find that the oft-
encountered confusion in definition stems in large part from
treating "process philosophy" as a distinct and unified philosophical tradition. An examination of the history of the movement, however, suggests the following: 1) rather than a distinct category, "process" in a broad sense--temporalism and
becoming, or the "event character" of reality--is characteristic of the enterprise of contemporary speculative philosophy
from Hegel onwards (as distinguished from contemporary con-
tinuations of classical and medieval traditions, such as Thom-
ism, or from the implicit Democritean and Parmenidean assumptions of much early Anglo-American analysis); and 2) insofar as process philosophy can be treated as a tradition (distinct from dialectical materialism, positivism, realism, logical empiricism, subjective idealism, monistic idealism, linguistic analysis, phenomenology, existentialism, and so forth),
it is not monolithic. Instead, the process tradition exhibits
internal divisions or "schools," focusing on different elements
of the a priori criteria specified by Hartshorne and Reck--not
to mention at least two more movements with a distinctive
internal self identity, which overlap the concerns of the major
"schools" that I delineate, and thus defy any tidy classification.

It is not surprising, then, that systematic ambiguity
should be encountered in the discussion of process philosophy,
nor is it surprising that one must resort to historical analysis
to sort out these concerns. To date, however, only Prof.
Hartshorne's brief essay "The Development of Process Philosophy" has been devoted exclusively to this task. That essay was not intended as a thorough analysis and review of
recent developments; indeed, the essay surveys personalities
and epochs from Ikhnaton of Egypt (c. 1370 B.C.E.) to the
present.21 It would appear, therefore, that a sustained historical treatment of process philosophy is long overdue.

In this volume I attempt to develop a set of inclusive criteria defining process philosophy, as these criteria
emerge in its historical genesis and development. This historical development is adumbrated through critical discussion of a
large body of secondary literature--journal articles, doctoral
dissertations, and some personal correspondence, as well as
books--encompassing almost two centuries of the history of
speculative thought in Europe and America. By and large
these selections individually either investigate or advocate a
variety of possible similarities between two or more process
philosophers or theologians, or among differing schools within

the process tradition itself. Few of the authors placed their own work in the context I have here developed since, for most of them, that context either did not exist or was only vaguely intuited or anticipated by the specific personalities, problems, or issues upon which they chose to focus.

In broad aggregate, the historical and bibliographical data assembled here suggest that contemporary process philosophy is characterized in large part by a recovery of salient elements of classical metaphysics: viz., an emphasis on change and becoming, together with a recognition that change requires a background of permanence in order to render it intelligible. That "permanence," however, is not the hypostasis of Parmenides, Plato, and Aristotle. Rather, what is permanent, as Heraclitus apparently discerned, is the rational principle of change--the structure, pattern, or organization, together with the purposiveness or "directedness" of process itself.

In addition, contemporary process thought reflects the abandonment in contemporary scientific theory of mechanistic and deterministic interpretations of causality as adequate explanations of natural phenomena. Instead, as was the case in Plato's Timaeus, the cosmos is more accurately portrayed as an "organism"--or rather, as a complex society or system of organisms. That is to say, process philosophers utilize the data and theories of contemporary science to argue for the replacement of the mechanistic by a revised teleological paradigm. [22]

By suggesting that process thought entails a reintroduction of teleological explanation, however, I do not intend the trivial "external" forms of teleology popularized, for example, in certain variations of eighteenth-century Deism. According to this view (ridiculed by Bacon, Voltaire, and Hegel), the principle of organization of the "world-machine" was entirely external to the world-system itself, while the "final cause" of such organization was conceived primarily in terms of its promotion of either divine or human well-being.

The modified "internal" teleology integral to contemporary process philosophy, by contrast, is drawn from the heuristic applications of teleology or "teleonomy" in contemporary biological sciences and statistical physics (especially quantum statistics). As a result, this contemporary form of teleological explanation tends towards pluralism, stressing finite, interacting centers of purposive activity, and bears a

strong resemblance to Aristotle's doctrine of "entelechy" or
"self-realizing end. " According to Aristotle's biology and
metaphysics, every organism possessed an ideal, internal
pattern or purpose, organizing its behavior, which it sought
more fully and adequately to realize in every phase of its
becoming. It was that pattern or principle of organization,
rather than any underlying "stuff" or "substance, " which
uniquely identified each organic form. In turn, each of those
individual vector purposes stood in some relation of valuation
to an ideal pattern or form of perfection for the universe as
a whole: "self-thinking thought, " which Aristotle identified
as God. It is in these various senses that process philosophy
represents simultaneously a completely contemporary interpretation of nature, as well as a recurrence of a modernized
variation of ancient Greek cosmology. [23]

In general, any philosophy qualifies as a "process"
philosophy if it (1) stresses that events or occasions of experience form the primary ontology, rather than static being,
unchanging substance, or irreducible atomic "simples"; (2)
employs a modified form of teleological explanation that is
both pluralistic and organic (or holistic), emphasizing both
discrete entities, and real, constitutive internal relations
among those entities comprising a larger organic system or
systems; and (3) discerns some sort of immanent pattern or
principle of organization which is generally exhibited in all
processes of change--a Concept or Notion, Principle of Concretion, or (in the terminology of classical metaphysics) a
logos. [24] Additional features resulting from these primary
foci include an emphasis on the importance of a doctrine of
time; the development of a concept of nature in which the
"bifurcation" of nature into mind and matter, subject and
object, is overcome; and an emphasis on freedom and creativity
as constitutive of all actual entities described by the metaphysical system.

In historical perspective, differing schools of process
philosophy may be distinguished by their different treatment
and relative emphasis of these concerns. Pragmatism, for
example, differs from other forms of process philosophy primarily by the ambiguity and caution shown regarding the acceptance of focus point (3) above. On Whitehead's analysis,
any refusal to accept (3) constitutes conceptual incoherence--
an "arbitrary disjunction of first principles"--in the metaphysics of pragmatism. [25] For James and Dewey, however, (3)
involves the unconditional surrender of human freedom and
creativity to some sort of Hegelian "absolute. " A willingness

to entertain analysis of, and eventually adopt some position regarding the issues cited in the preceding paragraph, however, aides in distinguishing process philosophy from other traditions of philosophical method and discourse. In the following sections, I briefly delineate and document four major schools of process philosophy, and at least two connecting "bridge" movements.

Part I: Process rationalism (or, the Whiteheadian school) originates primarily in response to the novel developments in relativity and quantum physics during the early part of the present century. Whitehead in particular exhibits the strong influence of early twentieth-century realism and empiricism. It is nonetheless clear that in this phase, his philosophy, Hartshorne's, and the philosophy of this school in general, is self-consciously rationalistic in the Spinozist (mathematical-deductive) sense, stressing the internal necessary coherence and generality of metaphysical first principles and subsequent deductions. This has prompted Prof. Hartshorne to label this school "neo-classical metaphysics." Process rationalists are further characterized for the most part by an uncompromising stress upon metaphysical pluralism and temporalism.

Part II: The older tradition of evolutionary cosmology ventures a variety of speculative metaphysical systems heavily influenced by the phenomenon of biological evolution. As a reflection of the historical origins of this school in pre-Darwinian romantic Naturphilosophie, the proponents of evolutionary cosmologies are often more descriptive, metaphorical and intuitive in their methodology, and hence less rigorously systematic than the more recent process rationalists. Concepts such as the "vital impulse" (élan vital), nisus, orthogenesis and "emergents" are used to designate questionable doctrines of causality in the evolutionary process, to call attention to the feature of creative novelty in evolutionary advance, and also in a metaphorical sense to designate organic inter-connectedness and holism in nature. The "emergent evolutionists" collectively reflect an underlying Lamarckian interpretation of evolution which, with the exception of Herbert Spencer, was developed in conscious opposition to the radical mechanism of neo-Darwinianism. The point at issue, however, was not the largely-discredited theory of inheritance of acquired traits, but instead the preservation of a larger consideration prompting that theory: viz., Lamarck's apparently broad use of the term "organism" to designate finite centers of modified purposive activity in the natural world--

organic systems adapting (and hence evolving) in response to
constantly fluxuating environmental stimuli.

Part III: A more controversial school of process philosophy arises as a result of a modern form of organic teleology (similar to Whitehead's "organic mechanism" in Science
and the Modern World) developed in Hegel's philosophy of nature in order to explain human mind and self-consciousness
as a supervenient phase of complexity in the larger arena of
nature and history. Hegel's organic teleology shows the influence of Goethe's early physical and biological theories,
which in turn reflect Lamarck's influence generally on Con-
tinental romantic Naturphilosophie. Hegel's use of organic
categories reveals a far greater role for freedom, time, and
radical contingency in nature and history than commonly understood either by the Hegelian left or right. Dialectic,
especially in Hegel's Science of Logic and Encyclopedia, reveals much in common with Whitehead's microscopic description of concrescence, and may indeed be portrayed as a first
attempt (historically) to formulate a "logic of process" in conscious opposition to the static and sterile implications of
Aristotelian formal logic.

Part IV: Certain philosophers associated with pragmatism and both British and American realism shared a desire to defend both pluralism and a real (even if finite) freedom. In a few cases, these concerns were supplemented with
a desire to reconcile a concept of God with the "brute facts"
of the natural world. In certain of these respects, James,
Fiske, and C. I. Lewis (among others) seem to have shared
concerns in common with certain of the evolutionary cosmologists, such as Morgan and Thomas Huxley. The concept of
"natural law" as "habit," especially in Peirce's philosophy,
produced a dynamic cosmology under the influence of evolutionist theories.

From the standpoint of temporalism, pluralism, and
creativity, the interpretations of Hegel and Whitehead sym-
bolize the doctrinal extremes of the process tradition as a
whole. Evolutionary cosmology--ranging from Lamarck, the
early Goethe, Robert Chambers, Bergson, C. Lloyd Morgan,
Jan Smuts, Teilhard de Chardin, and Julian Huxley, to Theodosius Dobzhansky, C. H. Waddington, W. A. Thorpe, Charles
Birch, and Rene Dubos--represents historically the earliest
and most enduring expression of process thought. Intermed-
iate or "transitional" formulations (in historical perspective)
are represented by pragmatists and realists, such as Peirce,
James, Fiske, Mead, Perry, Lewis, and Dewey.

Part V: In this final section, I attempt to discuss
those schools which systematically defy classification under
any single heading (other than their own), yet evidence clear
relevance for, and affinity with the process tradition as a
whole. These "bridge movements" include variations of personal idealism (e.g., E. S. Brightman, whose decidedly Hegelian orientation led to views very similar to Whitehead's own,
W. E. Hocking, and Josiah Royce, whose affinities with both
pragmatism and Whitehead's thought have only recently been
documented), and the "English" (both British and American)
Hegelians--particularly those for whom nature and time were
of real importance, such as Samuel Alexander, Bernard Bosanquet, R. G. Collingwood and Errol E. Harris.

Organization of Bibliographical Entries

The relevant bibliographical entries for each section
follow the notes for that section in every case. Citations
that have been annotated in a previous chapter are preceded
by an asterisk (*) and followed by the chapter reference and
entry number in square brackets, indicating where the anno-
tation may be found. A complete index to bibliographical entries by author is included at the end of the book.

For the most part, I do not attempt further annotations
of works whose contents or significance are discussed in some
detail in the text or notes. The arguments presented in each
chapter, however, obviously depend for support and documentation on both specific notes and the annotated selections following. As to form, in the absence of any clearly prescribed
standard, I endeavor to follow the MLA style recommendations
for notes and bibliographical entries with one exception: I
utilize two arabic numerals, separated by a slash(/), to indicate volume and issue number, respectively, for journals.

In order to illustrate and enhance the discussion of the
affinities and differences between the different schools of process philosophy, the arrangement of bibliographical data are dis-
played on a 4 x 4 matrix on the next page. Roman numerals designate the major schools. Bibliographical entries that compare
a given school with its predecessors in the discussion are indicated serially with arabic numerals. Thus, III:2 indicates bibliographical references comparing Hegelian idealism (III) with
evolutionary cosmologies (II), while IV:1 indicates those references that compare pragmatism and/or realism (IV) with process rationalism (I). For the reasons cited above, it has been

	Process Rationalism	Evolutionary Cosmology	Hegelian Idealism	Pragmatism & Realism
P. R.	I			
Ev. C.	II:1	II		
Heg. Id.	III:1	III:2	III	
Prag. /R.	IV:1	IV:2	IV:3	IV

necessary to relegate the bibliographical data for the "bridge movements" to a separate section (V).

Process rationalism (the Whiteheadian school) is treated first as the most familiar school, in order to facilitate comparisons with the earlier and less familiar schools of process thought. Thereafter, the order of treatment roughly parallels the chronological order of historical development.

NOTES

(1) Sterling P. Lamprecht, The Metaphysics of Naturalism (New York: Appleton-Century-Crofts, 1967), 112f.

(2) Alfred North Whitehead, Process and Reality (New York: Macmillan, 1929), hereafter designated as PR. Cf. PR, p. v.:
      "The writer who most fully anticipated the main positions of the philosophy of organism is John Locke in his Essay, especially in its later books." See also the entries under "Locke" in David Griffin's index to the Corrected Edition of PR, eds. D. R. Griffin and D. W. Sherburne (New York: The Free Press, 1978), 370f.

(3) For example, see A. N. Whitehead, Essays in Science and Philosophy (New York: Philosophical Library, 1948), p. 10:
      "I have never been able to read Hegel: I initiated my attempt by studying some remarks of his on mathematics which struck me as complete nonsense. It was foolish of me, but I am not writing to explain my good sense."

The same volume, p. 88, cites Whitehead's remarks on "Process and Reality" at Harvard in 1931,
at a symposium in honor of his seventieth birthday:
"... I have never read a page of Hegel. That is
not true. I remember when I was staying with Haldane at Cloan I read one page of Hegel. But it is
true that I was influenced by Hegel. I was an inti-
mate friend of McTaggart almost from the very first
day he came to the University [Trinity College, Cambridge, 1897], and saw him for a few minutes almost
daily, and I had many a chat with Lord Haldane about
his Hegelian point of view, and I have read books
about Hegel. But lack of first-hand acquaintance is
a very good reason for not endeavoring in print ...
to display any knowledge of Hegel. But as I said in
my book I admit a very close affiliation with Bradley."

Not all of Whitehead's references to Hegel are so
unflattering or uninformed; witness his extended anal-
ogy of his thrust in PR with Hegel's thought at the
conclusion of Part Two, ch. VIII (PR 254). I discuss Whitehead's understanding of and affinities with
Hegel in my book, Two Views of Freedom in Process
Thought (Chico, Cal.: Scholars Press, 1979).

(4) PR 63.

(5) R. G. Collingwood, The Idea of Nature (Oxford: The
Clarendon Press, 1945), 170.

(6) Cf. Prof. Ford's introduction to Two Process Philosophers: Hartshorne's Encounter with Whitehead (Tallahassee, Fla.: American Academy of Religion, 1973).

(7) Cf. PR vii, 105f. See also A. N. Whitehead, Science
and the Modern World (New York: Macmillan, 1925),
205ff. Hereafter designated SMW.

(8) Cf. the bibliography in Sec. IV:1 below.

(9) Process Studies 8/3 (Fall, 1978), 209f.

(10) For Whitehead's comments on Samuel Alexander, see
SMW xi; PR 65. For Henri Bergson, see SMW 74,
212ff.; PR vii, 49. For Bradley, see PR vii, viii,
304f. Note also A. N. Whitehead, Adventures of
Ideas (New York: Macmillan, 1933), 166, 253. Hereafter designated AI.

(11)   Samuel Alexander, "Hegel's Conception of Nature,"
       Mind o. s. 9/41 (1886), 499-502; and Space, Time
       and Deity, 2 Vols. (London: Macmillan, 1920).

(12)   E. g. , Milic Capek, writing on "Change" in the Encyclo-
       pedia of Philosophy, ed. Paul Edwards (New York:
       Macmillan & Free Press, 1967), vol. I, pp. 75-79,
       depicts contemporary process philosophy as the latest
       form of the Heraclitian position. Some similarities
       and differences of Heraclitus and contemporary proc-
       ess thought are explored in an article by James
       Wayne Dye, "Heraclitus and the Future of Process
       Philosophy," Tulane Studies in Philosophy 23 (1974),
       13-31.

(13)   The most authoritative treatment of Heraclitus to date
       is that of Prof. Philip Wheelwright, Heraclitus
       (Princeton, N. J. : Princeton University Press, 1959).
       Cf. especially his translation of Fragments 20, 23.
       This blend of the mythological and actual for the sake
       of symbolic representation is not itself objectionable.
       One sometimes wonders, however, whether Heraclitus
       does not profit from the underrepresentation of his
       surviving work--whether, indeed, were his full phi-
       losophy available to us, we might be found to have
       mistaken obscurity for profundity.

(14)   Andrew J. Reck criticizes this view of process on the
       grounds that "the experience of total process cannot
       even deliver the insight that it is in process." See
       "Substance, Process and Nature," Journal of Philos-
       ophy 55 (1958), 766. James K. Feibleman notes
       further that Whitehead's focus was rather on the mu-
       tual dependence of permanence and change. See
       "Why Whitehead Is Not a 'Process' Philosopher,"
       Tulane Studies in Philosophy 23 (1974), 48-59.

(15)   For a clear summary of this aspect of Russell's "final
       views," cf. My Philosophical Development, ed. A.
       Wood (New York: Simon & Schuster, 1959), 16-27.
       That this "final" view is, however, implicit in Rus-
       sell's earlier views can be demonstrated. Cf. "The
       Philosophy of Logical Atomism" (1918) in Logic and
       Knowledge, ed. C. Marsh (London: G. Allen & Un-
       win, 1956), 274-79; The Analysis of Mind (London:
       G. Allen & Unwin, 1921), 141ff. ; and Mysticism and
       Logic (New York: Doubleday, 1957), 124ff.

(16) Whitehead discusses his affinities with Buddhism briefly
      in PR, especially 519f., and in AI, pt. I:3. From
      the perspective of analytic philosophy, see H. H.
      Price's dramatic address for the American Philosoph-
      ical Association's Pacific Division meeting in 1962:
      "Appearing and Appearances," American Philosophical
      Quarterly 1/1 (January 1964), 3f. Cf. Hartshorne's
      discussion in Philosophers Speak of God, ed. Hart-
      shorne and Reese (Chicago: University of Chicago
      Press, 1953), 411-415. Cf. also John B. Cobb, Jr.
      and David Ray Griffin, Process Theology: An Intro-
      ductory Exposition (Philadelphia: Westminster Press,
      1976), 136-142.

(17) Cf. the Buddha's famous denunciation of speculative
      metaphysics as comprising "Questions which Tend
      not to Edification": Sutta 63, Majjhima-Nikaya.

(18) John Cobb and Lewis Ford, in their introduction to the
      inaugural issue of the journal Process Studies, cited
      the elusiveness of the term "process," and noted a
      list of philosophers from Buddha and Faustus Socinus
      to Whitehead: "Prospectus for Process Studies,"
      Process Studies 1/1 (Spring 1971), 7. Charles
      Hartshorne lists Bergson, James, Fechner, Alexan-
      der, Whitehead, Varisco, Scheler, Ward, Boutroux,
      W. P. Montague, Parker, Garnett, Hocking, Boodin,
      and others: Reality as a Social Process (Glencoe,
      Ill.; Boston: Free Press/Beacon Press, 1953), 131.
      Andrew J. Reck begins with Heraclitus, and in the
      modern period includes Spencer, Bergson, Alexander,
      George Herbert Mead, Whitehead, and Teilhard:
      Speculative Philosophy (Albuquerque: University of
      New Mexico Press, 1972), 185-232. Browning, Sib-
      ley, and Gunter, in their anthologies, include Berg-
      son, C. S. Peirce, William James, Alexander, C.
      Lloyd Morgan, John Dewey, G. H. Mead and White-
      head: Philosophers of Process, ed. Douglas Brown-
      ing (New York: Random House, 1965); Process Phi-
      losophy: Basic Writings, eds. J. R. Sibley & P.A.Y.
      Gunter (Washington, D.C.: University Press of Amer-
      ica, 1978).

(19) Andrew J. Reck lists ten categories: process, quality,
      relation, creativity, order, space, time, situation,
      sociality, and power: "Process Philosophy, A Cate-
      gorial Analysis," Tulane Studies in Philosophy 25

(1975), 58-91. Hartshorne expands his earlier list
of past process philosophers to include Hume, Marx,
Nietzsche, Berdyaev, and Schelling, suggesting there
is a case for including Hegel, Croce, Collingwood,
and Heidegger (although he does not state that case).
He lists fifteen "common theses (accepted, or at
least not denied, by all or most process thinkers),"
followed by a list of four special insights of Peirce,
and ten special insights each for Whitehead and Hartshorne himself: "Ideas and Theses of Process Philosophers," in Two Process Philosophers, ed. Lewis
S. Ford (Tallahassee, Fla.: American Academy of
Religion, 1973), 100-103. While the case is not ar-
guable here, not all of the "common theses" are accepted even by some alleged process thinkers; those
which are are non-unique, and can be reduced to ap-
proximately five or six distinct categories, indicated
later in this section.

(20)   This is the predominant methodology employed in the
classifications listed in n. 18 above, especially in
Browning, Sibley, and Gunter.

(21)   Charles Hartshorne, "The Development of Process Philosophy," in Philosophers of Process, ed. Douglas
Browning (New York: Random House, 1965), v-xxii.
Since completing this work, however, I have received
a copy of a new book by James R. Gray, Modern
Process Thought: A Brief Ideological History (Washington, D. C.: University Press of America, 1982).
While Gray does discuss the early origins of the
modern process tradition in the mechanist-vitalist
controversy in the late nineteenth century, his main
concern is to exhibit the subsequent historical development from Whitehead to contemporary process
theologians.

(22)   Cf., for example, J. M. Burgers, "The Measuring
Process in Quantum Theory," Reviews of Modern
Physics, 35 (1963), 145-150; "Causality and Antici-
pation," Science, 189 (July 1975), 194-198. Also
R. G. Collingwood, The Idea of Nature (Oxford: The
Clarendon Press, 1945). The most detailed analy-
sis of this issue may be found in the many works of
Prof. Errol E. Harris: cf. Nature, Mind and Mod-
ern Science (London: George Allen & Unwin, 1954);
Foundations of Metaphysics in Science (London: George

Allen & Unwin, 1965); "Teleology and Teleological
Explanation, " Journal of Philosophy, 56/1 (January
1, 1959), 5-25; "Mechanism and Teleology in Contemporary Thought, " Philosophy in Context, 2 (1973),
49-55; "Science, Metaphysics and Teleology, " The
Personal Universe, ed. Thomas Wren (Atlantic Highlands, N. J.: Humanities Press, 1975), 24-38.
Charles Hartshorne outlines and defends the use of
the category of "organism" in process philosophy in
a manner very similar to Harris: "A World of Organisms, " The Logic of Perfection and Other Essays
in Neoclassical Metaphysics (LaSalle, Ill.: Open
Court, 1962), 191-215.

(23) Obviously process philosophers do not intend merely to
revert to or reiterate that cosmology. Rather, the
modern tradition essentially recaptures the spirit of
that ancient worldview in an entirely contemporary
form. Cf. Milic Capek, "The Second Scientific Revolution, " Diogenes, 63 (1968), 114-133.

(24) Note that it is this more general principle, rather than
Hartshorne's specific reference to a doctrine of God
or of dipolar panentheism, which characterizes process philosophy as a whole. The dipolar theisms of
Whitehead and Hartshorne, as well as the dialectical
panentheisms of Hegel, Samuel Alexander, and (most
recently) Wolfhart Pannenberg, are merely special
cases, or logically-possible corollaries of this more
general category.

(25) PR 9.

INTRODUCTION: BIBLIOGRAPHY

---

1. Alexander, Samuel. "Hegel's Conception of Nature. "
    Mind (old series), 9/41 (1886).
        Argues that Hegelian dialectic is a process philos-
    ophy, but as a history of ideas, dialectic forms a
    "process not in time. "

2. _____. "Some Explanations. " Mind 30 (1921), 409-
    428.

A response to criticisms of C. D. Broad, indicating Alexander's divergence from Whitehead.

3. Browning, Douglas, ed. Philosophers of Process. New York: Random House, 1965.
   Following an introductory essay by Charles Hartshorne on the development of process philosophy, the anthology exhibits selections from Bergson, Peirce, James, Alexander, C. Lloyd Morgan, John Dewey, G. H. Mead, and Whitehead.

4. Burgers, J. M. "The Measuring Process in Quantum Theory." Reviews of Modern Physics, 35 (1963), 145-150.

5. _____. "Causality and Anticipation." Science, 189 (July 1975), 194-198.

6. Capek, Milic. "Toward a Widening of the Notion of Causality." Diogenes, 28 (1959), 63-90.
   Discusses the "career" of the deterministic interpretation of causality, from Greek philosophy through Newtonian-Laplacian mechanism. As this notion is incompatible with the perceived reality of temporal passage, it must be abandoned in terms of the wider notion of causality suggested in contemporary physics.

7. _____. "Change." Encyclopedia of Philosophy I. Ed. Paul Edwards. New York: The Free Press and Macmillan, 1967. Pp. 75-79.
   Heraclitus is cited as the sole representative of the "anti-substantialist trend in Greek philosophy." Contemporary process philosophy is depicted as the latest form of the Heraclitian position.

8. _____. "The Second Scientific Revolution." Diogenes, 63 (1968), 114-133.
   Discusses the broader significance of the transition from the mechanist-materialist assumptions of classical Newtonian physics, to the event-metaphysics of contemporary natural science.

9. _____. "Natural Sciences and the Future of Metaphysics." Main Currents, 28/3 (May-June 1972), 167-171.

9a. Cobb, John B., Jr. and Ford, Lewis S. "The Prospects

for Process Studies." Process Studies, 1/1 (Spring,
1971), 3-8.
    "Process philosophy" is defined as "any view which
treats reality as fundamentally temporal and creative,
such that becoming is more fundamental than being."
A list of contributors to the tradition is cited, from
Hegel to Whitehead.

10. _____, and Griffin, David Ray. Process Theology:
    An Introductory Exposition. Philadelphia: Westmins-
    ter Press, 1976.

11. Collingwood, Robin G. The Idea of Nature. Oxford:
    The Clarendon Press, 1945.
        Collingwood dates the transition to the contemporary
    view of nature as a purposive system with Hegel, and
    suggests that the recent exponents of this view include
    Bergson, Alexander, and Whitehead.

12. Dye, James Wayne. "Heraclitus and the Future of
    Process Philosophy." Tulane Studies in Philosophy,
    23 (1974), 13-31.
        The differences in method, form, and content be-
    tween classical Greek and modern philosophy are ex-
    amined in order to distinguish the concerns of Hera-
    clitus from those of contemporary process philosophers.
    "The proximate cause of process philosophy as it ex-
    ists today seems to have been the work of Darwin,
    which triggered a veritable avalanche of nineteenth-
    century evolutionist philosophies, sometimes original,
    sometimes disguised as Platonism or Hegelianism."

13. Feibleman, James K. "Why Whitehead Is Not a 'Proc-
    ess Philosopher.'" Tulane Studies in Philosophy, 23
    (1974), 48-59.
        Harsh criticism of the contemporary Whiteheadian
    "school," which "in honoring [has] demeaned White-
    head," and of the journal Process Studies, which re-
    flects Hartshorne's, rather than Whitehead's interests.
    Discusses Whitehead's focus on permanence amidst
    change, and makes much of the fact that, for White-
    head, the two were mutually dependent, that total proc-
    ess would be unintelligible.

14. Ford, Lewis S. Two Process Philosophers: Hartshorne's
    Encounter with Whitehead. "AAR Studies in Religion,
    5." Tallahassee, Fla.: American Academy of Religion,
    1973.

15. Gray, James R. Modern Process Thought: A Brief
     Ideological History. Washington, D. C. : University
     Press of America, 1982.
         Beginning with mechanism, vitalism and F. H.
     Bradley's "absolutism," the author traces (in effect)
     the parallel development of Whiteheadians and emer-
     gent evolutionists (such as Teilhard), illustrating the
     development of the contemporary process theologies
     of Christian, Meland, Pittinger, Cobb, and others.

16. Harlow, Victor Emmanuel. Bibliography and Genetic
     Study of American Realism. Oklahoma City, 1931.
         Documents the rise of realism in America (and
     later in Great Britain) in conjunction with pragmatism,
     as a reaction against Hegelianism. R. B. Perry's
     "half-realism," however, represented a re-assertion
     in a new guise of Bradley's view of sentience and
     reality. By 1930, naive, neo, and critical realisms
     had been transformed into "objective relativism, plu-
     ralism and organism," the chief exponent of which is
     A. N. Whitehead, who exhibited marked similarity to
     Hegel and Bradley. Thus, the history of realism in
     the United States illustrated the return to the very
     fount of idealism to which it had been consciously op-
     posed.

17. Harris, Errol E. Nature, Mind and Modern Science.
     London: George Allen and Unwin, 1954.
         A chapter on Hegel and Whitehead discusses the
     latter's strong affinity with Hegel and Bradley against
     dominant positivist-empiricist modes of thought. Com-
     pares Hegel's Absolute with Whitehead's "Consequent
     Nature."

18. _____. Foundations of Metaphysics in Science.
     London: George Allen and Unwin, 1965
         Includes a discussion of the contribution of White-
     head's thought to philosophy of nature, as well as a
     brief analysis of the problem of the status of mind in
     nature in his philosophy.

19. _____. "Teleology and Teleological Explanation."
     Journal of Philosophy, 56/1 (January 1, 1959), 5-25.

20. _____. "Mechanism and Teleology in Contemporary
     Thought." Philosophy in Context, 2 (1973), 49-55.

21. _____. "Science, Metaphysics and Teleology." The

Personal Universe. Ed. Thomas Wren. Atlantic
Highlands, N. J. : Humanities Press, 1975. Pp. 24-
38.

22. Hartshorne, Charles. Reality as a Social Process:
Studies in Metaphysics and Religion. Glencoe, Ill. ;
Boston: The Free Press/Beacon Press, 1953.
Author's preface and W. E. Hocking's foreword
trace the affinities of process thought with pragmatism
and American idealism (especially Royce). Both con-
fuse anglo-idealism's occasional concern for a "timeless absolute" with orthodox Hegelianism (which it is
not), and as a central doctrine of idealism (which it
is only for McTaggart and perhaps Bradley).

23. _____. "A World of Organisms." The Logic of
Perfection and Other Essays in Neoclassical Metaphysics. LaSalle, Ill. : Open Court, 1962. Pp. 191-215.
With reference to the roles of chance and purpose
in Darwinian evolution, the author argues for "organic
monism," the doctrine that the universe is comprised
of organisms, and is itself a cosmic organism.

24. _____. "Present Prospects for Metaphysics." The
Monist, 47 (1963), 188-210. Reprinted in Creative
Synthesis and Philosophic Method. London: SCM
Press, 1970. Pp. 43-56.
Whereas past metaphysical syntheses were often
divorced from experience and at odds with natural
science, the latter enterprise today constitutes the
chief impetus for re-thinking systematic and inclusive
conceptual structures along the lines of relativity and
indeterminism.

25. _____. "The Development of Process Philosophy."
Philosophers of Process. Ed. Douglas Browning.
New York: Random House, 1965.

26. _____. "Ideas and Theses of Process Philosophers."
Two Process Philosophers: Hartshorne's Encounter
with Whitehead. Ed. Lewis S. Ford. Tallahassee, Fla. :
American Academy of Religion, 1973. Pp. 100-103.

27. _____, and Reese, William L. Philosophers Speak
of God. Chicago: University of Chicago Press, 1953.

28. Lamprecht, Sterling P. The Metaphysics of Naturalism.
New York: Appleton-Century-Crofts, 1967.

29. Lovejoy, Arthur O. The Great Chain of Being. "The
    William James Lectures, 1933." Cambridge, Mass.:
    Harvard University Press, 1942.
        Lovejoy links Bergson and Whitehead and the idea
    of creative evolution with the past history of a natural
    theology of pantheism ("Plenitude of Nature"). A
    devastating historical critique of this view, which
    nonetheless fails to note that certain aspects of con-
    temporary process thought originate in a similar cri-
    tical rejection of the nature philosophy of naive ro-
    manticism.

30. Lucas, George R., Jr. Two Views of Freedom in
    Process Thought: A Study of Hegel and Whitehead.
    "AAR Dissertation Series, 28." Chico, Cal.: Scholars
    Press, 1979.
        A comparative analysis of the cosmologies of White-
    head and Hegel, utilizing freedom as the most impor-
    tant metaphysical category held in common by both.
    Demonstrates the similar grounding of freedom by
    both philosophers in doctrines of "organic mechanism"
    central to their respective philosophies of nature.
    Suggestions are offered regarding a broader definitional
    and historical understanding of "process philosophy"
    to accommodate these similarities.

31. Price, H. H. Perception. London: Methuen, 1932.

31a. _____. "Appearing and Appearances." American
    Philosophical Quarterly, 1/1 (January 1964), 3-19.

32. Reck, Andrew J. "Substance, Process and Nature,"
    Journal of Philosophy, 55 (1958), 766.

33. _____. Speculative Philosophy: A Study of Its Na-
    ture, Types and Uses. Albuquerque, N.M.: Uni-
    versity of New Mexico Press, 1972.
        Metaphysics and speculative philosophy are not
    sharply distinguished. Reck's discussion includes
    realism, idealism, materialism and process. Hera-
    clitus is portrayed as the spiritual ancestor of the
    evolutionary thought which launches contemporary
    process metaphysics: Spencer, Bergson, Alexander,
    Mead, Whitehead, and Teilhard.

34. _____. "Process Philosophy, a Categorial Analysis."
    Tulane Studies in Philosophy, 24 (1975), 58-91.
        Selects and analyzes ten categories that apply to

process thought from Plato and Aristotle to Alexander, Bergson, Dewey, Hartshorne, James, Mead, and Peirce: process, quality, relation, creativity, order, space, time, situation, sociality, power.

35. Russell, Bertrand. The Analysis of Mind. London: George Allen and Unwin, 1921.

36. _____. Mysticism and Logic. New York: Double-day, 1957.

37. _____. "The Philosophy of Logical Atomism." Logic and Knowledge. Ed. C. Marsh. London: George Allen and Unwin, 1956.

38. _____. My Philosophical Development, with an Appendix: Russell's Philosophy. Ed. A. Wood. New York: Simon and Schuster, 1959.

39. Sheldon, W. H. America's Progressive Philosophy. New Haven, Conn.: Yale University Press, 1942.
   Process philosophy in America is the culmination of a historical revolution in conceptual thought that begins with Galileo.

40. Sibley, Jack R., and Gunter, P. A. Y., eds. Process Philosophy: Basic Writings. Washington, D. C.: University Press of America, 1978.
   The preface by Charles Hartshorne defends the vitality of metaphysics in the twentieth century, and briefly assesses the significance of some pre-Whiteheadian process philosophers. The editors' introduction portrays modern process philosophy primarily as a reaction and response to evolutionist theories, devoted to combatting the static and mechanical aspects of traditional (pre-Darwinian) philosophy of science. The process tradition can no longer be restricted to Whitehead and his disciples, but rather represents "an amalgam of the insights of a great many philosophers." Selections include the works of Bergson, James, Whitehead, Wieman, Capek, Morgan, Smuts, and Hartshorne.

41. Wheelwright, Philip. Heraclitus. Princeton, N. J.: Princeton University Press, 1959.

42. Whitehead, Alfred North. Science and the Modern World. "Lowell Lectures, 1925." New York: Macmillan, 1925.

43. _____. Process and Reality. "Gifford Lectures,
     1927-28." New York: Macmillan, 1929.

44. _____. Adventures of Ideas. New York: Macmillan,
     1933.

45. _____. Essays in Science and Philosophy. New
     York: Philosophical Library, 1948.

46. _____. Process and Reality, Corrected Edition.
     Eds. David Ray Griffin and Donald W. Sherburne.
     New York: The Free Press, 1978.

PART I: PROCESS RATIONALISM

The Whiteheadian School

From the perspective of the interested outsider, the term
"process philosophy" customarily intends the metaphysical
approach initiated by Whitehead in Science and the Modern
World (1925), brought to maturity in Process and Reality
(1929), and seen throughout his "Harvard" writings until his
death in 1947. [1] Charles Hartshorne is recognized as the
subsequent standard-bearer of this tradition, to which he
made (and, at this writing, continues to make) substantial
original contributions. This, at least, is the view presented
in the major philosophical and theological interpretations of
Whitehead's work. [2]

This view is further reinforced in the quarterly journal Process Studies. The title itself suggests a concern for
the tradition of process philosophy; the journal masthead,
however, specifies that this term should be taken to apply
"primarily, though not exclusively, to the philosophy of Alfred North Whitehead and his intellectual associates, most
notably Charles Hartshorne." [3] Not surprisingly, this thrust
has fostered an unconscious tendency within this school to
view both earlier and contemporary philosophers and theologians, who articulate concerns similar in many respects to
Whitehead's, either as mere forerunners, or as contemporary
exponents of the Whiteheadian tradition. [4] As I have suggested, it is this unconscious tendency to assimilate predecessors into a single, unified tradition which has engendered
much troublesome confusion in the definition of process philosophy.

This tendency toward uncritical assimilation has been
effectively countered by recent research, including work by
Hartshorne himself. Throughout his career, Hartshorne has
graciously expressed his indebtedness to Whitehead, while

simultaneously maintaining both the pluralism of his own influences and interests, as well as his differences from Whitehead on many issues. These important historical and conceptual distinctions were carefully explored in a monograph
edited by Lewis Ford,[5] and dramatically underscored by
Hartshorne himself. In a recent article, he claimed that,
apart from Whitehead's "revolutionary doctrine" of prehension, he (Hartshorne) already had arrived at the remaining
process categories as a result of the influence of C. S.
Peirce, W. E. Hocking, and many others.[6] A similar point
regarding plurality and diversity within the Whiteheadian tradition already had been emphasized, in a different sense, by
Victor Lowe, who argued strenuously against over-eager and
uncritical comparisons of Whitehead's work with that of
earlier predecessors in the process tradition.[7]

A major point at issue regarding the classification of
Whitehead's "intellectual associates" is the definition of
"process" itself. The term is systematically ambiguous,
even among Whiteheadians. For Ivor Leclerc and Donald
Sherburne, process is understood as the identity of being
and becoming.[8] Strictly speaking, however, Whitehead's
phrase is that being is "constituted by" becoming.[9] Thus,
more recently, Jorge Luis Nobo has examined the ambiguity
of this phrase, and offered the neo-Aristotelian view that
being is produced by becoming. Nobo suggests that Whitehead specified not one, but two species of creative process:
"concrescence" (focusing on the epochal, atemporal event-
character of the genesis of occasions of experience), and
"transition" (the mode of causal efficacy of the immediate
past in the present giving rise to the experience of duration
or temporal passage).[10] Thus, while some focus on change
and becoming seems to characterize process philosophy as
a whole, this emphasis is not sufficient to specify the Whiteheadian school.

The prevailing perception of the Whiteheadian process
tradition--that events rather than substances form the primary
ontology--both pre-dates Whitehead and is indeed exhibited
in his thought. But for Whitehead, events are "epochal"--
atomic occasions of experience which "concresce" (come into
being) all at once, and are themselves the stubborn, irreducible facts. This flux is not more fundamental than endurance
or permanence; indeed, it exhibits elements of permanence,
both in the forms of definiteness ("eternal objects") ingredient
in each such epochal occasion, as well as in the structured
order of process itself. Thus, flux and endurance both are
properties that measure the degree of sameness or difference
between successive atomic occasions.[11]

The innovations of the Whiteheadian interpretation of "process" seem to be "epochalism" and the doctrine of prehension, rather than the common ascriptions of temporalism and the event-character of reality. [12] The former pair distinguishes Whitehead and his disciples within, the latter pair marks their continuity with the broader tradition of process philosophy. Further, as the discussion of Hartshorne's work reveals, it is by no means clear how far his "intellectual associates" have followed, or are willing to follow Whitehead in his particular interpretation of "process." [13] If one consequently wishes to speak meaningfully of a "Whiteheadian school" of process thought, one might be better served by stressing broader issues which are shared unambiguously with other contemporary process philosophers and theologians, and which distinguish them from the earlier phases of the tradition as a whole. As observed, "becoming" and "temporalism" are not such issues.

First, the "Whiteheadian school" represents a form of cosmology influenced principally by mathematical physics (primarily relativity theory, and to a leaser degree, quantum mechanics), [14] and only to a minor degree by evolutionary biology (which is more or less presupposed). This fact alone represents a sharp break with Whitehead's predecessors and evolutionist contemporaries in the larger tradition of process philosophy, in which analysis and development of evolutionist or historicist cosmologies formed the principal mode of philosophizing.

Secondly, and perhaps because of these differences of influence, this cosmology is highly rationalistic: emphasis is placed on the elucidation of an inclusive set of metaphysical first principles, which must show themselves to be both internally coherent and experientially adequate to the subsequent description of all aspects of experience--not merely human and historical experience, but natural phenomena as well. This approach is reminiscent of the pre-Kantian tradition of rationalism, as exhibited, for example, by Spinoza and Leibniz. Indeed, Whitehead strongly identified with this tradition. Again (as noted in later chapters) this approach contrasts sharply with the more descriptive, intuitive and non-systematic methods practiced by several earlier process philosophers.

A third characteristic Whiteheadian emphasis, to which his contemporary interpreters maintain a troubled allegiance, is his modified Platonic realism (the doctrine of "eternal objects"). Though this issue has considerably exercised the patience of persistent critics of Whitehead, [15] both the problem

and the importance of the doctrine pale in historical perspective. Such Platonism was perfectly in keeping with the realist tradition in Great Britain and America during the early
part of the twentieth century--a movement, once again, with
which Whitehead closely identified himself. [16] Apart from
its continued manifestation in the Whiteheadian tradition, the
realist doctrine of universals was never so much refuted as
abandoned as untenable, indefensible, and finally superfluous.
It is difficult, however, to identify a realist during the early
1900's who was not also a Platonist in some sense--as was
the case with Russell and G. E. Moore, whose own philosophical voyages are highly illustrative in this regard. [17] In my
judgment, Whitehead's critical realism is notably unique in
this period not because of its Platonic overtones, but rather
because of its Leibnizian substitution of a single species of
actual entities as events, in place of the chaotic ontological
plethora of entities introduced through the British neo-realist
"sense data" theory.

Perhaps most characteristic, however, is the stress
within this school on some form of real, but (in marked contrast to Bradley, Royce, and McTaggart) temporally asymmetrical internal relatedness--what Whitehead himself meant
by the phrase, "Philosophy of Organism."[18] The organic
interrelatedness of events, interpreted through a doctrine of
the asymmetrical relatedness of past to present, purports to
account simultaneously for the causal efficacy of the past
and for the exercise of creative freedom in the present.
While the whole universe, in principle, is present in (or
available to) every individual, epochal occasion, temporally
simultaneous occasions in the unison of becoming are isolated
causally from one another (according to the constraints of
relativity theory). Thus, the constitutive relations are not
between and among all actualities, or even all present actualities (as with Bradley), but are between an individual present effect (a Whiteheadian "actual entity") and its multitude
of past "causes" (the determinate past actualities, the "finished concrescences," or what Prof. George Kline has termed
"concreta"). [19] Further, these relations are asymmetrical
because they are "internal" (constitutive) only for one term
(the present concrescence), and are wholly external to the
remaining terms (the past actualities). Thus, in an admittedly
complicated, but characteristically precise fashion, Whiteheadians can claim both organic interrelatedness and freedom
by holding that a present effect literally creates itself out
of its own causes, thus accounting both for historical conditioning (the causal efficacy of the past) and creative freedom. [20]

This complex and intriguing resolution of the problem
of freedom and determinism is unique to Whitehead. Shorn
of the technical terminology, however, such a hypothesis
regarding the compatibility of causality and finite freedom in
a manner which accounts for both order and creative novelty
is characteristic not only of Whitehead and Hartshorne, but
(as the following bibliographical annotations will suggest) of
several other philosophers as well. These include the as-
tronomer-philosopher Sir Arthur S. Eddington; physicist-
philosophers Werner Heisenberg, Sir James Jeans, Louis
de Broglie, and David Bohm; and philosophers such as
F. S. C. Northrop (a student of Whitehead's), Milic Capek,
and Hans Jonas. To some degree, doctrines of organism,
creativity, and freedom are combined with the broader commitment to temporalism and the articulation of an event
(rather than a substance) metaphysics--all pursued in a rigor-
ous and systematic manner which might best be described
as "rationalist cosmologies." Indeed, out of deference to
Prof. Hartshorne and to the independent reputations of these
other distinguished representatives of this school, it seems
most appropriate to refer to this, the most familiar and contemporary school of process philosophy, as "process rationalism."[21]

NOTES

(1) A complete listing of these writings is included in the
     bibliography for this section. Victor Lowe cautions
     against stressing too strongly the different concerns in
     various stages of Whitehead's career, and argues for a
     continuity of interests and a sustained development of
     concerns from the logical-conceptual foundations of
     mathematics, through philosophy of science, to cos-
     mology. See "The Development of Whitehead's Phi-
     losophy," in The Philosophy of Alfred North White-
     head, ed. Paul A. Schilpp (Evanston, Ill.: North-
     western University Press, 1941), 15-124. Cf. also
     Lowe's Understanding Whitehead (Baltimore: Johns
     Hopkins University Press, 1962).

(2) Principal among the standard interpretations, in addition
     to Victor Lowe's book, include: Ivor Leclerc, White-
     head's Metaphysics: An Introductory Exposition (Lon-
     don: G. Allen & Unwin, 1958); William A. Christian,
     An Interpretation of Whitehead's Metaphysics (New
     Haven: Yale University Press, 1959); and from the
     standpoint of philosophical theology, John B. Cobb,
     Jr., A Christian Natural Theology (Philadelphia:

Westminster Press, 1965); and John B. Cobb, Jr. and
David Ray Griffin, Process Theology: An Introductory
Exposition (Philadelphia: Westminster Press, 1976).

(3) Process Studies, published by the Center for Process
Studies in Claremont, California and edited by Lewis
S. Ford, has published a wide variety of articles on
process philosophy and theology. A breakdown by
category, however, reinforces the emphasis on the
Whiteheadian-Hartshornian interpretation. From its
inception in the spring of 1971 through the spring of
1981, Process Studies published 141 articles, 92 of
which were explicit interpretations and analyses of
the Whiteheadian or Hartshornian perspective, and
many more of which reflected that perspective in
original philosophical investigations. The record on
criticisms, reviews, and bibliographical essays is
slightly more balanced: altogether, 90 such items
have been published, of which slightly more than one-
half have been focused explicitly on either Whitehead,
Hartshorne, or their immediate disciples. Indeed,
one critic polemicizes that the journal is entirely
Hartshornian in character, having lost all touch with
Whitehead: James K. Feibleman, "Why Whitehead
Is Not a 'Process' Philosopher," Tulane Studies in
Philosophy 23 (1974), 48-59. Given that even by 1974
the preponderance of articles had been addressed to
explicit interpretations of Whitehead, this charge
would seem difficult to sustain.

(4) Cf. Charles Hartshorne's preface to Process Philosophy:
Basic Writings, eds. Sibley and Gunter (Washington,
D.C. : University Press of America, 1978), 5. This
is the principal mode of assimilating such now-familiar
"process" figures as Bergson, James, Dewey and Alexander, as well as less familiar figures, such as the
Rumanian Orthodox theologian, Nicolai Berdyaev. For an
example of this sort of assimilation, consult: James W.
Dye, "Berdyaev on 'Creativity'," The Personalist 46
(Fall 1965), 459-467; and Charles Hartshorne, "Whitehead
and Berdyaev: Is There Tragedy in God?" Journal of Religion 37/2 (April 1957), 71-84.

(5) Two Process Philosophers: Hartshorne's Encounter with
Whitehead, ed. Lewis S. Ford (Tallahassee, Fla. :
American Academy of Religion, 1973).

(6) Charles Hartshorne, "Whitehead's Revolutionary Concept
of Prehension," International Philosophical Quarterly

19/3 (September 1979), 253-263. Hartshorne enumer-
ates a long list of his intellectual antecedents including Fechner, W. E. Hocking, Josiah Royce,
James, Bergson, and Alexander (to name but a few).
See Reality as a Social Process (Glencoe, Ill.;
Boston: Free Press and Beacon Press, 1953), 31,
131. The full significance of these claims is explored
below, especially sections III-V.

(7) "The Influence of Bergson, James and Alexander on
Whitehead," Journal of the History of Ideas, 10
(1949), 267-296.

(8) Leclerc, op. cit., 68-71; Donald Sherburne, ed., A
Key to Whitehead's Process and Reality (New York:
Macmillan, 1966), p. 28.

(9) PR 34f.

(10) This position is adumbrated in three articles by Prof.
Nobo: "Whitehead's Principle of Process," Process
Studies 4/4 (Winter 1974), 275-284; "Whitehead's
Principle of Relativity," Process Studies 8/1 (Spring
1978), 1-20; and "Transition in Whitehead: A Creative Process Distinct from Concrescence," International Philosophical Quarterly 19/3 (September 1979),
265-283.

(11) Cf. PR 114, 124; and J. L. Nobo, "Transition in Whitehead," loc. cit. I am indebted to Lewis Ford for
clarification of this point. Cf. his "Duration of the
Present," Philosophy and Phenomenological Research
35 (1974), 100-106.

(12) This view agrees with Hartshorne's assessment of Whitehead's unique contributions: "Ideas and Theses of
Process Philosophers," in Two Process Philosophers,
ed. Lewis Ford, op. cit., p. 102.

(13) In addition to the questions that Nobo's critical studies
have raised, the adequacy of the understanding of
epochalism by Whitehead's principal disciples is
raised in a controversial study by F. Bradford Wallack, The Epochal Nature of Process in Whitehead's
Metaphysics (Albany, N.Y.: SUNY Press, 1980).

(14) Cf. Lewis E. Akeley, "The Problem of the Specious
Present and Physical Time," Journal of Philosophy
22/21 (October 8, 1925), 561-573; and "Wholes and

Prehensive Unities for Physics and Philosophy,"
Journal of Philosophy 24/22 (October 27, 1927), 589-
608; both of which give early favorable assessments
of the compatibility of Whitehead's views with relativistic theories of space-time. A more recent
discussion by physicist Ian Barbour, Issues in Science
and Religion (Englewood Cliffs, N. J.: Prentice-Hall,
1966), shows marked deference for the views of
Whitehead, Hartshorne, and Teilhard. Another physicist, J. M. Burgers, searches for verification of
Whitehead's metaphysical assumptions in contemporary
science: Experience and Conceptual Activity (Cambridge, Mass.: M. I. T. Press, 1965). The distinguished relativity theorist John L. Synge demonstrated that Whitehead's assumptions regarding space
and time could be shown to yield the Schwarzchild dif-
ferential equations which serve as solutions to Einstein's
non-linear field equations: The Relativity Theory of
A. N. Whitehead (College Park, Md.: Institute for
Fluid Dynamics and Applied Mathematics, Univ. of
Maryland, 1951). A Hegelian assessment of the
physics and mathematics-dependence of Whitehead's
views is offered by Klaus Heipcke, Die Philosophie
des Ereignisses bei Alfred North Whitehead (Würz-
burg: Julius-Maximilians Universität, 1964). Finally,
two contrasting views of the influence of quantun
theory on, and its compatibility with, Whitehead's
philosophy are offered by Abner Shimony, "Quantum
Physics and the Philosophy of Whitehead," in Philosophy in America, ed. Max Black (Ithaca, N. Y.:
Cornell University Press, 1965), 240-261; and Victor
Guillemin, The Story of Quantum Mechanics (New
York: Scribners, 1968).
     During the past decade, the battle has been joined
primarily in the pages of Process Studies. For
recent discussions of Whitehead and relativity theory,
see Robert Andrew Ariel, "Recent Empirical Disconfirmation of Whitehead's Relativity Theory," and
Dean R. Fowler's critical reply in Process Studies
4/4 (Winter 1974), 285-290; and Dean R. Fowler,
"Whitehead's Theory of Relativity," Process Studies
5/3 (Fall 1975), 159-174. For recent discussions
on the grounding of Whiteheadian metaphysics in
quantum theory, see Henry Pierce Stapp, "Quantum
Mechanics, Local Causality, and Process Philosophy,"
and Charles Hartshorne, "Bell's Theorem and Stapp's
Revised View of Space-Time," Process Studies 7/3
(Fall 1977), 173-191; William B. Jones, "Bell's

Theorem, H. P. Stapp, and Process Theism," Process Studies 7/4 (Winter 1977), 250-261; and David Bohm, "The Implicate Order: A New Order for Physics," Process Studies 8/2 (Summer 1978), 73-102.

(15) Cf., for example, Edward Pols, Whitehead's Metaphysics (Carbondale, Ill.: University of Southern Illinois Press, 1967), which suggests that eternal objects are finally the only possible active agents in Whitehead's system, thus refuting Whitehead's doctrine of freedom. For a critical assessment of the subsequent controversy over Pols' claims, cf. my Two Views of Freedom in Process Thought, pp. 36-40.

(16) PR viii.

(17) See for example, John H. Muirhead, The Platonic Tradition in Anglo-Saxon Philosophy (London: G. Allen & Unwin, 1931); and V. E. Harlow, Bibliography and Genetic Study of American Realism (Oklahoma City, 1931; Kraus Reprints, 1971).

(18) Cf. SMW 116, 149-64, 212-220, et seq. This early view led to the development of the doctrine of prehensions, or "feelings" in PR.

(19) George L. Kline, "Form, Concrescence and Concretum: A Neo-Whiteheadian Analysis," Southern Journal of Philosophy 7/4 (Winter 1969), 351-360.

(20) Here again, a lengthy treatment of Whitehead's theory of freedom, as well as of objections to his view, may be found in Two Views of Freedom in Process Thought, pp. 20-40.

(21) I prefer this term to Prof. Hartshorne's suggested designation of "neoclassical metaphysics." The latter term is reminiscent of medieval philosophical theology, whereas others in this tradition of rationalist process cosmology are not concerned exclusively, or even primarily with philosophical theism, as is Prof. Hartshorne.

I. PROCESS RATIONALISM: BIBLIOGRAPHY

I shall not attempt to list exhaustive primary or secondary bibliographies for Whitehead, Hartshorne, or those who are principally their expositors, save as such work bears upon the historical and conceptual questions at issue in this essay. Comprehensive bibliographies of Whiteheadian and Hartshornian scholarship are available as follows:

Fowler, Dean R. "Bibliography of Dissertations and Theses on Charles Hartshorne." Process Studies, 3/4 (Winter 1973), 304-307.

Hartshorne, Dorothy C. "Charles Hartshorne: A Secondary Bibliography." Process Studies, 3/3 (Fall 1973), 179-227.

_____. "Charles Hartshorne: Primary Bibliography." Process Studies, 6/1 (Spring 1976), 73-93.

_____. "Charles Hartshorne: 1980 Bibliographical Addenda." Process Studies, 11/2 (Summer 1981), 108-150.

Ricards, Philip. "Addenda to Bibliography of Dissertations and Theses on Charles Hartshorne." Process Studies, 11/2 (Summer 1981), 151-52.

Woodbridge, Barry A., ed. Alfred North Whitehead: A Primary-Secondary Bibliography. "Bibliographies of Famous Philosophers, 3." Bowling Green, Ohio: Philosophy Documentation Center, 1977.

47. Akeley, Lewis E. "The Problem of the Specious Present and Physical Time." Journal of Philosophy, 22/21 (October 8, 1925), 561-573.
     Suggests some correlations and implications in mathematical physics of relativistic space-time, of Whitehead's concept of the "specious present."

48. _____. "Wholes and Prehensive Unities for Physics and Philosophy." Journal of Philosophy, 22/24 (October 27, 1927), 589-608.
     An exposition and defense, in terms of physics, of Whitehead's concepts of abstraction, interrelatedness and eternal objects, utilizing common physical phenomena. Through discussion of measurement in terms of

observables and physical interaction, the author illustrates that Whitehead's views do account for particularity and empirical, finite knowledge on one hand,
and for the intuition of prehensive unity, reciprocity,
and organic holism on the other.

49. Alexander, Samuel. Space, Time, and Deity. 2 Vols.
"Gifford Lectures, 1916-1918." London: Macmillan,
1920.
    Alexander's major formal break with British ideal-
    ism is rendered in detail. Metaphysics must be con-
    ceived as an inclusive, empirical science. Thus,
    while the basic spatio-temporal character of all ex-
    perience is asserted, in contrast to Kant and analogous
    to Bergson, this is not an a priori feature, but one
    discerned experientially. "Space-time" is a continuous
    interrelated complex of motion, characterized by a
    nisus or creative tendency. An "emergent" is an
    "organized pattern" which produces new qualitative
    syntheses that could not have been predicted from a
    prior knowledge of the constituent elements of the
    pattern before their organization. Life and conscious
    mind are examples of emergent features of biological
    evolution, but there is no reason to assume that the
    creative, temporal process has ended there. "Deity"
    is understood in two senses: the spacetime universe
    itself, "pregnant" with emergent qualities (possibili-
    ties); and the likely future evolution of the universe
    towards a higher, more complex stage of emergent
    experience, transcending human mind.

50. Alston, William P. "Internal Relatedness and Pluralism
    in Whitehead." Review of Metaphysics, 5 (1952),
    535-558.
    Argues that internal relatedness is incompatible
    with pluralism, and that none of Whitehead's other
    doctrines is sufficient to preserve a commitment to
    pluralism.

51. Ariel, Robert Andrew. "Recent Empirical Disconfirma-
    tion of Whitehead's Relativity Theory." Process
    Studies, 5/3 (Fall 1975), 159-174.

52. Barbour, Ian G. Issues in Science and Religion. Engle-
    wood Cliffs, N.J.: Prentice-Hall, 1966.

53. Bohm, David. "The Implicate Order: A New Order for
    Physics." Process Studies, 8/2 (Summer 1978), 73-
    102.

54. _____. Wholeness and the Implicate Order. London:
     Routledge and Kegan Paul, 1980.
         A distinguished quantum physics theorist gives
     credence to the view that pattern and process--the
     implicate order--constitute the optimal description of
     the real. Though influenced by Whitehead, Bohm in-
     dicates that his views differ from or surpass White-
     head's at several points.

55. Bohr, Niels. "Causality and Complementarity." Es-
     says 1958-1962 on Atomic Physics and Human Knowl-
     edge. New York: Vintage, 1966. Pp. 1-7.

56. Burgers, J. M. Experience and Conceptual Activity:
     A Philosophical Essay Based upon the Writings of
     Alfred North Whitehead. Cambridge, Mass.: M. I. T.
     Press, 1965.
         A physicist makes a comprehensive attempt to find
     verification for Whitehead's metaphysical principles in
     contemporary science.

57. Capek, Milic. "The Doctrine of Necessity Re-examined."
     Review of Metaphysics, 5/5 (1951), 40-55.

58. _____. "Relativity and the Status of Space." Re-
     view of Metaphysics, 9/2 (1955).

59. *_____. "Toward a Widening of the Notion of Cau-
     sality." Diogenes, 28 (1959), 63-90. [Intro, no. 6]

60. _____. The Philosophical Impact of Contemporary
     Physics. New York: D. Van Nostrand, 1961.

61. _____. "The Myth of Frozen Passage: The Status
     of Becoming in the Physical World." Boston Studies
     in the Philosophy of Science, 2 (1965), 441-463.

62. *_____. "The Second Scientific Revolution." Dio-
     genes, 63 (1968), 114-133. [Intro, no. 8]

63. _____, ed. The Concepts of Space and Time: Their
     Structure and Development. Boston: D. Reidel,
     1975.

64. Carella, Michael Jerome. "Heisenberg's Concept of
     Matter as Potency." Diogenes (Winter 1976), 25-37.
         Heisenberg's formulation of quantum theory de-
     stroyed the mechanistic world-view. Thus, in order

to express indeterminacy and probability in the "logical
syntax" of quantum theory, he was forced to revert
to Aristotle's idea of matter as "potency."

65. Christian, William A. An Interpretation of Whitehead's
Metaphysics. New Haven, Conn.: Yale University
Press, 1959.

66. Cobb, John B., Jr. A Christian Natural Theology,
Based on the Writings of Alfred North Whitehead.
Philadelphia: Westminster Press, 1965.

67. _____, and Griffin, David Ray. Process Theology:
An Introductory Exposition. Philadelphia: Westminster
Press, 1976.

68. Coolidge, M. L. "Purposiveness Without Purpose in
a New Context." Philosophy and Phenomenological
Research, 4/1 (September 1943), 85-93.

69. de Broglie, Louis. "L'Espace et le temps dans la
physique quantique." Revue de metaphysique et de
morale, 54 (1949), 119-120.

70. Donnelley, Strachan. "Whitehead and Hans Jonas: Organism, Causality and Perception." International
Philosophical Quarterly, 19/3 (September 1979), 301-
315.
    Whitehead's actual occasions could not experience
causal efficacy since, "as epochal, atomic, autonomous
subjects, they lack the requisite enduring bodies, even
if they together belong to and constitute such bodies."
For Jonas, the enduring organic forms are themselves
the stubborn, irreducible fact, and not merely appearances thereof.

71. Dye, James Wayne. Unity in Duality: An Examination
of the Metaphysics of Nicholas Berdyaev. Diss.
Tulane University, 1960.

72. _____. "Berdyaev on 'Creativity'." The Personalist,
46 (Fall 1965), 459-467.

73. Eddington, Sir Arthur S. Space, Time and Gravitation:
An Outline of the General Theory of Relativity. Cambridge University Press, 1920.

74. _____. The Nature of the Physical World. "Gifford

Lectures, 1927." New York: Macmillan, 1929.
Eddington suggests some possible interpretations of
Einstein that satisfy Whitehead's complaint against
non-uniform space-time. Whitehead's reinterpretation
of the "first principles" of physics appears correct:
quantum mechanics as formulated by Heisenberg represents a denial of determinism. Hegel's view of
planetary motion as a "free geodesic" is partially true.
The overall reinterpretation of relativity physics and
quantum mechanics yields an "event metaphysics,"
stressing the process of becoming, and the essential
dynamism of nature. In particular, the advent of
"wave mechanics" suggests that "matter" is nothing
more than an enduring temporal organization of events.

75. _____. Science and the Unseen World. "Swarth-
more Lectures, 1929." New York: Macmillan, 1929.

76. _____. The Philosophy of Physical Science. "Tar-
ner Lectures, 1938." Cambridge: Cambridge University Press, 1939.
Author describes his view as "selective subjectivism" or "structuralism"; i. e. , empirical "evidence"
is that which the observer selects. We are directly
aware that the world consists mainly of life, consciousness, and spirit. Since knowledge of the physical
world is synonymous with "selective subjectivism,"
idealists are right, and materialists are "dead wrong."

77. Emmet, Dorothy M. Whitehead's Philosophy of Organism. New York: Macmillan, 1932.

78. Eslick, Leonard J. "Substance, Change and Causality
in Whitehead." Philosophy and Phenomenological Research, 18 (1958), 503-513.
Author questions whether there can be true change
without "substance" of some sort enduring through
change, or whether there can be a meaningful doctrine
of efficient causation without substance. Hartshorne's
reply, "Whitehead on Process," 514-520, defends
against these charges.

79. *Feibleman, James K. "Why Whitehead Is Not a 'Process' Philosopher." Tulane Studies in Philosophy, 23
(1974), 48-59. [Intro, no. 13]

80. Felt, James W. "Whitehead and the Bifurcation of Nature." Modern Schoolman, 45 (1968), 285-298.

81. Ford, Lewis S. "The Duration of the Present." Phi-
    losophy and Phenomenological Research, 35 (1974),
    100-106.

82. _____, ed. Two Process Philosophers: Hartshorne's
    Encounter with Whitehead. Tallahassee, Fla.: Ameri-
    can Academy of Religion, 1973.

83. Fowler, Dean R. "Disconfirmation of Whitehead's Rela-
    tivity Theory--a Critical Reply." Process Studies,
    4/4 (Winter 1974), 288-290.

84. _____. "Whitehead's Theory of Relativity." Process
    Studies, 5/3 (Fall 1975), 159-174.

85. Guillemin, Victor. The Story of Quantum Mechanics.
    New York: Scribners, 1968.
        A thoughtful and thorough discussion of the interplay
    of science and philosophy, and the importance of meta-
    physics for testing the logical implications and con-
    sistency of hypotheses based upon observation   Sta-
    tistical laws are not equivalent to caprice; rather,
    they are like the governing automobile ordinances in
    a town constituted by the behavior of individual cars.
    A chapter on "Determinism, Free Will and the New
    Physics," warns against the misunderstandings of
    "freedom" in quantum mechanics. Discusses Planck
    (who defends both causality and free will) and Edding-
    ton (who argues only against the classical view of
    mechanistic determinism). Author praises the good
    sense of Whitehead for arguing that there is one sys-
    tem of laws (no dualism), which is inherently incom-
    plete, and a function of the complexity of the groups
    to which the laws apply. New combinations of en-
    tities (e. g., from atoms to molecules to cells) evoke
    new laws, with unanticipated results. But laws are
    always a function of the system they describe.

86. Hammerschmidt, William W. Whitehead's Philosophy
    of Time. New York: Russell and Russell, 1947.

87. *Harlow, Victor Emmanuel. Bibliography and Genetic
    Study of American Realism. Oklahoma City, 1931;
    New York: Kraus Reprints, 1971. [Intro, no. 16]

88. Hartshorne, Charles. "Contingency and the New Era in
    Metaphysics." Journal of Philosophy, 29 (1932), 429.

89. _____. Man's Vision of God and the Logic of Theism.
Hamden, Conn.: Archon Books, 1941.

90. _____. "Organic and Inorganic Wholes." Philosophy
and Phenomenological Research, 3 (December 1942),
127-136.

91. _____. "Whitehead's Metaphysics." Whitehead and
the Modern World. Boston: Beacon Press, 1950.
Pp. 25-41.

92. * _____. Reality as a Social Process: Studies in
Metaphysics and Religion. Glencoe, Ill.; Boston:
Free Press and Beacon Press, 1953. [Intro, no. 22]

93. _____. "Causal Necessities: An Alternative to
Hume." The Philosophical Review, 63 (1954), 479-
499.

94. _____. "Whitehead and Berdyaev: Is There Tragedy
in God?" Journal of Religion, 37/2 (April 1957), 71-
84.
Discusses important similarities between the philosopher and theologian. For both, God is the "su-
preme cause," who participates sympathetically in
the joys and sufferings of creatures.

95. _____. "Outlines of a Philosophy of Nature, I/II."
The Personalist, 39 (Summer/Autumn 1958), 239-
248/380-391.

96. _____. The Logic of Perfection, and Other Essays
in Neoclassical Metaphysics. LaSalle, Ill.: Open
Court, 1962.

97. * _____. "Present Prospects for Metaphysics." The
Monist, 47 (1963), 188-210. [Intro, no. 24]

98. _____. A Natural Theology for Our Time. La-
Salle, Ill.: Open Court, 1967.

99. _____. Beyond Humanism: Essays in the New
Philosophy of Nature. Lincoln: University of Ne-
braska Press, 1968.

100. _____. Creative Synthesis and Philosophic Method.
London: SCM Press, 1970.

101. _____. Whitehead's Philosophy: Selected Essays,
     1935-1970. Lincoln: University of Nebraska Press,
     1972.

102. _____. "Perception and the 'Concrete Abstractness'
     of Science." Philosophy and Phenomenological Re-
     search 34/4 (June 1974), 465-476.

103. _____. "Whitehead and Leibniz: A Comparison."
     Contemporary Studies in Idealism. Eds. Howie and
     Buford. Cape Cod, Mass.: Claude Stark and Co.,
     1975. Pp. 95-115.
     Panpsychism, the reality of process, and God
     as the ground of order are themes common to both
     philosophers, as well as to Peirce.

104. _____. "Bell's Theorem and Stapp's Revised View
     of Space-Time." Process Studies, 7/3 (Fall 1977),
     183-191.

105. _____. "Whitehead's Revolutionary Concept of Pre-
     hension." International Philosophical Quarterly,
     19/3 (September 1979), 253-263.
     Self-identity and endurance are but limited special
     cases of the causal influence of the past in the pres-
     ent. "Reality consists ... of successions of states
     or events causally related to predecessors, only
     some of which were in the same individual series.
     Causality is not stopped at the boundaries of so-
     called identity." Prehension is this experience of
     past events in the mode of causal efficacy--and thus,
     in a stroke, Whitehead is able to account for causal-
     ity, freedom, identity, and difference.

106. Heelan, Patrick A., S. J. Quantum Mechanics and
     Objectivity: A Study of the Physical Philosophy of
     Warner Heisenberg. The Hague: Martinus Nijhoff,
     1965.
     A detailed exposition of Heisenberg's views. He
     rejects the "facile positivism" of Bohr and the naive
     realism of most scientists; he even rejects the de-
     ductionism of Spinoza and Leibniz which influenced
     the elder Einstein. His critical realism and em-
     piricism are reminiscent of the idealism of Kant and
     Hegel. Causality in the classical sense is definitely
     rejected, as is any attempt to state the "absolute"
     meaning of phenomena apart from an observer. The
     attempts to resurrect causality in quantum mechanics

through Schroedinger's wave-functions in Hilbert space
do not correspond to causality in the actual world.

107. Heipcke, Klaus. Die Philosophie des Ereignisses bei
      Alfred North Whitehead. "Habilitationsschrift." Würz-
      burg: Julius-Maximilians Universität, 1964.
          Author's specific concern is to compare White-
      head's "philosophy of events" with developments in
      the theory of mathematical physics, especially in-
      cluding Bernoullis, Laplace, and Boole. The analy-
      sis, however, is "neo-Hegelian," utilizing traditional
      Hegelian metaphysical language and categories to
      develop a typology for Whitehead's philosophy. Bib-
      liography includes, as sekundärliteratur, R. G. Col-
      lingwood's Idea of Nature and Hegel's Phänomenologie
      des Geistes.

108. Heisenberg, Werner. Physics and Philosophy: The
      Revolution in Modern Science. "World Perspectives
      Series." Ed. Ruth Nanda Anshen. Introduction by
      F. S. C. Northrop. New York: Harper and Bros.,
      1958.
          Northrop's introduction discusses the necessary
      basis of any physical theory in speculative metaphys-
      ics. Heisenberg's ontology of potentiality "has an
      element in common with Whitehead." Discusses the
      mechanistic and teleological interpretations of cau-
      sality, and attacks Einstein and other "hidden vari-
      able" theorists as non-empirical, and not in accord
      with present experimental results. Heisenberg sug-
      gests that his interpretation of the Copenhagen em-
      phasis on "what really happens classically in a quan-
      tum event," has transformed that perspective to a
      new metaphysical basis, including a subjectivist bias:
      what happens depends upon who, when and how the
      event is observed. Cites Bohr: " ... in the drama
      of existence we are ourselves both players and spec-
      tators." Author discusses the Greek controversy
      over being and becoming, the one and the many,
      commenting "that modern physics is ... extremely
      near to the doctrines of Heraclitus." Finally, Heisen-
      berg details the dilemma of the Copenhagen school:
      its proponents desired to retain both materialism and
      dogmatic realism (Einstein, Schroedinger), but were
      forced to move away from materialism and substance.
      Recounts the dramatic failure of David Bohm's "hid-
      den variable" interpretation, and his subsequent con-
      version to Heisenberg's view.

109. _____. Introduction to the Unified Field Theory of
Elementary Particles. New York: John Wiley,
1966.

110. _____. Natural Law and the Structure of Matter.
"An Address Delivered on the Hill of Pnyx, Athens:
3 June, 1964." London: Rebel Press, 1970.
Emphasizes the Platonic-idealistic implications of
modern mathematical physics. What is "real" are
conceptual structures and laws, but not matter or
substance.

111. _____. Physics and Beyond. Trans. of Der Teil
und das Ganze. Munich: R. Piper Verlag, 1971.
"World Perspectives Series." Ed. Ruth Nanda An-
shen. New York: Harper and Row, 1971.
A series of conversations, relating differences
with Mach, Einstein, Paul Dirac, Pauli, Bohr and
others. Explains, in terms of their native pragmatist philosophy, why Americans seem more ready
and able to adjust to changes in physical theory:
unlike Europeans, they never treated "law" or "natural law" as an Absolute in the first place. Criticizes the naivete and dogmatism of the Vienna
Circle for their inability to perceive the profound
metaphysical importance of quantum mechanics.

112. _____. Across the Frontiers. Trans. Peter Heath.
"World Perspectives Series." Ed. Ruth Nanda An-
shen. New York: Harper and Row, 1974.
A series of essays on science, culture, ethics,
history, and religion reminiscent of Whitehead.
Discusses Goethe's fascination and fear regarding
science. His theory of colors and treatment of
botany indicate that nature exhibits a single, unified
principle, a basic structure or Idea. Heisenberg
compares this 19th-century view with the discovery
of DNA and the structuralism of elementary-particle
physics, and suggests a correspondence between the
primal structures discerned in modern nature, and
Plato's search for ultimate natural forms (e. g. , the
"tetrahedrons" of fire). Author cites Wolfgang Pauli's
discussion of civilization, in which culture is bounded
by two limiting principles, neither of which is encountered or verified in actual experience: 1) the
idea of an objective world, pursuing a regular course
in space-time, independent of any observer; and 2)
the subjective-mystical experience of non-dualistic
unity of the world and the observer.

113. Jeans, Sir James. The New Background of Science.
      Cambridge: Cambridge University Press, 1933.
      The author suggests that the conceptual and theore-
      tical revolutions in the "new physics" of the twen-
      tieth century call for a revision of accepted modes
      of thought about nature "away from the materialism
      and strict determinism which characterized nine-
      teenth-century physics."

114. _____. Physics and Philosophy. Cambridge: Cam-
      bridge University Press, 1943.
      In a context of a historical discussion of issues
      leading to the new scientific revolution of Planck,
      Rutherford, Bohr, Heisenberg, de Broglie, Dirac,
      and others, the author attempts to reformulate some
      of the main problems in philosophy in light of these
      recent discoveries.

115. Johnson, Allison H. "Whitehead's Philosophy of His-
      tory." Journal of the History of Ideas, 7 (1946),
      234-249.
      Whitehead's is an inclusive philosophy of history,
      recognizing the causal efficacy of great thinkers and
      their ideas, as well as the influence of economic
      forces and the physical environment.

116. Jones, William B. "Bell's Theorem, H. P. Stapp,
      and Process Theism." Process Studies, 7/4 (Winter
      1977), 250-261.

117. Journal of Philosophy, 46/11 (1969), 307-355.
      Several philosophers discuss the implications of
      relativity theory.

118. Kennard, Kenneth Clifton. Whitehead's Contribution
      to Contemporary Discussion of the Nature of Meta-
      physics. Diss. Northwestern University, 1966.

119. Kline, George L. "Form, Concrescence and Concre-
      tum: A Neo-Whiteheadian Analysis." Southern
      Journal of Philosophy, 7/4 (Winter 1969), 351-360.

120. Leclerc, Ivor. "Whitehead's Transformation of the
      Concept of Substance." Philosophical Quarterly, 3
      (1953), 225-243.
      A comparison of the doctrine of substance in
      Whitehead and Aristotle.

121. _____. Whitehead's Metaphysics: An Introductory
      Exposition. London: George Allen and Unwin,
      1958.

122. _____. The Nature of Physical Existence. New
      York: Humanities Press, 1972.

123. _____. "The Necessity Today of the Philosophy of
      Nature." Process Studies, 3/3 (Fall 1973), 158-
      168.

124. Lindeman, F. A. The Physical Significance of Quan-
      tum Theory. Oxford: The Clarendon Press, 1932.

125. Lowe, Victor Augustus. Conceptions of Nature in the
      Philosophical Systems of Whitehead, Russell and
      Alexander. Diss. Harvard University, 1935.

126. _____. "The Development of Whitehead's Philosophy."
      The Philosophy of Alfred North Whitehead. Ed.
      Paul A. Schilpp. Evanston, Ill.: Northwestern
      University Press, 1941. Pp. 15-124.

127. _____. "The Influence of Bergson, James and
      Alexander on Whitehead." Journal of the History of
      Ideas, 10 (1949), 267-296.
           This is an authoritative discussion of unique ma-
      terial, available nowhere else. Impact of his three
      predecessors was more that of encouragement or
      sympathy with Whitehead's views, rather than "in-
      dispensable influence." The relationships of White-
      head and Bergson are occasionally overstressed and
      erroneous. There was considerable difference be-
      tween the two as regards pluralism, and Bergson's
      dualistic interpretation of reason.

128. _____. Understanding Whitehead. Baltimore: Johns
      Hopkins University Press, 1962.

129. _____; Hartshorne, C.; and Johnson, A. H. White-
      head and the Modern World: Three Essays. Bos-
      ton: Beacon Press, 1950.

130. *Lucas, George R., Jr. Two Views of Freedom in
      Process Thought: A Study of Hegel and Whitehead.
      Chico. Cal.: Scholars Press, 1979. [Intro, no.
      30]

131. McGilvary, E. B. "Dual Review: Eddington's <u>Nature</u>
      <u>of the Physical World</u> and <u>Science and the Unseen</u>
      <u>World.</u>" <u>Journal of Philosophy</u>, 27/7 (March 27,
      1930), 180-194.
         Evaluates Eddington's interpretation of the "new
      epistemology" entailed by quantum mechanics and
      Heisenberg's indeterminism. Eddington's discussion
      of quantum theory itself is lucid, but the reviewer
      complains that his espousal of panpsychism and
      theism bears no relation to his discussion at large,
      and is supported only by the vaguest passages. There
      appears to be more enthusiasm than care in Edding-
      ton's philosophy.

132. Martin, R. M. "On Hartshorne's 'Creative Synthesis'
      and Event Logic." <u>Southern Journal of Philosophy</u>,
      7/4 (Winter 1971), 399-410.

133. Muirhead, John H. <u>The Platonic Tradition in Anglo-</u>
      <u>Saxon Philosophy</u>. London: George Allen and Un-
      win, 1931.
         A detailed account of Hegelian idealism in Eng-
      land, the growth of personalism, and Bradley's
      philosophy. Author's thesis regarding American
      idealism is that James' famous anti-Hegelian article
      in <u>Mind</u> (1882), "On Some Hegelians," persuaded two
      young disciples of Hegel that Hegel must be "recast
      in a new form." These were Josiah Royce and
      C. S. Peirce. Discusses the affinities of Whitehead
      with Bradley on feelings, intuitions, and interrelated-
      ness. Whitehead, process philosophers, and Hegel
      continue the tradition of Plato in the West, with
      their respective philosophies of organism.

134. Murphy, A. "The Anticopernican Revolution." <u>Journal</u>
      <u>of Philosophy</u>, 26 (1929), 281-299.

135. Nobo, Jorge Luis. "Whitehead's Principle of Process."
      <u>Process Studies</u>, 4/4 (Winter 1974), 275-284.

136. _____. "Whitehead's Principle of Relativity." <u>Proc-</u>
      <u>ess Studies</u>, 8/1 (Spring 1978), 1-20.

137. _____. "Transition in Whitehead: A Creative Proc-
      ess Distinct from Concrescence." <u>International Philo-</u>
      <u>sophical Quarterly</u>, 19/3 (September 1979), 265-283.

138. Northrop, F. S. C. "The Theory of Relativity and the

First Principles of Science." Journal of Philosophy, 25/16 (August 2, 1928), 421-435.

Follows Eddington, Weyl, and Whitehead: Einstein's theory raises questions of interpretation, including an apparent transition to anti-materialism and the "mathematical idealism" of Plato. The new physics affirms these as primary: change, becoming, and events. Remaining central questions include an adequate interpretation of "change" in the absence of "matter" undergoing changes.

139. _____. "The Macroscopic Atomic Theory: A Physical Interpretation of the Theory of Relativity." Journal of Philosophy, 25/17 (August 16, 1928), 449-467.

Relativity entails an atomic theory, but the microscopic theory alone is insufficient. "Macroscopic" entities are also required to account for structure, organization, continuity and change. The "macroscopic atoms" are "organisms," or finite wholes: atoms, molecules, cells, organisms, the solar system and space-time universe exhibit properties not found entirely in their microscopic constituents.

140. _____. "Concerning the Philosophical Consequences of the Theory of Relativity." Journal of Philosophy, 27/8 (April 10, 1930), 197-210.

Relativity is a physical theory, referring to measurements (rods and clocks) attached to molar bodies in definite frames of reference. Nonetheless, the theory has tremendous philosophical implications, first clearly articulated by Whitehead in his attempt to develop a conceptual scheme more in keeping with the findings of relativity: viz., events and becoming. Differences between Whitehead, Eddington, and Einstein are explored.

141. _____. "The Unitary Field Theory of Einstein and Its Bearing on the Macroscopic Atomic Theory." The Monist, 40/3 (July 1930), 325-338.

Whitehead's concern with Einstein's relativity theory was that the non-uniformity of space-time destroyed both the meaning of measurement and the possibility of measuring. Thus, a metaphysical critique of the first principles of science became necessary. Einstein's subsequent attempts at a unified field theory seem to answer these concerns, and support a "macroscopic atomic theory" similar to the Greek view, without concepts of absolute space, time, or matter; rather, events are primary.

142. _____. "The Relation Between Time and Eternity."
     Proceedings of the 7th International Congress of
     Philosophy. Ed. Gilbert Ryle. Oxford: Oxford
     University Press, 1931. Pp. 100-105.

143. _____. Science and First Principles. New York:
     Macmillan, 1931.
     Mainly a detailed interpretation of relativity phys-
     ics and its philosophical interpretations.

144. _____. "Whitehead's Philosophy of Science." The
     Philosophy of Alfred North Whitehead. Ed. P. A.
     Schilpp. Evanston, Ill.: Northwestern University
     Press, 1941.

145. _____. Logic of the Sciences and the Humanities.
     New York: Macmillan, 1947.

146. _____. Man, Nature and God: A Quest for Life's
     Meaning. New York: Simon and Schuster, 1962.

147. Palter, Robert M. Whitehead's Philosophy of Science.
     Chicago: University of Chicago Press, 1960.

148. Peters, Eugene. Hartshorne and Neoclassical Meta-
     physics. Lincoln: University of Nebraska Press,
     1970.

149. Pols, Edward. Whitehead's Metaphysics: A Critical
     Examination of Process and Reality. Carbondale,
     Ill.: University of Southern Illinois Press, 1967.

150. Prior, A. N. Past, Present and Future. Oxford:
     Oxford University Press, 1967.

151. Reese, W. L., ed. Process and Divinity: The Hart-
     shorne Festschrift. LaSalle, Ill.: Open Court,
     1964.

152. Schilpp, Paul Arthur, ed. The Philosophy of Alfred
     North Whitehead. Evanston, Ill.: Northwestern
     University Press, 1941.

153. Schlegel, Richard. "Quantum Physics and Human
     Purpose." Zygon, 8/4 (September-December 1973),
     200-220.

154. Sherburne, Donald W., ed. A Key to Whitehead's
     Process and Reality. New York: Macmillan, 1966.

155. Shimony, Abner. "Quantum Physics and the Philosophy
     of Whitehead." Philosophy in America. Ed. Max
     Black. Ithaca, N.Y.: Cornell University Press,
     1965. Pp. 240-261.
     Demonstrates that Whitehead was relatively un-
     familiar with then-current developments in quantum
     theory, and suggests certain critical difficulties
     facing the philosophy of organism in reconciling its
     metaphysics with quantum mechanics.

156. Stapp, Henry Pierce. "Quantum Mechanics, Local
     Causality, and Process Philosophy." Process Studies,
     7/3 (Fall 1977), 173-182.

157. Synge, John L. The Relativity Theory of A. N. White-
     head. College Park, Md.: Institute for Fluid Dy-
     namics and Applied Mathematics, University of Mary-
     land, 1951.
     A formal mathematical treatment of Whitehead's
     theory of relativity, as compared with Einstein's.
     Intends to examine the claim of Eddington that
     Whitehead's theory can be shown to yield the same
     Schwarzchild differential equations which serve as
     the solution to Einstein's field equations in the General
     Theory of Relativity, without resorting to the non-
     linear differential equations of the General Theory.
     Synge demonstrates mathematically that Eddington's
     claim is indeed correct, then illustrates some of
     the differences between the Whiteheadian and the
     Einsteinian theories. For Whitehead, space and
     time are not arbitrarily non-uniform, as for Ein-
     stein: further, "c" is not constant throughout.
     Both theories yield identical results at the point of
     the Schwarzchild singularity, $r = km$. There is further
     formal agreement between the two theories with
     respect to particle orbits and light trajectories.

158. Wallack, F. Bradford. The Epochal Nature of Process
     in Whitehead's Metaphysics. Albany, N.Y.: State
     University of New York Press, 1980.
     A revisionist interpretation of the Whiteheadian
     "actual occasion," showing unintentional affinities
     with Northrop and Jonas: viz., that actual occasions
     can be any of a wide variety of macroscopic, en-
     during objects; they are not merely restricted to
     quantized, microscopic temporary phenomena.

159. Whitehead, Alfred North. Science and the Modern

World. "Lowell Lectures, 1925." New York: Macmillan, 1925.

160. _____. Religion in the Making. "Lowell Lectures, 1926." New York: Macmillan, 1926.

161. _____. Symbolism: Its Meaning and Effect. "Barbour-Page Lectures, 1927." New York: Macmillan, 1927.

162. _____. The Function of Reason. Princeton, N.J.: Princeton University Press, 1929.

163. _____. Process and Reality. "Gifford Lectures, 1927-28." New York: Macmillan, 1929.

164. _____. Adventures of Ideas. New York: Macmillan, 1933.

165. _____. Nature and Life. Chicago: University of Chicago Press, 1934.

166. _____. Modes of Thought. New York: Macmillan, 1938.

167. _____. "Mathematics and the Good." The Philosophy of Alfred North Whitehead. Ed. Paul Arthur Schilpp. Evanston, Ill.: Northwestern University Press, 1941. Pp. 666-681.

167a. _____. The Aims of Education. New York: Macmillan, 1959.

168. _____. The Interpretation of Science: Selected Essays. Ed. A. H. Johnson. Indianapolis, Ind.: Bobbs-Merrill, 1961.

169. Whittemore, Robert C. "The Americanization of Panentheism." Southern Journal of Philosophy, 7/1 (Spring 1969), 25-35.
     Discusses the definition of panentheism, and criticizes some of Hartshorne's views on this issue. Other American panentheists include John Fiske, Josiah Royce, and Whitehead.

170. [No entry.]

171. Wilcox, John T. "A Question from Physics for Certain Theists." Journal of Religion, 61 (1961), 293-300.

PART II: EVOLUTIONARY COSMOLOGY

The development of "evolutionary cosmologies," from the stand-point of the history of process thought, is by far the most significant and revealing episode in the genesis of the larger process tradition. The history of this distinctive school spans, and in a very real sense is, the history of modern speculative metaphysics in the process tradition in Europe and America.

Evolutionary cosmology is the milieu in which and from which Hegel formulated his dialectical concept of human historical and cultural evolution, even while rejecting as untenable then-current theories of natural evolution. His views in turn fathered both the personalist and English Hegelian traditions so akin in many respects to Whitehead.[1] Evolutionary cosmology deeply influenced, and indeed is strongly manifested in many representatives of the pragmatist tradition, notably C. S. Peirce, John Fiske, and to a slightly lesser degree in James and Dewey.[2] And the influence of this school, as mediated through Bergson, C. Lloyd Morgan, Jan Smuts, and Samuel Alexander, forms the background for the contemporary speculation of Whitehead, Hartshorne, Eddington, Heisenberg, and others in the school of process rationalism.

Finally, despite its profound influence on and strong similarities with these other schools of process thought, one finds in the troubled history of evolutionary cosmologies the sources of confusion and ambiguity in the process tradition as a whole--including the origins of many of the romanticized, idealized and fanciful interpretations of science and nature which frequently discredit the larger process tradition in the eyes of its more analytically-inclined critics.

Darwin's ability to exhibit biological evolution as a credible naturalistic[3] theory in 1859 provided, to be sure,

substantial impetus as well as a profound challenge to speculative thinkers. But the school of evolutionary cosmology
considerably antedates his work. Indeed, in the strangely-
persistent atmosphere of crisis and controversy still surrounding this issue, it seems prudent to recall that Darwin's contribution was not the evolutionary perspective, but the hypothesis of natural selection pertaining to the cause or means
of evolutionary development. Those who wave the flag of
religious orthodoxy must some day come to terms with the
fact that the question, then and now, was not whether, but
how evolution occurs. Their adversaries, waving the flag
of Galileo, however, must likewise come to terms with the
fact that Darwinism and neo-Darwinism represent merely
one family of alternative, scientifically credible and testable
hypotheses concerning the role of specific forms of causation
in the process of evolutionary development.[4] It is speculation
concerning the philosophical and theological implications of
the latter issue which, over the past two centuries, has
spawned the variety of evolutionary cosmologies considered
here as modes of process thought.[4a]

Roughly speaking, the period of evolutionary cosmologies
begins with Maupertuis, Diderot, Lamarck, Goethe and Robert
Chambers,[5] and spans some two centuries to its recent mani-
festations in the work of Teilhard de Chardin, Julian Huxley,
C. H. Waddington, Theodosius Dobzhansky, W. H. Thorpe,
and Rene Dubos.[6] Along the way, the movement in its
growth, demise, and resurgence includes a number of diverse
figures: 1) the ponderous English syncretist Herbert Spencer,
whose blending of Lamarck, Thomas Malthus, mechanistic
determinism and English utilitarianism under the auspices of
nineteenth-century progressivism helped to bring forth the
compelling monstrosity known as "social Darwinism";[7] 2)
the later Darwin, troubled by the apparent mathematical im-
probability of his earlier views on random variation, and
driven toward a degree of Lamarckian "process" interpretation of evolutionary development; 3) Darwin's friend, the
brilliant naturalist Thomas Huxley, who rejected both determinism and social Darwinism; and 4) the familiar "emergent
evolutionists" of the late nineteenth and early twentieth centuries, including Henri Bergson, Jan Smuts, Lecomte du
Noüy, and C. Lloyd Morgan.

Allowing for the tremendous variation in views which
these and lesser exponents of the school represent over so
long a span of time, the central thrust of the school--its
unifying thread--is symbolized in the attitude of its principal
founder, the French biologist Jean Baptiste Lamarck (1744-

1829). While the term "Lamarckism" normally conjures up
repugnant visions of "Aristotelian vitalism" and outmoded
theories regarding the inheritance of acquired traits in the
minds of contemporary biologists, this, as Charles Coulston
Gillispie notes, is both to miss and to misrepresent the significance of Lamarck's views.

> For Lamarck's theory of evolution was the last
> attempt to make a science out of the instinct, as old
> as Heraclitos [sic] and deeply hostile to Aristotelian
> ["substance"] formalization, that the world is flux
> and process, and that science is to study, not the
> configurations of matter, nor the categories of
> form, but the manifestations of that activity which
> is ontologically [more] fundamental [than] bodies in
> motion and species of being.... In both organic
> and inorganic nature, there is nothing but process
> linking the individual ... and the system or organi-
> zation ... into which it is temporarily cast. [8]

Lamarck, and most subsequent proponents of evolutionary cosmology, are further exhibited as exponents of
variations of the "Great Chain of Being'--that Romantic idea
of natural process and the "plenitude of nature," of which
A. O. Lovejoy has written so lucid and devastating a history. [9]

Gillispie suggests that this is no longer a familiar, or
even a recognizable point of view--although this is hardly the
case. Lovejoy, for example, suggested in the concluding chapter
of his William James Lectures that the creative evolution of
Bergson and Whitehead perpetuated a temporalized version of
the "Chain of Being" metaphysical tradition in the twentieth
century. Indeed, if anything, this Romantic view of nature--
with which Whitehead expressed so strong a sympathy[10]--
currently enjoys an unprecedented renaissance in the latter
part of the twentieth century. [11]

This broad interpretation of Lamarckism exerts an
obvious subsequent influence, not only on the school of evolutionary cosmology, but on the entire tradition of process
philosophy as well. This historical influence of Lamarckism
presents a profound challenge in the form of a formidible
dilemma, for the contemporary pursuit of process philosophy.
What is perhaps less adequately recognized is that the Lamarckian roots of process thought pose an equally serious
dilemma as well for critics of process thought from the
perspective of Anglo-American analytic philosophy. With

respect to the arguments represented in the bibliographical
selections accompanying this section, I shall endeavor to
state this dilemma as clearly as possible, in terms of four
main observations.

First, contemplating their present image in the mirror
of history, process philosophers cannot help but notice that
they are contemporary bearers of a longstanding metaphysical
tradition. The continuation of themes articulated by Diderot,
Lamarck and their romantic contemporaries to the present--
including interconnectedness or "organism," the teleological
order of nature, freedom, novelty, and progress--are not
only impressive but embarrassing precisely for their historical continuity. Those in the school of process rationalism,
for example, pride themselves on the alleged empirical bases,
as well as the internal coherence and logical rigor of their
speculations. The historical grounding of their cherished
themes in a tradition which is frequently portrayed as anti-
empirical, anti-intellectual or anti-rational, metaphorical
and romantically and fancifully descriptive, constitutes something of a scandal. Under the aegis of neo-Darwinians in
science, and analytic philosophers from G. E. Moore onwards, the ideas of order, structure, purpose, internal relatedness and freedom have been under heavy attack as (in
the words of Bertrand Russell), "those qualities which gov-
ernesses love." Little wonder, then, that the articulation
of these same themes, albeit on quite different grounds, is
nonetheless dismissed as so much speculative nonsense--a
mere anachronism, a throwback to the worst traditions of
nineteenth-century speculative thought.

Contemporary process philosophers, lacking a clear
historical self-understanding, have been particularly susceptible
to such criticisms, even as they have been frequently puzzled
by, and often even ignorant of them. They have assumed
that critics would examine process arguments on their own
merits, when in fact their views have been classified by
critics utilizing historical rather than logical categories.
Process views accordingly are dismissed as part of a tradition already proven unacceptable in the eyes of such critics.

Second, and as a consequence of this first observation, contemporary process thinkers in the rationalist tradition might be led to take refuge in their newfound history.
For if it is indeed the case that there are similarities between the two schools, so are there marked, distinctive differences.

The school of evolutionary cosmology had its birth in
the Romantic reaction to Newtonian-Laplacian science. If
it was the case, as Wordsworth had charged, that biologists
"murder to dissect," so it was perceived the case that mathe-
maticians, physicists, and logicians trivialized in order to
analyze. In Lamarck and Goethe, as in Hegel, one senses
a profound frustration with the reductionist and mechanistic
approaches to nature, yoked with the suspicion that the most
profound truths of nature escape this methodology.

Though many were theists, Lamarck and his followers
were no more hospitable to the old Christian "creationist"
hypothesis than they were to the "petty analysts." Instead,
their movement represents a recurrence to that mystical
tradition of the unity and benevolence of the cosmos as portrayed in Plato's Timaeus. And they were, by and large,
persuaded that mathematical and "mechanical" conceptualiza-
tions of this cosmos were nought but impoverished abstractions which failed to do justice to the experiential reality of
unity, harmony, creativity, purpose, and order.

These evolutionary cosmologists were, then, pantheists
in the tradition of Spinoza, the Greeks, and Sankara. Their
"science" was finally the science of Romantic mysticism,
rather than of the practicing scientists of their day, laboring
under the tutelage of Galileo, Newton, and Laplace. Small
wonder then, the hostility shown toward process thought by
the intellectual descendants of the latter group in early twentieth-century realism and logical empiricism. And how far
removed from the sensibilities of Whitehead, Hartshorne,
Eddington, Heisenberg, and Bohm--who perceived themselves
as members of this latter realist-logical empiricist camp,
dissenting merely over the implications of the delivery of
the empiricist approach.

The different emphases of evolutionary cosmologies
are best illustrated in contrast to Whitehead. Evolutionary
cosmologies tended to advocate the directedness and final
convergence of the evolutionary process, which for Whitehead was open-ended, entirely contingent, and indeterminate
regarding outcome. The evolutionists stressed the underlying
unity of evolutionary process, while Whitehead was a pluralist.
Process was itself continuous in evolution, whereas for Whitehead it was temporally quantized--epochal. Interestingly
enough, where Whitehead embraced the Platonism inherent
in the realist approach, there is no hint of any such doctrines
in the school of evolutionary cosmology, which tended toward

an explicit Aristotelianism and nominalism. What fascinated
Bergson, for example, was the experience of change, together with the observation (or intuition) of novelty and transi-
toriness or impermanence. Whitehead's doctrine of "eternal objects," as related to actual entities and their subjective aims, by
contrast, accounts for our experience of endurance, repetition
of pattern and form, and the ongoing causal efficacy of determinate actuality. Finally, the theism of the evolutionary
cosmologists, where manifested, tended more toward traditional
pantheism, rather than toward Whitehead's variation of panentheism.

     The major differences between the two schools, in
sum, are a tendency in evolutionary cosmologies toward
ontological (as well as epistemological) monism, and a stubborn (and perhaps unwarranted) faith in the unity, progress,
and convergence of evolution itself. These are hardly irreducible differences; indeed, in many respects, these are
disagreements among friendly colleagues. [12] But these differences do give a certain credence to the demand that the
rationalist school be judged independently, on the basis of its
unique contributions to the larger process tradition.   The
differences result from rather different assumptions about
the role of scientific investigation and explanation, as
well as from the divergent origins of the rationalist school
in contemporary physical and mathematical, rather than in
eighteenth- and nineteenth-century biological, sciences.

     Third, the process philosopher might well reverse
the challenge of his analytic critics, who tend to dismiss
his conjectures (especially those originating within the school
of evolutionary cosmology) as so much muddleheaded, un-
supportable nonsense.

     What, after all, is the adequate interpretation of na-
ture?   How are the natural world and the role of the human
agent in it finally to be understood?   And who is qualified
to deliver on this question?   Is it always the case that what
is the case can be said with precise logical clarity--or, as
Hegel and his followers in existentialism have claimed, is
it not sometimes the case that the most profound, complex
and significant truths defy such rigid and tidy conceptualiza-
tion?

     The criticisms I have suggested against the evolution-
ary cosmologists finally run the risk of simply dismissing
the members of this school as intellectually incompetent.   It
is surely possible that Bergson was mistaken on the issues of

élan vital and durée real, or that Morgan and Teilhard took
unwarranted liberties with biological evidence to build their
respective cases for emergence, progress, and evolutionary
convergence. What surely is not the case is that these and
other members of this school of process philosophy were
merely muddleheaded visionaries.

What is singularly frustrating in these analytic attacks
is their failure to account both for defection from their own
ranks, and for the intellectual prowess and consummate scientific expertise of many of those whom they criticize. While
it is surely the case, as Sir Julian Huxley noted,[13] that
Bergson was not fully competent in biology, his views cannot
be so easily dismissed without taking account of his articulate
defenders, who have accused Lovejoy, Russell, and other
critics of a serious misreading of Bergson, and defended
Bergson's conclusions regarding biology and physics.[14] When
one finds among the evolutionary cosmologists such competent
scientists as Rene Dubos, Theodosius Dobzhansky, Pierre
Teilhard, C. H. Waddington, W. H. Thorpe, and Charles
Birch it would seem prima facie that the school of evolutionary cosmology (as well as the tradition of process philosophy
as a whole) poses a dilemma regarding the adequate interpretation of nature equally as great for analytic philosophers as
that posed for process philosophy by the sharp and telling
criticisms of those same analytic thinkers.[14a]

It is apparent, then, that the issues joined in criticism
(often leading to unfortunate mutual antagonism) are genuine
dilemmas between legitimate philosophical approaches, not
merely cases of speculative thinkers proceeding stubbornly
in blind ignorance of allegedly "decisive" criticisms of their
efforts. This factor has been appreciated more clearly on
occasion by actual practitioners of the sciences these two
philosophical traditions seek to interpret. As a result, many
of those scientists are reluctant to lend support to either
side--revealing a disdain on their part for the relatively
trivial nature of much of what poses as "philosophy of science" in the analytic tradition, as well as a healthy skepticism regarding over-eager speculation on the "broader"
significance of their work.[15]

Fourth and finally, much of the debate just described
pertaining to the school of evolutionary cosmology was initiated by the neo-Darwinians in biology, in an effort to purge
their discipline of the last vestiges of outmoded Aristotelianism and Romantic, anthropomorphic fancy. This can be
portrayed (as Gillispie attempts to do) as a last-ditch defense

of the old Romantic Naturphilosophie against the final triumph
of the Newtonian-Darwinian worldview:

> Deep interests, then have been bound up with the
> view of nature which Lamarck expressed, deep
> interests and deep feelings.... And if one looks
> behind Lamarck into the 18th-century sense of na-
> ture, there too it will appear how his evolutionary
> theory is to be taken as a link between the En-
> lightenment and romanticism, and not as a way
> station between the Newtonian spirit and the Dar-
> winian.... Lamarck's writings are the last, though
> one of the most explicit, of a whole series of at-
> tempts, some sad, some moving, some angry, to
> escape the consequences for naturalistic humanism
> of Newtonian theoretical physics. For the signifi-
> cance of Newtonian physics for human affairs is
> that it has none. [16]

This challenging historical assessment illustrates the
effects which neo-Darwinist and analytic critics have achieved:
to portray the debate over cosmology as radically polarized,
and as settled in favor of the mechanist-reductionist interpretation.

In point of fact, such a view simply will not sustain
a careful analysis in its own right. We have had occasion
here to observe that the broad questions of cosmology and
philosophy of nature which the evolutionary cosmologists
joined not only remain unsettled, but are perhaps livelier in
the late twentieth century than at any time since the Roman-
tic-Transcendentalist period. The cosmological questions
will not disperse because they are lively, entertaining, vitally
important--and, in principal, answerable. [17] Indeed, the
interpretations offered by the neo-Darwinists are not so radically different from the Lamarckian tradition as is often
thought. A comparatively recent study for the University of
Chicago Centennial argues that, from the standpoint of contemporary science, Darwin and Lamarck both were correct
in stressing the different aspects of what turns out to be a
dialectical interaction between naturalistic contraints (Darwin) and organic self-activity (Lamarck). [18] A distinguished
Princeton biologist and president of the American Philosophical Association earlier had cited the final sanction of neo-
Darwinists in the replacement of "trivial, external teleology"
with the contemporary doctrines of holism, organism, and
reciprocal interdependence characteristic of the contemporary
biological and philosophical view. [19]

Through its own historical metamorphoses, then,
evolutionary cosmology is just as validly alive and contemporary as a distinctive school of process thought today as
when it originated in the controversies of eighteenth- and
nineteenth-century biological science.[20]

NOTES

(1) See below, parts III and V.

(2) Part IV below.

(3) "Naturalism" should not be confused here with the mechanistic and deterministic turn of some of the later
neo-Darwinians, such as Weismann and Lankester.
Darwin believed that random variation and natural
selection could account for evolutionary change, without appeals to vitalistic variations of "final cause."
At first he did not directly engage the larger "organism" and environmental holism questions of Lamarck.
Lacking the knowledge of Father Gregor Mendel's
studies of genetic inheritance, however, he was hard-
pressed to account for the relative endurance, stability,
and transmission of novel, successful traits on the
basis of a "blending" theory of genetic inheritance.
As Loren Eisley illustrates, this problem pushed Darwin further toward a Lamarckian position in later
years, emphasizing the holistic relation of organism
and environment in the production and transmission of
novelty. Cf. Loren Eisley, Darwin's Century: Evolution and the Men Who Discovered It (Garden City,
N. Y. : Doubleday, 1958), 199-231; see also Philip G.
Fothergill, Historical Aspects of Organic Evolution
(New York: Philosophical Library, 1953). For Dar-
win's views on teleology and "design" arguments in
evolution, consult his correspondence with Asa Gray
(Nov. 26, 1860) and a Dutch student (April 2, 1873):
The Life and Letters of Charles Darwin, ed. Francis
Darwin (New York: D. Appleton & Co. , 1888); Vol.
II, p. 146; Vol. I, p. 276; respectively.

(4) E. g. , to the current controversy between proponents of
neo-Darwinian "gradualism" and the implicitly neo-
Lamarckian thesis of "punctuated equilibrium" advocated by Harvard biologists Stephen Jay Gould and
Peter Williamson, one must add the most recent,
explicitly-Lamarckian, but fully testable hypothesis

of "formative causation" offered by Cambridge biologist
Rupert Sheldrake. These kinds of discussions and
debates ought not to be confused (as they frequently
are) with attacks upon evolution proper, or upon Darwin. Sheldrake, for example, is as critical of vitalistic as he is of mechanistic metaphysical intrusions
upon the domain of science. Cf. A New Science of
Life: The Hypothesis of Formative Causation. London: Blond & Briggs, 1981.

(4a) Cf. Loren Eisley, op. cit.; also Bentley Glass, Owsei
Temkin, and W. L. Strauss, Jr., eds: Forerunners
of Darwin: 1745-1859 (Baltimore: Johns Hopkins
University Press, 1959).

(5) Diderot, Lamarck, and Goethe all apparently employed
the term "organism" as a category of teleological
explanation in the contemporary "process" sense,
which Prof. Charles C. Gillispie summarizes, and
sharply criticizes as innately hostile to the rationality
of science: "Lamarck and Darwin in the History of
Science," in Glass, Temkin, Strauss, op. cit., 265-
291. These criticisms overlook the significant fact,
however, that this reformulation of the ancient Greek
notion of "organic" teleological explanation was intended
by all three men as an attack upon the deistic "external" design-final cause teleology in vogue among
their contemporaries, which itself followed from the
kind of mechanistic views of efficient causation which
Gillispie himself espouses, and attributes to Darwin.
Diderot may perhaps be credited with pioneering this
attack upon mechanistic teleology, while Lamarck is
among its most vigorous and significant exponents,
in turn influencing Goethe's views. See Lester G.
Crocker, "Diderot and Eighteenth-Century French
Transformism" pp. 114-143; Bentley Glass, "Maupertuis, Pioneer of Genetics and Evolution," pp. 51-83;
Arthur O. Lovejoy, "The Argument for Organic Evolu-
tion before the Origin of Species, 1830-1858," pp. 356-
414; and Prof. Gillispie's article cited earlier; in
Glass, Temkin, Strauss, op. cit. Cf. also Willy Hartner, "Goethe and the Natural Sciences," in Geothe:
A Collection of Critical Essays, ed. Victor Lange
(Englewood Cliffs, N.J.: Prentice-Hall, 1968), pp.
145-160. Joseph LeConte argues that Lamarck had
directly influenced Goethe, in Evolution: Its Nature,
Its Evidences, and Its Relation to Religious Thought
(New York: D. Appleton & Co., 1888). For an over-

view of the "Lamarckian" period in French and English
evolutionist thought, see C. Leon Harris, Evolution:
Genesis and Revelations, with Readings from Empe-
docles to Wilson (Albany, N. Y. : State University of
New York Press, 1981) chs. 5 and 6. For Robert
Chambers, see Milton Millhauser, Just Before Darwin
(Middletown, Conn.: Wesleyan University Press, 1959).
For the influence of Lamarck and Chambers on romantic and post-romantic biology generally, see Owsei
Temkin, "The Idea of Descent in Post-Romantic German Biology, 1848-1858," pp. 323-355; Arthur O.
Lovejoy, "Schopenhauer as an Evolutionist," pp. 415-
437; and Lovejoy's article on the history of evolution
cited earlier, pp. 356-414; in Glass, Temkin, Strauss,
op. cit.

(6)   E. g. , H. James Birx, Pierre Teilhard de Chardin's
Philosophy of Evolution (Springfield, Ill. : Thomas,
1972); Theodosius Dobzhansky, Mankind Evolving: the
Evolution of the Human Species (New Haven, Conn. :
Yale University Press, 1964); Rene Dubos, The Torch
of Life: Continuity in Living Experience (New York:
Simon & Schuster, 1962); Sir Julian Huxley, Evolu-
tion: the Modern Synthesis (New York: Harper and
Bros. , 1943); C. H. Waddington, The Strategy of the
Genes (New York: Macmillan, 1957); W. H. Thorpe,
Purpose in a World of Chance: A Biologist's View
(Oxford: Oxford University Press, 1978).

(7)   E. g. , in The Factors of Organic Evolution (New York:
Appleton, 1887) and Principles of Sociology (London,
1876). I do not mean to blame Spencer exclusively
for this foolishness. Darwin himself and, indeed, a
great many well-meaning but supercilious Victorian
scientists and philosophers (with the notable exception
of Alfred Wallace) supported this most unfortunate
example of the "naturalistic fallacy." Cf. Charles
Darwin, The Descent of Man, 2nd ed. (New York:
H. M. Caldwell, 1874), 642f. Cf. also John C.
Greene, Darwin and the Modern World View (Baton
Rouge, La.: Louisiana State University Press, 1961),
especially 97f. ; and Richard Hofstadter, Social Darwinism in American Thought, 1860-1915 (Philadelphia:
University of Pennsylvania Press, 1945).

(8)   "Lamarck and Darwin in the History of Science," in
Glass, Temkin, Strauss, op. cit. , 268f. , 272. In the
course of this brief historical survey and analysis, as

indicated above, Gillispie raises sharp criticisms and profound challenges to the adequacy of the process interpretation of nature.

(9) Arthur O. Lovejoy, The Great Chain of Being (Cambridge, Mass.: Harvard University Press, 1942).

(10) Cf. Science and the Modern World (SMW), ch. V: "The Romantic Reaction."

(11) Inasmuch as responsible, ecological (or holistic) metaphors for nature are often, at this writing, held hostage by a ridiculous array of popular fads, this "renaissance" is at best a mixed blessing for process philosophy.

(12) This is illustrated, for example, in the congenial contemporary debate among several process philosophers regarding whether or not Teilhard qualifies as a legitimate member of the tradition. Cf. Ian G. Barbour, "Five Ways of Reading Teilhard," The Teilhard Review, 3 (1968), 3-20, and "Teilhard's Process Metaphysics," Journal of Religion, 49 (April 1969), 136-159; Ewert Cousins, "Process Models in Culture, Philosophy and Theology," in Process Theology, ed. Ewert Cousins (New York: Newman Press, 1971); Robert T. Francoeur, Perspectives in Evolution (Baltimore: Helicon, 1965), and Evolving World, Converging Man (New York: Holt, Rinehart & Winston, 1970); Anthony Hanson, ed., Teilhard Reassessed (London: Darton, Longman & Todd, 1970); John Stephen Homlisk, God and the Cosmos According to Teilhard de Chardin and Alfred North Whitehead (Diss., McMaster University, 1975); Francis J. Klauder, Aspects of the Thought of Teilhard de Chardin (N. Quincy, Mass.: Christopher, 1971); and David B. Richardson, "The Philosophies of Hartshorne and Chardin: Two Sides of the Same Coin?" Southern Journal of Philosophy, 2 (Fall 1964), 107-115.

(13) Op. cit., p. 457f.

(14) Cf. Milic Capek, "Bergson's Theory of Matter and Modern Physics," Revue Philosophique, 77 (1953), and Bergson and Modern Physics: A Re-interpretation and Re-evaluation (Dordrecht, Holland: D. Reidel Publ. Co., 1971); Louis deBroglie, "The Con-

cepts of Contemporary Physics and Bergson's Ideas
on Time and Motion," in Bergson and the Evolution
of Physics, ed. P. A. Y. Gunter (Knoxville: University of Tennessee Press, 1969); for the critical com-
ment on Lovejoy's, Russell's and Santayana's "specious" interpretations of Bergson, cf. the editor's
introduction, p. 31f.; finally, David A. Sipfle, "Henri
Bergson and the Epochal Theory of Time," also in
the Gunter anthology.

(14a) Such problems in the formulation of an adequate philosophy of nature are the subject of a recent book by
Prof. Charles Birch (Biology, University of Sydney)
and John B. Cobb, Jr. (Theology, Claremont Graduate School), entitled: The Liberation of Life: From
the Cell to the Community (Cambridge: Cambridge
University Press, 1981).

(15) Cf., for example, the cautious assessments of the
following biologists: Francis Elliot, "The Creative
Aspect of Evolution," International Philosophical
Quarterly, 6 (June 1966), 230-247; Rayomnd J. Nagor,
The Wisdom of Evolution (Garden City, N. Y. : Double-
day, 1963); Ledyard G. Stebbins, The Basis of Pro-
gressive Evolution (Chapel Hill: University of North
Carolina Press, 1968). For this caution in historical
perspective, cf. the distinguished nineteenth-century
American naturalist Joseph LeConte, Evolution: Its
Nature, Its Evidences, and Its Relation to Religious
Thought (New York: D. Appleton & Co., 1888).

(16) C. C. Gillispie, loc. cit., p. 279.

(17) See Francis Elliott, "The Creative Aspect of Evolution,"
loc. cit.

(18) R. W. Gerald, "Becoming: The Residue of Change,"
in Evolution After Darwin, vol. II, ed. Sol Tax
(Chicago: University of Chicago Press, 1960), pp.
255-267.

(19) Edwin Grant Conklin, Man: Real and Ideal (New York:
Scribners, 1943).

(20) For an account of the Lamarckian resurgence in the
mid-20th century, consult: E. Aguirre, "Aspectos
filosóficos y teleológicos de la evolución," Review
of the University of Madred, 8 (1959), 445-531;

George W. Stocking, Jr. , "Lamarckianism in American Social Science: 1890-1955," Journal of the History of Ideas, 23/2 (April-June, 1962), 239-256; and C. H. Waddington, The Strategy of the Genes (New York: Macmillan, 1957). As mentioned in n. 4 above, the present controversy regarding "gradualism" versus "punctuated equilibrium," in a purely naturalistic sense, is a current example of this Lamarckian resurgence in biology. It is unfortunate that the concept "Lamarckism" has come to be associated in a purely polemical sense with such specious nonsense as Lysenkoism in the early U. S. S. R. , rather than with such substantive scientific disputes. Cf. C. Leon Harris, op. cit. , ch. 9.

II.   EVOLUTIONARY COSMOLOGY: BIBLIOGRAPHY

I do not attempt to provide in this work a comprehensive bibliography for the most prominent members of this school, Henri Bergson and Pierre Teilhard de Chardin. Interested readers are referred to the following:

Gunter, P. A. Y. Henri Bergson: A Bibliography. "Bibliographies of Famous Philosophers. " Bowling Green, Ohio: Philosophy Documentation Center, 1974.
McCarthy, Joseph M. Pierre Teilhard de Chardin: A Comprehensive Bibliography. "Garland Reference Library of the Humanities, Vol. 158. " New York: Garland Publishing Co. , 1981.

172.   Ackoff, Russell L. , and Emery, Fred E. On Purposeful Systems. Chicago: Aldine, 1972.

173.   Agar, W. E. "The Concept of Purpose in Biology. " The Quarterly Review of Biology, 13 (1938), 255-273.
          An analysis of the concept of purpose in evolution, focusing on the ambiguous experimental results of tests for Lamarckian hereditary properties.

174.   _____. A Contribution to the Theory of the Living Organism. 2nd ed. Cambridge: Cambridge University Press, 1951.

175. Aguirre, E. "Aspectos filosóficos y teleológicos de
      la evolución." Review of the University of Madrid,
      8 (1959), 445-531.

176. Armagnac, Christian d'. "De Bergson à Teilhard.
      La nature, l'homme et Dieu." Etudes, 320 (1964),
      166-177.

177. Ashforth, Albert. Thomas Henry Huxley. New York:
      Twayne, 1969.

178. Ayala, F. J. "Teleological Explanations in Evolution-
      ary Biology." Philosophy of Science, 37/1 (March
      1970), 1-15.

179. _____, and Valentine, James W. Evolving: The
      Theory and Processes of Organic Evolution. Menlo
      Park, Calif. : The Benjamin/Cummings Publ. Co. ,
      1979.

180. Barthelemy-Madaule, Madeleine. "Introduction à la
      methode chez Bergson et Teilhard de Chardin."
      Actes du 10 Congres des Sociétés philosophie de
      langue française. "Congres Bergson." Paris: Ar-
      mand Colin, 1959. Pp. 211-216.
          Compares the similar need of Bergson and Teil-
      hard to return to the "great metaphysical questions,"
      and to discover the true ground of Being and Truth.

181. _____. "Introduction à un rapprochement entre
      Bergson et Teilhard de Chardin." Les études berg-
      soniennes, 5 (1960), 65-81.

182. _____. "Bergson et Teilhard de Chardin." La
      parole attendue. Paris: Editions du Seuil, 1963.
      Pp. 116-131.

183. _____. Bergson et Teilhard de Chardin. Paris:
      Editions du Seuil, 1963.

184. Benz, Ernst. Evolution and Christian Hope. Trans.
      H. G. Frank. New York: Doubleday, 1966.
          A historical view of Christian concepts of creation
      and eschatological hope as these changed from the
      early church fathers to Teilhard. Argues that a
      continuous evolution of these concepts results in and
      supports Teilhard's views.

185. Bergson, Henri. <u>Duration and Simultaneity.</u> Trans.
     Leon Jacobson. Indianapolis, Ind.: Bobbs-Merrill,
     1964.

186. _____. "Cours du College de France: Philosophie
     moderne." <u>Archives du Collège de France,</u> 5 (1905),
     90; 7 (1907), 80.
     These notes document and discuss Bergson's
     courses, taught on Spencer's <u>First Principles</u> and
     <u>Principles of Psychology.</u>

187. _____. <u>Time and Free Will: An Essay on the
     Immediate Data of Consciousness.</u> Trans. F. L.
     Pogson. New York: Macmillan, 1910.

188. _____. <u>Matter and Memory.</u> Trans. N. M. Paul
     and W. S. Palmer. New York: 1911.

189. _____. <u>Creative Evolution.</u> Trans. Arthur Mitchell.
     New York: Henry Holt, 1913.
     Darwin's mechanistic interpretation of evolution
     fails to account for the emergence of novelty and
     ever-greater complexity in the evolutionary process.
     These are, rather, the manifestations of a radically
     creative vital impulse or life-force, discerned by
     means of intuitive introspection of living experience.

190. _____. <u>The Two Sources of Morality and Religion.</u>
     Trans. R. A. Audra and C. Brereton. New York:
     Henry Holt, 1935.

191. _____. <u>The Creative Mind.</u> Trans. Mabelle Andi-
     son. New York: Philosophical Library, 1946.

192. Biondi, A. "Teilhard and Bergson." <u>Teilhard Review,</u>
     (1973), 82-85.

193. Birch, L. Charles. "A Biological Basis for Human
     Purpose." <u>Zygon,</u> 8 (1973), 244-260.
     A biologist utilizes the categories of process
     philosophy to suggest new approaches to the concept
     of human purpose based upon an understanding of
     evolution.

194. _____, and Cobb, John B., Jr. <u>The Liberation of
     Life: From the Cell to the Community.</u> Cambridge:
     Cambridge University Press, 1981.
     The mechanistic model of life, dominant in the

Western world, is rejected in favor of a holistic,
organic, or "ecological" model, applicable from the
cell to human communities. The implications of
this view in a variety of fields are explored.

195. Birx, H. James. Pierre Teilhard de Chardin's Phi-
      losophy of Evolution. Springfield, Ill. : Thomas,
      1972.
      The four central principles of Teilhard's philosophy
      are monistic idealism, the evolution of consciousness
      to greater complexity, the existence of "critical
      thresholds" of consciousness, and the "Ω-point" as
      the goal of all reality. In comparing Teilhard with
      a large number of other evolutionary cosmologists,
      Birx suggests that Teilhard has gone "far beyond
      any other philosopher of evolution in trying to recon-
      cile the special sciences, philosophy, and theology."

196. Bjelland, Andrew G. "Bergson's Dualism in 'Time
      and Free Will.'" Process Studies, 4/2 (Summer
      1974), 83-106.

197. Blair, Thomas Albert. Two Evolutionary Theories:
      Neo-Darwinism and Teilhard de Chardin. Diss. St.
      John's University, 1972.

198. Bloch, B. G. "Koncepja ewolucji zycia u H. Bergsona
      i P. Teilharda de Chardin." [The Concept of Evolu-
      tion of Life According to Bergson and Teilhard de
      Chardin.] Studia philosophiae christianae, (1969),
      218-228.

199. Boulding, Kenneth E. Ecodynamics: A New Theory
      of Societal Evolution. Beverly Hills, Cal. : Sage,
      1978.

200. Buffon, Cuvier Lacepede. A Natural History of the
      Globe, of Man, and of Quadrupeds. 2nd ed. New
      York: J. P. Peaslee, 1834.

201. Bustos-Fierro, Raul. "Spencer et Bergson." Homenaje
      à Bergson. Córdoba, Argentina: Imprenta de la
      Universidad, 1936.

202. Cannon, H. Graham. "Darwin and Lamarck." Main
      Currents, 15 (May, 1959), 106-110.

203. Capek, Milic. "Process and Personality in Bergson's

Thought." Philosophical Forum, 17 (1959-60), 25-42.

204. Carr, H. W. The Philosophy of Change: A Study of the Fundamental Principles of the Philosophy of Bergson. London: Macmillan, 1914.

205. Carter, George Stuart. A Hundred Years of Evolution. New York: Macmillan, 1957.

206. Collins, James. "Darwin's Impact on Philosophy." Thought, 24 (June, 1959), 184-248.
    Darwin challenged the progressivism of the Enlightenment, and effectively destroyed Paley's version of teleology, leading to the agnosticism of Spencer and Thomas Huxley. Cites influence of Darwin on Peirce, Bergson, and Teilhard.

207. Conklin, Edwin Grant. The Direction of Human Evolution. New York: Scribners, 1922.

208. Crepin, Julien. "Zwei Vertreter der Evolutionslehre: Bergson und Teilhard de Chardin." Perspektiven der Zukunft, 3 (1969), 5-7.

209. Crocker, Lester G. "Diderot and Eighteenth-Century French Transformism." Forerunners of Darwin: 1745-1859. Eds. Bently Glass, Owsei Temkin, and W. L. Strauss. Baltimore: Johns Hopkins University Press, 1959. Pp. 114-143.

210. Crusafont Pairo, Miguel. "Neodarwinismo y ortogeneticismo: un intento de conciliación." Atlantida, 16 (1965), 395-401.

211. Darwin, Charles. On the Origin of Species. (1859) Cambridge, Mass.: Harvard University Press, 1964.

212. _____. The Descent of Man. New York: H. M. Caldwell, 1874.

213. Darwin, Erasmus. Zoonomia. Third Edition. London, 1801.
    Pt. I contains Charles Darwin's grandfather's first explicit ideas on biological evolution, suggesting independently a theory similar to Lamarck's.

214. Darwin, Francis, ed. The Life and Letters of Charles Darwin. 2 Vols. New York: D. Appleton, 1888.

215. D'Aurec, Pierre. "De Bergson spencerien à l'auteur
      de l'Essai." Archives de Philosophie, 17/1 (1947),
      102-121.
        Chronicles Bergson's early intellectual develop-
      ment, including the influence of Herbert Spencer.

216. Delaney, C. F. "Bergson on Science and Philosophy."
      Process Studies, 2/1 (Spring 1972), 29-43.

217. Delfgaauw, Bernard. Evolution: The Theory of Teil-
      hard de Chardin. Trans. Hobert Hoskins. Intro.
      by Bernard Towers. New York: Harper & Row,
      1969.

218. Devaux, Andre-A. "Bergson et Teilhard de Chardin."
      Cahiers Universitaires Catholiques, 2 (November
      1964), 116-120.

219. Dewey, John. "Evolution and Ethics." The Monist,
      8/3 (April 1898), 321-341.

220. _____. "The Evolutionary Method as Applied to
      Morality: Its Scientific Necessity." Philosophical
      Review, 11/2 (March 1902), 107ff.

221. _____. "The Philosophical Work of Spencer."
      Philosophical Review, 13/2 (March 1904), 159ff.

222. _____. The Influence of Darwin on Philosophy and
      Other Essays in Contemporary Thought. New York:
      Henry Holt, 1910.
        Dewey claims that Darwin's impact on philosophy
      shifted its focus from permanence to change and
      process, from design to the role of chance and ran-
      domness, and from finality regarding ultimate (and
      unanswerable) questions to the empirical or instru-
      mental approach to practical problems.

223. _____. "Spencer and Bergson." Edited with French
      trans. by Gérard Deledalle. Revue de Metaphysic
      et de Morale, 70/3 (1965), 325-333.
        An analysis of the close relationships in the thought
      of Spencer and Bergson.

224. Diderot, Denis. Pensées sur l'interpretation de la
      Nature. Paris, 1754.
        Hints at the transformist hypothesis concerning
      the evolutionary development of new species.

225. Dobzhansky, Theodosius. Evolution, Genetics and Man. New York: John Wiley, 1955.

226. _____. The Biological Basis of Human Freedom. New York: Columbia University Press, 1956.

227. _____. "Variation and Evolution." Proceedings of the American Philosophical Society, 103 (1959), 252-263.
A process view of evolution: the process of evolution is not random, but directed through the activity and the production of novelty by finite organisms.

228. _____. Mankind Evolving: The Evolution of the Human Species. New Haven, Conn.: Yale University Press, 1964.
A distinguished biologist and theorist of evolution assesses sympathetically but critically the contributions of Teilhard.

229. _____. The Biology of Ultimate Concern. New York: New American Library, 1967.

230. _____. "Teilhard de Chardin and the Orientation of Evolution." Zygon, 3/3 (1968), 242-258.

231. _____. Genetics and the Evolutionary Process. New York: Columbia University Press, 1970.

232. _____; Ayala, F. J.; Stebbins, G.; Valentine, J. Evolution. San Francisco: W. H. Freeman, 1977.

233. _____, and Thorpe, W. H. "Wissenschaftlicher über Teilhard--der Paläontologe J. Piveteau, Paris; der Biologe T. Dobzhanski, New York; der Verhaltensforscher W. H. Thorpe, Cambridge." Perspektiven der Zukunft, 3 (1970), 2-6.

234. Driesch, Hans. The Science and Philosophy of Organism. London: Adam and Charles Black, 1908.

235. _____. The History and Theory of Vitalism. Trans. C. H. Ogden. New York: Macmillan, 1914.

236. Dubos, Rene. The Torch of Life: Continuity in Living Experience. New York: Simon & Schuster, 1962.
Discusses purpose, the "open future" of possibilities and adventure as intergral themes, as well as

the resurgence and viability of teleological explanation in biology. Notes with amusement the attempts
of colleagues in biology, such as Jacques Monod,
to deny what they simultaneously employ so effectively
as forms of teleological explanation.

237. _____. Beast or Angel: Choices That Make Us
Human. New York: Scribners 1974.

238. Eisley, Loren. Darwin's Century: Evolution and the
Men Who Discovered It. Garden City, N. Y. : Doubleday, 1958.
A thorough and scholarly historical analysis of
Darwin's significance, the controversies between
later neo-Lamarckians and neo-Darwinists, and the
contributions of Gregor Mendel, Thomas Huxley,
Haeckel, Wallace, Weissman and others of Darwin's
contemporaries. Especially strong on the assessment of Darwin and Lamarck.

239. Elliot, Francis. "The Creative Aspect of Evolution."
International Philosophical Quarterly, 6 (June 1966),
230-247.
A biochemist surveys the knowledge of biochemical
evolutionary processes, and finds reason to affirm
spontaneity, but in a manner which is deliberately
creative rather than chaotically random. The influence of Teilhard is cited.

240. Eto, Taro. "Ningen jitsuzon no fuan to sentaku--
Teilhard de Chardin no genshogakuteki kosatsu ni
okeru." [Anxiety and Choice in Human Existence
According to the Phenomenological Analysis of Teilhard de Chardin.] Ningenron no shomondai. [Prob-
lems of Anthropology.] Tokyo: Sophia University,
1968. Pp. 91-127.

241. Fellows, Otis E. , and Milliken, Stephen F. Buffon.
New York: Twayne Publ. , 1972.

242. Fisch, Max H. "Evolution in American Philosophy."
Philosophical Review, 56 (July 1947), 357-373.

243. Forsyth, T. M. "Creative Evolution in its Bearing
on the Idea of God." Philosophy, 25 (1950), 195-
208.

244. Fothergill, Philip G. Historical Aspects of Organic

<u>Evolution</u>. New York: Philosophical Library, 1953.
A dry, encyclopedic treatment of history, debates
and controversies surrounding evolution. Argues
that Darwin was midway between the later neo-Darwinist and neo-Lamarckian positions. True Darwinism thus contains portions of Lamarck's theory.
Darwin's vitalist views are correlated with Bergson,
and compared in turn with Aristotle's <u>entelechia</u>, as
representative of modern attempts to generalize
evolutionist theories to include the entire cosmos.

245. Francoeur, Robert T. <u>Perspectives in Evolution</u>.
Baltimore: Helicon, 1965.

246. _____. Evolving World, Converging Man. New
York: Holt, Rinehart & Winston, 1970.
A well-known biologist, cultural psychologist and
philosopher gives a sympathetic assessment of Teilhard's views.

247. Furlong, Guillermo. "Carlos Darwin y Teilhard de
Chardin." <u>Anales de la Academia Argentina de</u>
<u>geografía</u>, 3 (1959), 15-19.

248. Gabriel, Leo. "Evolution und Zeitsbegriff, von H.
Bergson zu Teilhard de Chardin." <u>Wissenschaft und</u>
<u>Weltbild</u>, 15 (1962), 31-36.

249. Gerald, R. W. "Becoming: The Residue of Change."
<u>Evolution After Darwin</u>. 3 Vols. "The University
of Chicago Centennial." Ed. Sol Tax. Chicago:
University of Chicago Press, 1960. Pp. 255-267.

250. Gillispie, Charles Coulston. <u>Genesis and Geology</u>.
Cambridge: Harvard University Press, 1951.

251. _____. "Lamarck and Darwin in the History of
Science." <u>Forerunners of Darwin: 1745-1859</u>. Eds.
Bently Glass, Owsei Temkin, and W. L. Strauss.
Baltimore: Johns Hopkins University Press, 1959.
Pp. 265-291.

252. Glass, Bentley. "Maupertuis, Pioneer of Genetics
and Evolution." <u>Forerunners of Darwin: 1745-1859</u>.
Eds. Glass, Temkin, Strauss. Baltimore: Johns
Hopkins University Press, 1959. Pp. 51-83.

253. _____; Temkin, Owsei; Strauss, W. L., Jr.;

eds. Forerunners of Darwin: 1745-1859. Baltimore: Johns Hopkins University Press, 1959.
Important essays on the intellectual history of
evolutionist theories, as well as evolutionist cosmologies, assessing the contributions of Diderot, Buffon,
Maupertuis, Lamarck, Kant, Schopenhauer, Goethe,
and many others.

254. Goldschmidt, Richard. The Material Basis of Evolution. New Haven, Conn.: Yale University Press,
1940. Rev. ed. 1982.

255. Gosztonyi, Alexander. "Bergson und Teilhard." Perspektiven der Zukunft, 2 (1972), 7-9.

256. Grant, Verne. Organismic Evolution. San Francisco:
W. H. Freeman, 1977.
Harshly critical of Bergson, Teilhard and "orthogenesis," which is not a scientific hypothesis, but
"mystical name-calling." There is no scientific
evidence whatever for orthogenesis in any of its
variations in the modern theory of synthetic evolution.
Orthoselection, stressing organic-environment interaction of sufficient duration to reveal trends which
follow environmental shifts, replaces ortho-genesis.
The latter anachronism is still of interest to literary
intellectuals and religious philosophers intent on
discerning the working of purpose in the evolutionary
process.

257. Grau, Joseph A. Morality and the Human Future in
the Thought of Pierre Teilhard de Chardin. Madison,
N.J.: Fairleigh Dickinson Press, 1976.

258. Greene, John Coulton. "Biology and Social Theory in
the Nineteenth Century: August Comte and Herbert
Spencer." Critical Problems of the History of Science. Ed. Marshall Claggett. Madison, Wisc.:
University of Wisconsin Press, 1959.

259. _____. Darwin and the Modern World View. Baton
Rouge, La.: Louisiana State University Press, 1961.

260. Guitton, Jean. "Teilhard et Bergson." Profils paral-
leles. Paris: Fayard, 1970. Pp. 401-457.

261. Gunn, J. A. Bergson and His Philosophy. London:
Methuen, 1920.

262. Haber, Francis C. "Fossils and the Idea of a Process
      of Time in Natural History." Forerunners of Dar-
      win: 1745-1859. Eds. Glass, Temkin, Strauss.
      Baltimore: Johns Hopkins University Press, 1959.
      Pp. 222-264.

263. Habermehl, Lawrence LeRoy. Value in the Evolution-
      ary World: Views of Samuel Alexander, C. Lloyd
      Morgan, and Pierre Teilhard de Chardin. Diss.
      Boston University, 1967.

264. Haldane, J. S. Mechanism, Life and Personality.
      London: John Murray, 1913.

265. Hardy, Sir Alister. The Living Stream. New York:
      Harper & Row, 1965.

266. Harris, C. Leon. Evolution: Genesis and Revelations,
      with Readings from Empedocles to Wilson. Albany,
      N. Y.: State University of New York Press, 1981.
          Biographical and critical analysis of historical
      topics and issues in evolution, coupled with useful
      selections from important primary sources.

267. Hartner, Willy. "Goethe and the Natural Sciences."
      Goethe: A Collection of Critical Essays. Ed. Victor
      Lange. Englewood Cliffs, N. J.: Prentice-Hall,
      1968. Pp. 145-160.

268. Hofstadter, Richard. Social Darwinism in American
      Thought, 1860-1915. Philadelphia: University of
      Pennsylvania Press, 1945.

269. Hull, David L. Darwin and His Critics. Cambridge,
      Mass.: Harvard University Press, 1973.

270. Huxley, Sir Julian. Evolution: The Modern Synthesis.
      London: Harper & Bros, 1943.
          Bergson's "vital impulse" can serve as a sym-
      bolic, but not as a scientific description of evolution.
      Bergson was a writer of great vision, but little bio-
      logical understanding. C. Lloyd Morgan's principle
      of "organic selection" replaces the Lamarckian em-
      phasis on inheritance of acquired traits, by partici-
      pating in molding environments to favor selection and
      survival of certain genetic traits. Thus, evolutionary
      change is not completely at random.

271. _____. Evolution in Action. New York: Harper
      & Bros., 1953.

272. _____, and Kettlewell, H. B. D. Charles Darwin
      and His World. New York: The Viking Press, 1965.

273. Huxley, Thomas Henry. Man's Place in Nature. New
      York: D. Appleton, 1903.

274. Irvine, William. Apes, Angels and Victorians. New
      York: McGraw-Hill, Inc., 1955.

275. Isaye, Gaston. "Bergson et Teilhard de Chardin."
      Bulletin de la Société française de philosophie, 53
      (1959), 167-169.
      The role of Bergson's "intuition" in aspects of
      Teilhard's thought is examined.

276. Jantsch, Erich. The Self-Organizing Universe: Sci-
      entific and Human Implications of the Emerging
      Paradigm of Evolution. New York: Pergamon,
      1980.
      A sophisticated evolutionary process cosmology
      by a distinguished Viennese physicist and general
      systems theorist.

277. _____, and Waddington, C. H., eds. Evolution and
      Consciousness: Human Systems in Transition. Read-
      ing, Pa.: Addison-Wesley, 1976.

278. Johnstone, James. The Philosophy of Biology. Cam-
      bridge: Cambridge University Press, 1914.

279. Koestler, Arthur, and Smythies, J., eds. Beyond
      Reductionism: New Perspectives in the Life Sci-
      ences. London: Hutchinson, 1969.

280. Kopp, Joseph V. Teilhard de Chardin: A New Syn-
      thesis of Evolution. Glen Rock, N.J.: Paulist
      Press, 1964.

281. Krutch, Joseph Wood. The Great Chain of Life. Bos-
      ton: Houghton Mifflin, 1956.

282. Lamarck, Jean Baptiste Pierre Antoine de Monet de.
      Philosophie zoologique. Trans. Hugh Elliot. New
      York: Macmillan, 1914.

Describes evolution in transformist terms, as a
response of individual organisms to new needs created
by the environment.

283. LeCam, Lucian M., ed. Proceedings of the Sixth
Berkeley Symposium on Mathematical Statistics and
Probability. Berkeley: University of California
Press, 1972.
Essays discuss the statistical aspects of Darwinian and non-Darwinian evolution. By the latter term
is meant only theories such as the "random drift"
of genetic mutations (Sewall Wright) rather than the
orthogenesis or telefinalism of Lamarck, Osborn,
and Teilhard.

284. LeConte, Joseph. Evolution: Its Nature, Its Evidences,
and Its Relation to Religious Thought. New York:
D. Appleton, 1888.
A remarkably thorough, balanced and impartial
account of evolutionist theories, evidence and implications by a distinguished nineteenth-century American geologist and professor of natural history. Refers
briefly to the effect of Lamarck's Philosophy of Zo-
ology (1809) on Goethe and Comte. Vitalism is
decisively rejected, as is any implied logical connection between evolution and materialism. Suggests
in conclusion a necessary outline for any future natural theology.

285. LeMorvan, Michael. Pierre Teilhard de Chardin:
Priest and Evolutionist. London: Catholic Truth
Society, 1965.
An 18-page tractate defending Teilhard's synthesis
of evolution and Christian thought.

286. Lewes, George Henry. The Life of Goethe. New
York: E. P. Dutton, 1864.

287. Licorish, R. F. "Bergson's Creative Evolution and
the Nervous System in Organic Evolution." Lancet,
182 (February 10, 1912), 391f.
This medical article criticizes Bergson's doctrine
from a Lamarckian perspective.

288. Lovejoy, Arthur O. The Great Chain of Being. "William James Lectures, 1933." Cambridge, Mass.:
Harvard University Press, 1942.

289. _____. "Buffon and the Problem of Species." Fore-
     runners of Darwin: 1745-1859. Eds. Glass, Tem-
     kin, Strauss. Baltimore: Johns Hopkins University
     Press, 1959. Pp. 84-113.

290. _____. "Kant and Evolution." Forerunners of
     Darwin: 1745-1859. Eds. Glass, Temkin, Strauss.
     Baltimore: Johns Hopkins University Press, 1959.
     Pp. 173-206.

291. _____. "The Argument for Organic Evolution Be-
     fore the Origin of Species, 1830-1858." Forerunners
     of Darwin: 1745-1859. Eds. Glass, Temkin, Strauss.
     Baltimore: Johns Hopkins University Press, 1959.
     Pp. 356-414.

292. _____. "Schopenhauer as an Evolutionist." Fore-
     runners of Darwin: 1745-1859. Eds. Glass, Tem-
     kin, Strauss. Baltimore: Johns Hopkins University
     Press, 1959. Pp. 415-437.

293. McDougall, William. Modern Materialism and Emerg-
     ent Evolution. London: Methuen, 1934.
     An unfavorable analysis of Lloyd Morgan's thesis
     of emergent evolution by a colleague in biology, who
     accuses Morgan of disguised materialism.

294. McGinnis, Thomas Michael. Julian Huxley's Evolution-
     ary Ethics: Its Account of the Ethical 'Ought'. Diss.
     St. Louis University, 1971.
     Compares Teilhard's concept of the open future
     and teleology with Huxley's use of modern "synthetic"
     evolution as possible grounds for moral philosophy.

295. McKinney, H. Lewis. Wallace and Natural Selection.
     New Haven, Conn.: Yale University Press, 1972.

296. Malinow, Carlos A. "Finalidad y determinismo en los
     sistemas evolutivos de Pierre Teilhard y Henri Berg-
     son." Dialogos, 2/4 (1965), 111-131.

297. Maupertuis, Pierre-Louis Moreau de. The Earthly
     Venus (1745). Trans. S. B. Boas. New York,
     1966.
     Discusses origins of new races or species through
     chance variations, preserved in favorable environ-
     ments, and transmitted via genetic "particles" to
     descendents.

298. Melsen, Andreas Gerardos Maria van. Evolution and
      Philosophy. Pittsburgh, Pa.: Duquesne University
      Press, 1965.

299. Millhauser, Milton. Just Before Darwin: Robert
      Chambers and Vestiges. Middletown, Conn.: Wes-
      leyan University Press, 1959.
      Discussion of the origins and influence of Cham-
      bers' Vestiges of the Natural History of Creation,
      a work of "popular" science whose larger purpose,
      in light of Lamarck's efforts, was to re-assess the
      meaning of science for humankind.

300. Millikin, Robert Andrews. Evolution in Science and
      Religion. New Haven, Conn.: Yale University
      Press, 1927.

301. Montague, William P. "A Materialistic Theory of
      Emergent Evolutionism." Essays in Honor of John
      Dewey. New York: Holt, Rinehart & Winston,
      1929. Pp. 257-273.
      Against mechanism, vitalist dualism and emergent
      evolutionism (principally that of Samuel Alexander),
      Montague argues that evolutionary emergence and
      personal freedom can be explained wholly in terms
      of naturalistic, physical categories.

302. Morgan, Conway Lloyd. Instinct and Experience.
      London: Methuen, 1885.

303. _____. "Three Aspects of Monism." The Monist,
      4/3 (April 1894), 321-332.
      Attempts to correct confusion over discussion of
      monism by attributing three meanings to the term:
      1) as the opposite of the dualism of subjective ideal-
      ism, monism implies that subjects and objects are
      distinguishable aspects of one reality; 2) as applied
      to organism and evolution, monism implies that man
      and nature are not distinct or wholly unrelated; 3)
      as applied to psychology and epistemology, monism
      implies the identity of physical brain states and con-
      sciousness.

304. _____. "Physical and Metaphysical Causation."
      The Monist, 8/2 (January 1898), 230-249.

305. _____. "Philosophy of Evolution." The Monist,
      8/4 (July 1898), 481-501.

306.   _____. "Vitalism." The Monist, 9 (1899), 179-
        196.
        Protests against the anti-scientific, dualistic mys-
        ticism of most proponents of vitalism. Discusses
        some of the alleged "mysteries" (such as chiral
        asymmetry in organic molecules), exposes the vacuity
        of "vitalist" explanations of these phenomena, and
        presents some purely naturalistic explanations that
        might account for peculiar organic observations.

307.   _____. "Biology and Metaphysics." The Monist,
        9/4 (July 1899), 538-562.

308.   _____. Interpretation of Nature." The Contemporary
        Review, 87 (May 1905), 609-627.

309.   _____. Spencer's Philosophy of Science. Oxford:
        The Clarendon Press, 1913.
        Spencer is portrayed as an advocate of a highly
        unsatisfactory, scientifically obscurantist vitalism.

310.   _____. Emergent Evolution. London: Williams
        and Norgate, 1923.
        Mechanistic views of evolution cannot account for
        novelty. Traditional vitalistic views are scientifically
        unsound. An "emergent" is an entirely novel event
        in the evolutionary process, whose appearance can-
        not be explained in terms of rearrangement of pre-
        viously-existing biological components. By contrast,
        "resultants" are new qualities which can be so ex-
        plained, and thus represent evolutionary continuity.
        The totality of evolutionary development is com-
        prised of both the continuous and the discontinuous
        processes.

311.   _____. "A Philosophy of Evolution." Contemporary
        British Philosophy, Vol. I. Ed. J. H. Muirhead.
        London: George Allen & Unwin, 1924. Pp. 271-
        306.
        Morgan outlines the differences between his thesis
        of emergent evolution, and the earlier views of
        Samuel Alexander and Henri Bergson, suggesting his
        own antecedents are primarily the influence of Thomas
        Huxley.

312.   _____. Life, Mind and Spirit. London: Williams
        and Norgate, 1926.

313.　　　　　. "Mind in Evolution." Creation by Evolution.
　　　　Ed. Frances Mason. New York: Macmillan, 1928.
　　　　Contrasts evolution with "dissolution" (entropy).
　　　　Reality consists entirely of different states of flowing
　　　　events, which exhibit an upward and progressive ad-
　　　　vance. Minds are products of this creative process,
　　　　whose culmination is God. Morgan cites with ap-
　　　　proval both Whitehead's Science and the Modern
　　　　World, and Jan Smuts' Holism and Evolution.

314.　　　　　. Mind at the Crossroads. London: Williams
　　　　and Norgate, 1929.

315.　　　　　. The Emergence of Novelty. London: Wil-
　　　　liams and Norgate, 1933.

316.　　　　　. "The Ascent of Mind." The Great Design.
　　　　Ed. F. Mason. New York: Macmillan, 1934. Pp.
　　　　115-134.

317. Nagor, Raymond J. *"From the Fact of Evolution to
　　　　the Philosophy of Evolutionism." The Thomist, 24
　　　　(April-October 1961), 463-501.

318.　　　　　. The Wisdom of Evolution. Garden City,
　　　　N. Y.: Doubleday, 1963.
　　　　A biologist and Catholic priest supports evidence
　　　　for biological evolution, but cautions against over-
　　　　eager philosophical and theological interpretations,
　　　　such as Teilhard's.

319. Neville, Robert C. "Nine Books by and about Teil-
　　　　hard." Journal of the American Academy of Re-
　　　　ligion, 37/1 (1969), 71-82.

320. Noble, Edmund. Purposive Evolution. New York:
　　　　Henry Holt, 1926.
　　　　Defends an organic, holistic view of nature and
　　　　evolution, but criticizes Bergson's vitalism and te-
　　　　leology as useless. Many uses of teleology exhibit
　　　　merely man's "ineradicable tendency to read into
　　　　the universe and its processes the life, will, con-
　　　　sciousness or personality ... which he finds in him-
　　　　self."

321. Northrop, F. S. C. "Evolution in Its Relation to the
　　　　Philosophy of Nature and the Philosophy of Culture."
　　　　Evolutionary Thought in America. Ed. S. Pearsons.

New Haven, Conn.: Yale University Press, 1950.
Pp. 44-84.

322. Noüy, Lecomte du. Human Destiny. New York:
      Longmans, Green & Co., 1947.
      An internationally-renowned French scientist offers
      an assessment of the improbable, "anti-chance" as-
      pects of the evolutionary process, suggesting his
      thesis of "telefinalism."

323. Oresme, Nicolas de. "Darwin y Teilhard de Chardin."
      Abside, 29 (1965), 336-341.

324. Osborn, Henry F. The Origin and Evolution of Life.
      New York: Scribners, 1923.

325. Paradis, James G. T. H. Huxley: Man's Place in
      Nature. Lincoln: University of Nebraska Press,
      1978.
      A critical edition of Huxley's seminal philosophical
      work of evolutionary cosmology.

326. Paskai, Laszlo. "Weltbild und Teleologie bei Teilhard.
      Zur Rolle der Teleologie in einer konvergierenden
      Evolution." Acta teilhardiana, 1 (1970), 24-31.

327. Pomeau, Rene. Diderot: Sa Vie, Son Oeuvre. France:
      Presses Universitaires de France, 1967.

328. Potter, Van R. "Teilhard de Chardin and the Concept
      of Purpose." Zygon, 3 (December 1968), 367-376.

329. Sellars, Roy Wood. "Emergent Evolution: the New
      Philosophy of Nature." Scribner's Magazine, 87
      (January-June 1930), 316-325.
      Emergent evolutionism, a hypothesis held by a
      growing number of English and American scientists
      and philosophers, offers a viable alternative both to
      scientific mechanism and philosophic dualism.

330. Sheldrake, Rupert. A New Science of Life: The Hy-
      pothesis of Formative Causation. London: Blond
      & Briggs, 1981.
      A British biologist attacks the hidden vitalism
      and telefinalism inherent in the supposed naturalistic
      attempts at genetic reductionism, criticizing as well
      the privileged position of ad hoc metaphysical assump-
      tions of mechanism and materialism in the present

practice of biological science. He distinguishes
energetic causation (i. e. , efficient or mechanical
causation) from a new hypothesis of "formative"
causation, depicting the cumulative power of the
past. In so doing, Sheldrake proposes a new type
of physical field which might play a role in the development of new forms in evolution. What distinguishes this revised suggestion of Lamarckian "emergent evolution," however, is that Sheldrake proposes
a number of testable consequences of his theory,
and re-interprets the past results of neo-Lamarckian
experiments by William McDougall, F. A. E. Crew,
and W. E. Agar, suggesting that these collectively
tend to confirm his new hypothesis of formative
causation.

331. Sherrington, Sir Charles. Goethe on Nature and on
     Science. Cambridge: Cambridge University Press,
     1949.

332. Simpson, George G. The Meaning of Evolution. New
     Haven, Conn. : Yale University Press, 1949.

333. _____. The Major Features of Evolution. New
     York: Columbia University Press, 1969.

334. Smuts, Jan C. Holism and Evolution. New York:
     Macmillan, 1926.
     An uncompromisingly pluralistic statement of the
     holistic evolution hypothesis. The universe is dy-
     namic; its fundamental character is to be active in
     the production of finite wholes. Such activity is not
     purposive or directed (beyond the individual patterns
     of organization and maintenance of the wholes them-
     selves), and Smuts accordingly rejects any notion
     of finalism or all-inclusive holism.

335. Spencer, Herbert. First Principles. London: 1862.

336. _____. Principles of Biology. London: 1864.

337. _____. Principles of Psychology. London: 1870.

338. _____. Principles of Sociology. London: 1876.

339. _____. The Factors of Organic Evolution. New
     York: Appleton, 1887.

340. Stansfield, William D. The Science of Evolution. New
      York: Macmillan, 1977.

341. Stebbins, G. Ledyard. Processes of Organic Evolution.
      "Concepts of Modern Biology Series." Englewood
      Cliffs, N. J.: Prentice-Hall, 1966.

342. _____. The Basis of Progressive Evolution. "Har-
      relsen Lectures." Chapel Hill: University of North
      Carolina Press, 1968.
      A noted biologist interprets contemporary theories
      and prospects for evolutionism. Very flattering of
      Teilhard's approach, as "one of the first evolution-
      ists to recognize the need for broadening our outlook
      beyond the organic realm."

343. Steward. J. N. "Evolution and Process." Anthropology
      Today. Ed. A. L. Kroeber. Chicago: University
      of Chicago Press, 1953. Pp. 313-326.

344. Stocking, George W., Jr. "Lamarckianism in Ameri-
      can Social Science: 1890-1955." Journal of the
      History of Ideas, 23/2 (April-June 1962), 239-256.
      Discusses in particular Herbert Spencer's broad
      neo-Lamarckianism, and its influence on American
      social thought in the 1890's.

345. Taschdjian, Edgar. "Dobzhansky and Teilhard." Cross
      Currents, 17 (1967), 360-363.

346. Tax, Sol, ed. Evolution After Darwin. 3 Vols. "Uni-
      versity of Chicago Centennial." Chicago: University
      of Chicago Press, 1960.

347. Teilhard de Chardin, Pierre. The Phenomenon of Man.
      Trans. Bernard Wall. Introduction by Sir Julian
      Huxley. New York: Harper, 1955.

348. _____. The Appearance of Man. Trans. J. M.
      Cohen and Robert Francoeur. New York: Harper,
      1956.

349. _____. The Vision of the Past. Trans. J. M.
      Cohen. New York: Harper, 1957.

350. _____. The Future of Man. Trans. Norman Denny.
      New York: Harper, 1959.

351. _____. Human Energy. Trans. J. M. Cohen.
      London: Collins, 1962.

352. _____. The Activation of Energy. Trans. Rene
      Hague. New York: Harcourt Brace Jovanovich,
      1963.

353. _____. Man's Place in Nature. Trans. Rene
      Hague. New York: Harper & Row, 1963.

354. _____. Science and Christ. Trans. Rene Hague.
      New York: Harper & Row, 1965.

355. _____. Christianity and Evolution. Trans. Rene
      Hague. New York: Harcourt Brace Jovanovich,
      1969.
          Of Teilhard's voluminous, posthumously published
      writings, the preceding nine volumes are most crucial
      for understanding his theories regarding convergent
      evolution, process, and the integration of evolution-
      ary cosmology with philosophy and theology. The
      original French language editions are all published
      by Seuil Publishers, Paris.

356. Temkin, Owsei. "The Idea of Descent in Post-Roman-
      tic German Biology: 1848-1858." Forerunners of
      Darwin: 1745-1859. Eds. Glass, Temkin, Strauss.
      Baltimore: Johns Hopkins University Press, 1959.
      Pp. 323-355.

357. Thompson, J. Arthur. "The Influence of Darwinism
      on Thought and Life." Science and Civilization.
      Ed. F. S. Marvin. Oxford: Oxford University
      Press, 1923. Pp. 213-220.

358. _____. Concerning Evolution. "Terry Lectures."
      New Haven, Conn.: Yale University Press, 1925.
          A professor of natural history at the University
      of Aberdeen argues against Paley's "external" tele-
      ology in favor of organic holism and interdependence.
      He cites the British biologist C. Lloyd Morgan and
      the German personalist philosopher Hermann Lotze
      to suggest that evolution discloses a "sublime cosmic
      process ... towards more dominance of mind."

359. United Nations Educational, Scientific and Cultural Or-
      ganization. Science and Synthesis: An International
      UNESCO Colloquium on the 10th Anniversary of the

deaths of Albert Einstein and Pierre Teilhard de
Chardin. The Hague: Martinus Nijhoff, 1971.

360. Vandel, Albert. "L'importance de L'Evolution creatice
dans la genèse de la pensée moderne." Revue de
Theologie et de Philosophie, 9/2 (1960), 85-108.
Traces the philosophy of evolution from Lamarck,
including Bergson's contribution. Analyzes Bergson's
influence on Teilhard.

361. Waddington, C. H. The Strategy of the Genes. New
York: Macmillan, 1957.
Chronicles the Lamarckian resurgence in biology,
and the teleological re-interpretation of evolution.

362. _____. "Practical Consequences of Metaphysical
Beliefs on a Biologist's Work." Towards a Theoretical Biology. 2 Vols. Ed. C. H. Waddington. Chicago: Aldine, 1968. Vol. II, Pp. 72-81.

363. _____. The Evolution of an Evolutionist. New
York: Cornell University Press, 1975.

364. Walker, Charles. "M. Bergson's Creative Evolution."
Lancet, 182 (February 17, 1912), 456f.
Letter criticizes Bergson's alleged "failure to
understand Darwin," and criticizes an earlier Lancet
article by R. F. Licorish [no. 287] for its "neo-
Lamarckian" interpretation of Bergson.

365. Wallace, Alfred Russell. Social Environment and Moral
Progress. New York: Funk and Wagnalls, 1913.
Wallace's final work, in which he "solves" the
problem of accounting for the evolution of the human
brain via a hypothesis of natural selection alone.
Since the brain is vastly superior, now and in the
remote past, to the mere requirements of survival,
it can be accounted for only by postulating a "divine
influx, which at some point in his evolution at once
raised man above the rest of the animals."

366. Weierich, Andre Jean. The Relationship of Teilhard
de Chardin's Law of Complexity-Consciousness to the
Mechanism-Vitalism Debate in Biology. Diss. Oregon
State University, 1971.

367. Wilkie, J. S. "Buffon, Lamarck and Darwin: the
Originality of Darwin's Theory of Evolution." Dar-

win's Biological Work. Ed. P. R. Bell. Cambridge:
Cambridge University Press, 1959. Pp. 262-307.

368. Wilkinson, Elizabeth M. "Goethe's Conception of Form."
Goethe: A Collection of Critical Essays. Ed. Victor
Lange. Englewood Cliffs, N. J.: Prentice-Hall,
1968. Pp. 110-131.

369. Willoughby, Leonard A. "Unity and Continuity in
Goethe." Goethe: A Collection of Critical Essays.
Ed. Victor Lange. Englewood Cliffs, N. J.: Pren-
tice-Hall, 1968. Pp. 161-178.

370. Zirkle, Conway. Evolution, Marxian Biology and the
Social Scene. Philadelphia: University of Pennsylvania Press, 1959.

II. 1. EVOLUTIONARY COSMOLOGY AND
PROCESS RATIONALISM: BIBLIOGRAPHY

---

371. *Alexander, Samuel. Space, Time and Deity. "Gifford
Lectures, 1916-1918." London: Macmillan, 1920.
[I, no. 49]

372. Baltazar, Eulalio. "Evolutionary Perspectives and the
Divine." Traces of God in a Secular Culture. Ed.
George F. McLean. Staten Island, N. Y.: Alba
House, 1973. Pp. 143-165.
    Contrasts an eschatological view of "convergent
time" based on Teilhard, with the Greek view of
timeless eternity, and the Whiteheadian process view
of time as pure succession or change and perpetual
becoming.

373. Balz, Albert G. A. "Evolution and Time." Essays
in Honor of John Dewey. New York: Holt, Rinehart & Winston, 1929.
    Cites Alexander, Bergson, and Whitehead: "Evolu-
tion is not an answer to the question of temporal
creativity," rather it is a problem. "Time cannot
be taken seriously if reality be one vast evolution."
This view would entail a return to the Leibnizian
pre-established harmony and set laws of development,

which preclude freedom, novelty and pluralism--and
thus are irrelevant to time.

374. Barbour, Ian G. "Five Ways of Reading Teilhard."
      The Teilhard Review, 3/1 (1968), 3-20.

375. _____. "Teilhard's Process Metaphysics." Journal
      of Religion, 49/2 (April 1969), 136-159.
      Compares the similarities and differences of White-
      head and Teilhard: both suggest that the world is
      evolutionary process; that entities are temporal proc-
      ess in relationships; and note the reciprocal God-
      world interaction. Whitehead is pluralistic, while
      Teilhard is a monist. Teilhard attempts to reconcile
      human freedom with divine determinism, while White-
      head stresses absolute freedom. Whitehead denies
      the possibility of forecasting the outcome of evolution-
      ary process, while Teilhard emphasizes evolutionary
      convergence.

376. Birch, L. Charles. Nature and God. Philadelphia:
      Westminster Press, 1965.
      Biologist suggests that process philosophy and
      theology provide the key for reconciling Darwinian
      and post-Darwinian evolution with biblical creation-
      ism.

377. _____. "Purpose in the Universe: A Search for
      Wholeness." Zygon, 6 (1971), 4-27.
      Article discusses creative evolution, purpose and
      the unity of nature as perceived in Darwin, Teilhard,
      and Whiteheadian process thought.

378. _____. "Participatory Evolution: The Drive of
      Creation." Journal of the American Academy of Re-
      ligion, 11 (1972), 147-163.
      Varieties of possible evolutionary perspectives
      are examined by an evolutionary biologist in the light
      of contemporary process thought.

379. * _____, and Cobb, John B., Jr. The Liberation of
      Life: From the Cell to the Community. Cambridge:
      Cambridge University Press, 1981. [II, no. 194]

380. Burgers, J. M. Reflections on the Concept of Life.
      Santa Monica, Cal.: Rand Corp., 1969.

381. Capek, Milic. "Bergson's Theory of Matter and Modern

Physics." Revue Philosophique, 77 (1953); also in
Bergson and the Evolution of Physics. Ed. P. A. Y.
Gunter. Knoxville: University of Tennessee Press,
1969.
Argues that contemporary physics fully supports
Bergson's concepts of matter, time, and novelty.
Notes similarities in the views of Bergson and White-
head regarding time, the theory of matter as "vi-
bratory," and the definition of enduring material en-
tities in terms of series of events.

382. _____. Bergson and Modern Physics: A Re-interpretation and Re-evaluation. Dordrect, Holland:
D. Reidel Publishing Co., 1971.
Several of Capek's essays in this volume discuss
the similarities of Bergson and Whitehead.

383. Cesselin, Felix. La philosophie organique de Whitehead. Paris: Presses Universitaires de France,
1950.
Discusses the roots of Whiteheadian process thought
in William James, Bergson, Alexander, and Aristotle.

384. *Collingwood, Robin G. The Idea of Nature. Oxford:
The Clarendon Press, 1945. [Intro, no. 11]

385. Conklin, Edwin Grant. Man: Real and Ideal. New
York: Scribners, 1943.
Cites Darwin, Huxley, and Weissmann and other
neo-Darwinists to argue in favor, not of "trivial"
teleology, but of holism, organism, and biological
interdependence. Agrees with Alexander, Whitehead,
and John Dewey that there is no dualism in nature:
conscious personality is the product of biological
evolution, whence mind and body are but aspects of
a single, unified nature.

386. Cousins, Ewert. "Process Models in Culture, Philosophy and Theology." Process Theology. Ed. Ewert
Cousins. New York: Newman Press, 1971.
Suggests that Whitehead and Teilhard are the two
major spokesmen for process philosophy and theology
in the twentieth century.

387. Curtis, Charles J. "Process Theology: Teilhard de
Chardin." Contemporary Protestant Thought. Mil-
waukee, Wisc.: Bruce, 1970.

388.   deBroglie, Louis. "The Concepts of Contemporary
       Physics and Bergson's Idea on Time and Motion"
       (1947). Bergson and the Evolution of Physics. Ed.
       P. A. Y. Gunter. Knoxville: University of Ten-
       nessee Press, 1969. Pp. 45-62.
            A brilliant and influential physicist and formulator
       of the concept of wave-particle duality assesses the
       influence of Bergson on his thought. Compares
       Heisenberg's uncertainty principle and Bohr's "com-
       plementarity" with Bergson's view of the dynamic
       aspect of matter, in which change is primary. Sug-
       gests that duration, freedom, novelty, non-localiza-
       tion, and anti-materialism characterize the contem-
       porary view in physics.

389.   Devaux, Philippe. "Le bergsonisme de Whitehead."
       Revue Internationale de Philosophie, 56-57/15 (1961),
       217-236.
            Discusses Bergson's influence on Whitehead, and
       the similarities in their metaphysical positions.

390.   Foley, Leo A. "Cosmos and Ethos." New Scholasti-
       cism, 41 (1967), 141-158.
            Whitehead and Teilhard are cited as restoring
       the "Greek vision" of the cosmos to contemporary
       thought.

391.   Ford, Lewis S. The Lure of God. Philadelphia:
       Fortress Press, 1978.
            Discusses the inadequacy of the neo-Darwinian
       explanation of evolutionary advance solely in terms
       of interplay between chance, random variation and
       natural selection. Essentially there are no reasons
       offered as to why complexity should be as favored
       as it is in fact in evolutionary history. Indeed phy-
       sical evidence (entropy) suggests the opposite. Ford
       compares the process doctrine of God with a revised
       form of neo-Lamarckism, in terms of the "social"
       transmission of novelty as habit in subsequent events.

392.   Francoeur, Robert T. "The Process of Evolution and
       'Panpsychism' in Teilhard de Chardin." American
       Benedectine Review, 12 (1961), 206-219.

393.   Gunter, P. A. Y., ed. Bergson and the Evolution of
       Physics. Knoxville: University of Tennessee Press,
       1969.

Collected essays by Louis deBroglie, Milic Capek, and others provide a vigorous re-interpretation and defense of Bergson's importance.

394. _____. "Bergsonian Method and the Evolution of Science." Bergson and the Evolution of Physics. Ed. P. A. Y. Gunter. Knoxville: University of Tennessee Press, 1969. Pp. 3-42.
Bergson's discovery of "duration" ("lived-time") helped throw off the influence of Spencer's mechanism. Time and space are radically different: time is heterogeneous, not homogeneous, like space. It is non-uniform, organic, unique, and the realm of unpredictable possibility. Gunter suggests that Bergson influenced William James, Whitehead, Heidegger, and Marcel. He argues that the major criticisms of Bergson by Lovejoy, Russell, and Santayana are based upon serious misreadings. Bergson is not just a "mishmash of undigested science and indigestible poetry." Rather, he represents an important anticipation of contemporary physical theory.

395. _____. "The Heuristic Force of Creative Evolution." Southwestern Journal of Philosophy, 1/3 (1970), 111-118.

396. _____. "Bergson's Theory of Matter and Modern Cosmology." Journal of the History of Ideas, 32/4 (October-December 1971), 525-542.

397. Hanson, Anthony, ed. Teilhard Reassessed. London: Darton, Longman & Todd, 1970.
Teilhard agrees with Bergson, Whitehead, and Alexander on panpsychism, the existence of God, and the problem of evil. They differ over the concept of God (Teilhard's is wholly Christian), and eschatology.

398. *Hartshorne, Charles. "A World of Organisms." The Logic of Perfection and Other Essays in Neoclassical Metaphysics. LaSalle, Ill.: Open Court, 1962. Pp. 191-215. [Intro, no. 23]

399. Hélal, Georges. "La cosmologie: un nouvel examen de sa nature et de sa raison d'être." Dialogue, 8/2 (1969).
Whitehead's cosmology thoroughly reflects contemporary developments in modern physics; its antece-

dents in Bergson, Alexander and Hegel are assessed;
the merits of such comprehensive worldviews are
extolled in comparison to analytic philosophies of
"logical atomism."

400. Homlish, John Stephen. The Cosmos and God According to Pierre Teilhard de Chardin and Alfred North
Whitehead. Diss., McMaster University, 1974.
Compares the cosmologies of Whitehead and Teilhard to discern whether these are consistent with
their respective theologies. The principal inconsis-
tency is Teilhard's retention of "classical theism"
through divine immutability.

401. Hurley, Patrick J. "Bergson and Whitehead on Freedom." Proceedings of the American Catholic Philosophical Association, 50 (1976), 107-117.
Illustrates a difference in the two views of freedom: for Bergson, freedom is equated with radical
novelty to avoid mechanism. For Whitehead, freedom involves the envisagement of pure possibilities
(eternal objects).

402. Kaufmann, Alvin H. Elan Vital, Nisus and Creativity
as Treated in the Thought of Henri Bergson, Samuel
Alexander, and A. N. Whitehead. Diss. Boston
University, 1952.
Compares the élan vital of Bergson, the nisus of
Alexander, and the creativity of Whitehead. The
former two are mystical concepts, whereas White-
head's is both rational and empirically-grounded.
Charges that Whitehead failed to make clear the re-
lation of creativity to actual entities.

403. Klauder, Francis J. Aspects of the Thought of Teilhard de Chardin. N. Quincy, Mass.: Christopher,
1971.
Compares Teilhard with Aquinas, Bonaventure,
and Whitehead. Evolution portrayed as progress
toward a divine goal, as a manifestation of the creative power and intelligence of God who creates according to the Whiteheadian model.

404. Levi, Albert William. "Substance, Process, Being.
A Whiteheadian-Bergsonian View." Journal of Philosophy, 55 (1958), 749-761.

405. _____. "Bergson or Whitehead?" Process and

Divinity: The Hartshorne Festschrift. Eds. W. L.
Reese and E. Freeman. LaSalle, Ill.: Open Court,
1964. Pp. 139-159.
Corrects the author's earlier identification of
Whitehead and Bergson (above), by suggesting that
the two held radically different views of time and
process. Bergson is a dualist regarding personal
vs. natural time, whereas "Whitehead's relentless
panpsychism denies all natural bifurcation."

406. McCarthy, John Willadams. The Naturalism of Samuel
Alexander. New York: Kings Crown Press, 1948.
Alexander's evolutionary emergence in Space, Time
and Deity is compared with Aristotle and Spinoza.

407. Meland, Bernard Eugene. "From Darwin to Whitehead: A Study in the Shift in Ethos and Perspective
Underlying Religious Thought." Journal of Religion,
40 (1960), 229-245.
Discusses the development and gradual shift in
evolutionary perspectives among Darwin, Lotze, and
Bergson, as compared with Whitehead.

408. _____. "The New Realism in Religious Inquiry."
Encounter, 31/4 (Autumn 1970), 311-324.
Traces "Christian realism" to James, Bergson,
and Whitehead, and suggests the relations of process
theology with other modes of thought.

409. *Morgan, C. Lloyd. Emergent Evolution. "Gifford
Lectures, 1922." London: Williams and Norgate,
1923. [II, no. 310]

410. Overman, Richard H. Evolution and the Christian
Doctrine of Creation. Philadelphia: Westminster
Press, 1967.
Whitehead's thought provides the conceptual scheme
for a synthesis of evolution and Christian doctrine,
including the perspectives of Darwin, Lamarck and
Teilhard.

411. Pemberton, Harrison J. The Problem of Personal
Identity with Special Reference to Whitehead and Berg-
son. Diss. Yale University, 1953.
Claims that Whitehead's view of personal identity
is inadequate, but capable of reformulation utilizing
Bergson and Plato.

412. Prigogine, Ilya. From Being to Becoming: Time and
      Complexity in the Physical Sciences. San Francisco:
      Freeman, 1980.
          A distinguished chemist and general systems theorist
      synthesizes evolution and process thought.

413. Richardson, David B. "Philosophies of Hartshorne and
      Chardin: Two Sides of the Same Coin?" Southern
      Journal of Philosophy, 2 (Fall 1964), 107-115.

414. Rideau, Emile. The Thought of Teilhard de Chardin.
      Trans. Rene Hague. New York: Harper & Row,
      1967.
          Traces the influence of Bergson and Julian Huxley
      on Teilhard's thought. Reinforces the view that
      Teilhard, like Morgan, Whitehead, and Heisenberg,
      came to his "process" view of nature more through
      his studies of science than through the influence of
      other philosophers.

415. Rose, Mary C. Three Hierarchies of Value: A Study
      in the Philosophies of Value of Henri Bergson, Alfred
      North Whitehead, and Søren Kierkegaard. Diss.
      Johns Hopkins University, 1949.

416. Rust, Eric. Evolutionary Philosophies and Contem-
      porary Theology. Philadelphia: Westminster Press,
      1969.
          Under this heading, Rust discusses the theological
      impact of Whitehead, Hegel, Teilhard, Collingwood,
      and Hartshorne.

417. Singerman, Ora. "The Relation Between Philosophy
      and Science: A Comparison of the Positions of Berg-
      son and Whitehead." Iyyun, 9/2 (April 1968), 65-91.
          This article, in Hebrew, discusses primarily the
      comparative sociologies of Whitehead and Bergson.

418. Sipfle, David A. "Henri Bergson and the Epochal
      Theory of Time." Bergson and the Evolution of
      Physics. Ed. P. A. Y. Gunter. Knoxville, Tenn. :
      University of Tennessee Press, 1969. Pp. 275-294.
          Details many of the similarities in the positions
      of Whitehead and Bergson, and rejects the widespread
      view that Bergson's was a continuous theory of time.
      Rather, time is quantized in an organic system, as
      in Whitehead.

419. Stahl, Roland C. The Influence of Bergson on White-
      head. Diss. Boston University, 1950.
      Traces numerous influences on Whitehead by Berg-
      son, as well as numerous modifications of Bergson's
      ideas by Whitehead.

420. _____. "Bergson's Influence on Whitehead." The
      Personalist, 36/3 (1955), 250-257.
      Argues with careful justification and documenta-
      tion, that Bergson's influence on Whitehead was con-
      siderable.

421. Stallknecht, Newton P. Studies in the Philosophy of
      Creation: With Especial Reference to Bergson and
      Whitehead. Princeton, N.J.: Princeton University
      Press, 1934.

422. Stiernotte, Alfred P. "Process Philosophies and Mys-
      ticism." International Philosophical Quarterly, 9
      (1969), 560-571.
      An analysis of Teilhard's philosophy.

423. Thatcher, Adrian. "Three Theologies of the Future:
      Moltmann, Teilhard de Chardin, and A. N. White-
      head." Baptist Quarterly, 25 (1974), 242-250.

424. Thorpe, W. H. Purpose in a World of Chance: A
      Biologist's View. Oxford: Oxford University Press,
      1978.
      A condensation of the author's Gifford Lectures,
      published earlier as Animal Nature and Human Na-
      ture (1974). Argues that biologists should abandon
      their exclusive focus on inadequate modes of reduc-
      tionistic explanation in a manner parallel to the move
      away from such modes of explanation in the physical
      sciences. Discusses the role of "purposive" explana-
      tion in contemporary biology, especially in ethology
      and the study of "animal speech." Asserts that
      Whitehead's work provides an acceptable philosophical
      framework for these discussions.

425. Whitehead, Alfred North. The Concept of Nature.
      "Tarner Lectures." Cambridge: Cambridge Univer-
      sity Press, 1920.
      Whitehead acknowledges an indebtedness to Berg-
      son, even at this early stage of his thought, in his
      chapter on "Time."

426. _____. Science and the Modern World. "Lowell
     Lectures." New York: Macmillan, 1925.
     Rejects Bergson's élan vital, as well as the Berg-
     sonian tendency towards anti-rationalism; ch. 3.

427. Whitla, William. "Sin and Redemption in Whitehead
     and Teilhard de Chardin." Anglican Theological Re-
     view, 47 (1965), 81-93.

428. Young, Henry James. Two Models of the Human Fu-
     ture: A Study in the Process Theism of Teilhard
     and Whitehead. Diss. Hartford Seminary Foundation,
     1974.
     Argues for the superiority and consistency of
     Whitehead over Teilhard, who lapses back into "per-
     manence and substantivalism." Teilhard perceives
     creativity as a temporary phase, while Whitehead
     perceives it as the ultimate metaphysical principle.
     Teilhard's "omega-point" is inconsistent with his
     scientific-evolutionary model of becoming. White-
     head avoids this pitfall by portraying the future as
     an open-ended process of creativity involving the
     dialectical interplay of God and the world.

PART III: HEGELIAN IDEALISM

The history of idealism spans a far greater period, and accordingly exhibits an even greater internal diversity, than evolutionary cosmology. The most familiar forms of idealism--subjective and monistic--are widely perceived as hostile to a process interpretation of nature, owing to the decidedly-inferior status of the flux of natural forms as "external" (i. e. , non-mental or non-spiritual) phenomena. One may trace the principal source of these views in Western Europe to Plato, and in South Asia to the Vedanta systems based upon philosophical interpretations of the Upanishads. The latter exert their influence on Western thought in many ways, as exhibited in the morose monistic idealism of Schopenhauer, and more recently in the mystical monism of F. H. Bradley.

Idealistic philosophies may or may not embrace an epistemological dualism (such as those of Plato, Kant, and Bradley), but they are similar in stressing an ontological monism which emphasizes that ultimate reality most closely resembles the experiences of rational consciousness (or alternatively, of mystical spirituality). As with Sankara and the earlier Plato, the flux of natural processes is, by contrast, only a partial and misleading appearance of that underlying timeless and all-inclusive reality. [1]

Owing to the apparent dominance of such anti-process views under the heading of idealism, it may seem strange to attempt a discussion of idealism in a work devoted to process philosophy. Nonetheless it appears to be the case that the process tradition owes a considerable debt--and indeed is similar in many respects--to traditions of idealism other than the two just mentioned. Although close students of the literature of idealism might wish to press the comparisons even further, in this section I limit discussion to three variations of idealism that qualify as schools of process thought: Hegelian idealism (which I discuss here), personal idealism, and for want of a more precise term, what we shall call "English" Hegelianism[2] (both of which I postpone for Part V below).

Due to a residual confusion concerning this issue among many philosophers, it is important to note that these three traditions were not at all affected by G. E. Moore's famous "refutation" of idealism.[3] Moore's essay analyzed a rather limited and trivial variation of subjective idealism advocated on quasi-religious grounds by A. E. Taylor, and mistakenly attributed to Berkeley.[4] As puzzled idealists of other persuasions then and now have noted,[5] there seems to be less conflict and greater agreement on substantive themes than such hostile and programmatic adversaries have been willing to acknowledge. Indeed, it seems the case that idealists and their critics alike often have failed to appreciate the remarkable diversity of views included under the umbrella of idealism.[6]

A large measure of the blame for this melancholy state of affairs may be laid at the feet of Hegel. For it is Hegel who symbolizes the idealist movement, especially for its hostile English-language critics, despite the fact that he held few of the views attributed to him by such critics. The problem is further complicated by an unfortunate tendency to interpret Hegel through the eyes of later critics (such as Kierkegaard),[7] or to attribute to him directly the positions of his later admirers (who themselves distinguished their views from Hegel's). In Great Britain, for example, the emphasis by McTaggart and Bradley on Hegel's Logic, together with a deliberate de-emphasis of his extensive philosophy of nature, led to a rather obscure ontology and theology which was later the focus of attacks against "Hegelian" idealism, as J. N. Findlay has illustrated.[8] What is particularly fascinating and frustrating in this regard is the profound differences of such views from those of other "English Hegelians," such as Bernard Bosanquet, R. G. Collingwood, H. H. Joachim, and Samuel Alexander.[9]

Rather than further dignify this embarrassing intellectual travesty, it would be well to adumbrate those views actually developed by Hegel in his own writings which suggest his historical interest for process philosophers.

We must remind ourselves, for example, that Hegel was a harsh critic of German-French romanticism and its accompanying Naturphilosophie, as advocated by Schelling and F. Schlegel. This, together with the paucity of empirical

evidence in its support, accounts for Hegel's decisive rejection in the early nineteenth century of Lamarckian-romanticist
theories of <u>natural</u> evolution and progressivism. [10] Yet Hegel
adapted those views to firmer empirical ground in the process
of interpreting historical and cultural evolution, and so developed the first clear concept of "historical process."[11]

Hegel's view of natural science was shaped primarily
by an acquaintance with the life sciences, rather than the
physical sciences. In this he shared much in common with
early representatives of evolutionary cosmology--indeed, his
views of science were profoundly influenced by, even as they
were sympathetic to, the "organic" views of Goethe. We
have had occasion already to note Lamarck's broad influence
in such circles.

As a result, while eschewing the idea of a real, temporal evolution in his philosophy of nature, Hegel nonetheless
developed an "organic teleology" applicable throughout the
natural realm, as an alternative to the Newtonian metaphysics
of mechanism and causal determinism. Hegel's theory of
teleological explanation bears a striking resemblance in many
respects to Whitehead's first metaphysical synthesis of "organic mechanism" in <u>Science and the Modern World.</u> [12]
Hegel's theories of organic purpose and historical-evolution-
ary process exerted profound subsequent influence on later
thinkers, including Marx, Croce, Collingwood, and Royce,
as well as many philosophers in the school of evolutionary
cosmology.

Specifically, in the <u>Science of Logic</u>, the term "organism" is treated as if it were a general metaphysical category. Individual "units" or quanta of being are "organisms,"
in a sense not to be confused with biological organisms,
which are but one special case of the former. Organisms
are distinguished by the immanence (or "innerness") of the
<u>Begriff</u> or Concept, which is Hegel's somewhat obscure way
of indicating that organisms are internally-governed, self-
determining entities. [13]

In considering three successively more complex descriptions of process or activity (mechanism, "chemism,"
and teleology), Hegel concludes that mechanistic and deterministic models do not account for the behavior of organisms.
He argues that, from an external perspective at least, an
organism is certainly capable of purely "mechanical" behavior; but he adds, "to that extent it is not a living being...."
When an organism is regarded solely as a mechanical system

subject to strict deterministic causality, "then the Concept
is regarded as external to it and it is treated as a <u>dead</u>
thing."[14]

What characterizes a living entity, by contrast, is
the immanence of its pattern or principle of organization of
its activity. Organisms are characterized for Hegel (in a
manner very similar to Whitehead) by process, immanent
purposiveness, subjectivity and feeling, self-determination,
"conditioned" or partial self-creation, and freedom.[15] Organisms are defined by Hegel so as to apply in the realm of
nature to describe biological entities (including human beings), as well as in the realm of <u>Geist</u> to characterize cultural, political, and finally religious institutions (such as
the church).[16]

Likewise, in the portions of his <u>Encyclopedia</u> devoted
to the philosophy of nature, Hegel argues that it is the <u>Beg-
riff</u> itself which is objectified and immanent in nature. The
<u>Naturphilosophie</u> narrates the emergence of the Concept in
the progression of more complex forms in nature, culminat-
ing in organisms, whose behavior is governed according to
an inner "concept" or Idea. As such, organisms are subject
to teleological description, within which mechanism is sub-
lated.[17]

Thus, I find that Hegel's doctrine at this phase of its
development may be classified as an early form of what
Whitehead later called "organic mechanism," indicating that
the mechanical and chemical functions which an entity per-
forms may be understood only in terms of the purposive
organization of those functions toward the survival and main-
tenance of the entity as a whole. Mechanical and chemical
functions of entities are organized according to this purpose,
and are conditioned further by the interdependence and reciprocal internal relatedness among the entities (i. e., within
an organic system).

This organic teleology forms the connecting link in
the transition from inorganic nature (nominally subject, in
Hegel's view, to mechanistic description) to the realm of
Spirit, where events are described in terms of their freedom and interdependence.[18] Thus, an understanding of nature is not peripheral, but rather integral to Hegel's whole
system, narrating as it does this gradual transition from
necessity to the freedom constitutive of real being.

Such views strongly influenced, and were perceived by

many as fully compatible with, the developing traditions of
evolutionary cosmology later in the nineteenth century. [19]
Until quite recently, the affinities of Hegelian idealism and
the school of process rationalism have been largely overlooked. William Ernest Hocking, to be sure, offered a
charming account of Whitehead's growing interest in Hegelian
themes as a result of the influence of Josiah Royce and other
Hegelians during Whitehead's tenure at Harvard. [20] But the
parallels that may be drawn between Whitehead and Hegel,
in accordance with Whitehead's own comments (see "Introduction," n. 3 above), are more to be described as "surprising
similarities," than as having issued from any direct influence.
On the other hand, these many similarities have a historical
genealogy which we have partially reconstructed, extending
from Lamarck, Goethe, and Hegel at the beginning of the
nineteenth century, through Bergson's evolutionary cosmology,
to the cosmologies of Alexander, Bradley, and the "process"
views of William James--all of which Whitehead does acknowledge.

R. G. Collingwood, in his recounting of the development of the philosophy of nature, suggests that the contemporary view of nature is characterized by a recovery of a
modified form of teleological explanation, replacing the outmoded and discarded model of mechanism that had been the
paradigm for classical physics. Collingwood dates this transition to the modern view of nature with Hegel and suggests
that this view is developed subsequently by Bergson, Alexander, and Whitehead. [21] Errol Harris concurs with this
view of the importance of "internal" or modified teleological
explanation in contemporary science, and suggests further
that despite his ignorance of this as a Hegelian tradition
Whitehead himself represents its most contemporary expon-
ent. [22]

Beyond such general comments, however, very few
thorough or systematic studies of the relationship between
Hegelian Idealism and Whiteheadian process rationalism have
been published. In 1937 Gregory Vlastos suggested that
Whitehead and Hegel both were "dialectical" philosophers,
concerned with understanding the processes of becoming.
The major difference, he noted, was that Hegel's dialectic
was "homogeneous": i. e. , all the categories of existence
were derived in terms of <u>Geist</u>. Whitehead's "heterogeneous"
dialectic, by contrast, was a variation of the Hegelian dialectic based upon diverse categories of existence derived from
"eternal objects" and "actual entities. "[23]

Robert Whittemore, inspired by Collingwood and Harris, offered a number of comparisons in an article discussing "Hegel's 'Science' and Whitehead's 'Modern World'."[24] Specifically, he suggested that Whitehead's notion of "process" corresponded closely with Hegel's understanding of "dialectic," and that both embraced panentheism. A more helpful comparison, I feel, is that Hegel intended in his use of dialectic a perpetual, interactive process akin to what Whitehead intended by the term "concrescence."[25]

More recently, Daniel Day Williams highlighted important similarities in the respective attempts by Hegel and Whitehead to develop a philosophical interpretation of Christian faith and of religion in general.[26] In the introduction to his anthology, Alfred North Whitehead: Essays on His Philosophy, George L. Kline suggested that there were interesting similarities in the respective attempts by Whitehead and Hegel to overcome the subject-object dualism in Western thought by developing an understanding of "objectivity" that was purely relative. He also suggested certain linguistic parallels in their uses of "concrete" and "abstract" as value-laden terms to describe the relative "actuality" of any given entity or concept.[27] These points were taken up again by Professor Kline in a paper for an Eastern Division meeting of the American Philosophical Association. Kline added at this point a comparison of Hegel's pivotal notion of the Begriff with Whitehead's understanding of "concrescence"--both of which represented the teleological nature of process or becoming.[28]

In the annotated bibliography immediately following, I cite works that discuss the process doctrines in idealism, interpret Hegel's philosophy of nature, trace the Hegelian influence on later idealists, and discuss the similarities and differences between the Hegelian school of process thought and the schools of process rationalism and evolutionary cosmology.

NOTES

(1) The sweeping and inaccurate generalization that such views were characteristic of "Greek metaphysics" deserves unraveling. For the present, it is worth noting that the view that process, flux and change are unreal and illusory is challenged by Plato himself in later dialogues, especially the Sophist, Parmenides, and the Timaeus. Aristotle's so-called "substance" metaphysics in reality reflects this concern of the

later Plato over the relative status of permanence
and change--indeed, the Metaphysics represents a
profound attempt to do justice to both experiences. Cf.
Daniel A. Dombrowski, Plato's Philosophy of History
(Washington, D. C. : University Press of America, 1981).

(2) Richard Kroner applies the term to British Hegelians
from Stirling to Collingwood and Mure. Cf. "Mure
and Other English Hegelians," Review of Metaphysics,
7/1 (September 1953), 64-73. I use the term more
broadly to include the American Hegelians as well,
including Howison, Palmer, Royce, and the early
Dewey, among others.

(3) G. E. Moore, "The Refutation of Idealism," (1903); re-
printed in Moore's Philosophical Studies (London:
Routledge & Kegan Paul, 1922), 1-30. James B.
Pratt, reviewing a 1932 Festschrift in honor of Josiah
Royce for the Journal of Philosophy, evidences a bitter
frustration with the apparently elusive diversity of
"idealisms," and attempts via a tour de force to de-
fine idealism exclusively to fit Moore's refutation:
"Is Idealism Realism?" Journal of Philosophy, 30/7
(March 30, 1933), 169-178.

(4) Berkeley, of course, did advocate the view that esse est
percipi. But his variation of pan-personalism is not
threatened by the obvious inconsistencies of mere so-
lipsism which Moore points out. This misunderstanding provides yet another example of the dilemma discussed in the introductory remarks of this work, that
is, philosophers often make poor intellectual historians.

(5) Cf. Contemporary Idealism in America, ed. Clifford
Barrett (New York: Macmillan, 1932); Bernard Bosanquet, "Realism and Metaphysics," The Philosophical
Review, 26/1 (January 1917), 4-15; Edgar S. Brightman, "The Definition of Idealism," Journal of Philosophy, 30/16 (August 3, 1933); also note Clifford Barrett's reply to James Pratt (n. 3 above) in this same
volume of the Journal of Philosophy: "Is Idealism
Realism?" pp. 421-429.

(6) The diversity and richness of contemporary idealism is
attested by both idealists and non-idealists: cf. E. S.
Brightman, "Modern Idealism," Journal of Philosophy,
17/20 (September 23, 1920), 533-550; A. C. Ewing,

ed. , The Idealist Tradition from Berkeley to Blanshard (Glencoe, Ill. : The Free Press, 1957); W. E.
Hocking, "Theses Establishing an Idealistic Metaphysics by a New Route," Journal of Philosophy, 38
(December 1941), 688-689; and John Howie and Thomas
O. Buford, eds. , Contemporary Studies in Philosophical Idealism (Cape Cod, Mass. : Claude Stark, 1975).

(7)   Alan Brinkley, for example, exposes such a process of
misinterpretation being transmitted as valid interpretation: he blasts Samuel Alexander for abandoning Hegel and popularizing the notion that Bergson
was the first to "take time seriously." Through
careful textual analysis, Brinkley shows that Hegel,
despite such current misconceptions, developed a
profound and completely contemporary doctrine of
time.   See "Time in Hegel's Phenomenology," Tulane Studies in Philosophy, 9 (1960), 3-15.

(8)   Cf. J. N. Findlay, Hegel: A Re-examination (Oxford:
Oxford University Press, 1958); also "Hegel's Use
of Teleology," The Monist, 48/1 (January 1964),
1-17.

(9)   See Part V (B) below.

(10) It is well to note that no less respected an evolutionist
than Thomas Huxley also claimed to have rejected
evolutionary theories until seeing solid empirical
evidence in support of such views, as provided in
Darwin's Origin of Species. It is remarkable irony
that Hegel's rejection of what, in 1820, was perceived as a fanciful and scientifically unsound theory
should earn for him the reputation of enmity toward
science. Those unfamiliar with Hegel's work would
be profoundly instructed by considering his similar,
sensible rejection of then-current and highly popular
pseudo-sciences, such as physiognomy and phrenology,
in his Phenomenology of Spirit (1807). Cf. also the
comments of Errol E. Harris, "Hegel and the Natural Sciences," in Beyond Epistemology, ed. F. G.
Weiss (The Hague: Martinus Nijhoff, 1974), 129-153;
and Charles Taylor, Hegel and Modern Society (Cambridge: Cambridge University Press, 1979).

(11) Cf. Wolfe Mays, "Temporality and Time in Hegel and
Marx," Study of Time II: Proceedings of the Second
Conference of the International Society for the Study

of Time (Berlin: 1975), 98-113; and Joseph A.
O'Hare, The Meaning of Action in the Phenomenology
and Logic of Hegel (Diss., Fordham University,
1968).

(12) J. N. Findlay discusses "organic and teleological levels"
in Hegel's concept of nature: cf. Language, Mind
and Value (London: G. Allen & Unwin, 1963), 217-
231. Following this example, I discuss "organic
mechanism" in Hegel's Naturphilosophie in my Two
Views of Freedom in Process Thought: A Study of
Hegel and Whitehead (Chico, Cal.: Scholars Press,
1979), 88-107.

(13) Hegel's Science of Logic, trans. A. V. Miller (London:
G. Allen & Unwin, 1969), 762.

(14) Ibid., 766.

(15) This list of comparisons between "life as generalized
ontological category" in Hegel and "units of living
process" in Whitehead is developed by Prof. George
L. Kline: "Life as Ontological Category: A Whiteheadian Note on Hegel," in Art and Logic in Hegel's
Philosophy, eds. Schmitz and Steinkraus (New York:
Humanities Press, 1980), 158-162. As Hegel pro-
ceeds to define the basic units of "life" as "organisms," I understand him to be using the latter term
in a broad (perhaps metaphorical) sense, as Whitehead does in Science and the Modern World.

(16) Cf., for example, the Philosophy of Right, Sec. 267
and 269, in which Hegel refers to the "organism of
the State"; cf. also Encyclopedia Sec. 539. In a
similar vein, Whitehead refers to a factory as an
organism in SMW 287.

(17) I briefly discuss Hegel's use of Goethe's "scientific"
theories, as well as his polemical relationship to
German Romantic Naturphilosophie in the Encyclopedia. Cf. Two Views of Freedom in Process
Thought, pp. 99-107.

(18) Cf. Tsuyoshi Iwabuchi, "The Concept of Nature in Hegel's
Philosophy of Spirit," Meijo-Shogaku, 25 (1976), 1-20.

(19) Cf. the annotated selections in the bibliography, Part
III:2, below.

(20) "Whitehead As I Knew Him," Journal of Philosophy, 58
     (1961), 505-516. In addition to Whitehead's acknow-
     ledgment of the influence of F. H. Bradley, and this
     further influence of Royce and Hocking, the follow-
     ing anecdote, attributed to Prof. Peter Bertocci
     (for which I am indebted to Prof. Tyler Thompson)
     suggests the lesser influence of Whitehead's colleague
     at Boston University, Prof. Edgar Sheffield Bright-
     man: "Whitehead was giving a paper at a colloquim
     at which Brightman was present. At the conclusion
     of the session Brightman, a highly competent Hegel
     scholar, argued at some length with Whitehead to the
     effect that Whitehead's position in the paper just
     read was identical with that of Hegel. Whitehead
     was not initially receptive to this suggestion. After
     lengthy debate, however, Whitehead threw up his
     hands in frustration and exclaimed: 'Well, if that
     is what Hegel meant, then I agree with him! My
     problem is, I never could understand Hegel!'"

(21) Cf. The Idea of Nature (Oxford: Oxford University
     Press, 1945), 14-16, 121f., 136-141, 158-174.

(22) Nature, Mind and Modern Science (London: George
     Allen & Unwin, 1954), 416f. See above, "Introduc-
     tion," n. 22 for Harris's work on teleology and tele-
     ological explanation in science.

(23) "Organic Categories in Whitehead," Journal of Philos-
     ophy, 34 (May 1937), 253-263. I find this comment
     somewhat puzzling, as Hegel's dialectic is hardly
     homogeneous with respect to Geist. I believe that
     Vlastos' criticism is based upon the fundamental
     misinterpretation of Hegel as an unqualified monist.

(24) Philosophy, 31/116 (January 1956), 36-54.

(25) Cf. Two Views of Freedom in Process Thought, pp. 72,
     129ff.

(26) "Philosophy and Faith: A Study in Hegel and White-
     head," in Our Common History as Christians: Es-
     says in Honor of Albert C. Outler, eds. J. Deschner,
     L. T. Howe, and K. Penzel (New York: Oxford
     University Press, 1975), 157-175. A similar point
     regarding the importance and mutual similarity of
     Hegel's and Whitehead's use and critique of religious
     symbolism was made in a Master's thesis by James

Robert Kuehl, Actuality as Spirit: A Study in Hegel
and Whitehead (Evanston, Ill.: Northwestern University, 1964).

(27) Englewood Cliffs, N. J.: Prentice-Hall, 1963.

(28) Society for the Study of Process Philosophies/American
Philosophical Association (Washington, D. C.: December 28, 1977). My own response to Prof. Kline's
paper at this meeting stressed basic agreement with
these several points he had developed, but suggested
that dialectic corresponds to concrescence, while
Begriff is more to be compared with the subjective
aim of each Whiteheadian "actual occasion."

III.   HEGELIAN IDEALISM: BIBLIOGRAPHY

Part III is concerned only with entries that reflect
upon (or criticize) the notion of Hegel as a process thinker.
A complete bibliography of writings on Hegel and his philosophy can be found in Kurt Steinhauer's recent compilation:
Hegel Bibliography/ Bibliographie (Munich: K. G. Sauer,
1980).

429. *Alexander, Samuel. "Hegel's Conception of Nature."
     Mind, old series, 9/41 (1886). [Intro, no. 1]

430. Allan, George. "The Gods Above, the Stones Beneath:
     An Essay on Historical Existence." Soundings, 51
     (1968), 448-464.
         A process philosopher comments on Hegel and the
     dialectical-teleological rhythm in the historical proc-
     ess of the rise and fall of civilizations and cultures.

431. Barrett, Clifford, ed. Contemporary Idealism in
     America. "Festschrift in Memory of Josiah Royce."
     New York: Macmillan, 1932.
         Contains essays by W. E. Hocking, Brightman,
     and other idealists. Editor's introduction argues
     that idealism tends toward an organic view of the
     universe, of spirit, and of value, and stresses the
     fact that every actual existent is an experience or
     feeling.

432. _____. "Is Idealism Realism?" Journal of Philosophy, 30/16 (August 3, 1933), 421-429.
A reply to criticisms of the above anthology by
James Pratt (no. 525, below). Argues that Moore
refutes only Berkeleyan "mentalism," not Platonic
or objective idealisms. The difference of idealism
from critical realism is that the latter utilizes re-
ductionism to explain reality, whereas idealism is
holistic, stressing the organic unity of whole and
parts.

433. Bartos, Jaromir. "Die dialektische Umgestaltung des
Begriffs 'Zufall' in Hegels Philosophie." Die Kate-
gories des Zufälligen in der Geschichte des philo-
sophischen Denkens. Prague, Czechoslovakia, 1965.

434. Bosanquet, Bernard. "Realism and Metaphysics."
Philosophical Review, 26/1 (January 1917), 4-15.
A denial that the differences in metaphysical
claims between "speculative philosophy" (idealists
such as Hegel, Green, Caird and Wallace) and realism are nearly so great as realists suggest. Both
seek to banish essential doubt about whether knowledge is really knowledge, and take what presents
itself as it comes. Bosanquet implies that, through
Bradley, the term "idealism" has taken on a negative and misleading connotation, and should be abandoned. This might lead to a re-integration of realism with "speculative philosophy."

435. Brecht, Stefan Sebastian. The Place of Natural Science
in Hegel's Philosophy. Diss. Harvard University,
1959.

436. Brightman, Edgar S. "Modern Idealism." Journal
of Philosophy 17/20 (September 23, 1920), 533-550.
A summary of the history, doctrine, and status
of idealism principally in America in the period
1910-20, defending the "vigor" of idealism, despite
its critics. "Bergson ... although hard to classify,
is in the broad sense an idealist, influenced by the
personalist Renouvier." Technical philosophical
idealism can be divided into four schools: 1) Platonic; 2) Berkeleyan (mentalism); 3) Personalism
(Bowne, Pringle-Pattison, Lotze, T. H. Green);
4) Logical or Organic (Hegel). The first school ad-
heres to the principle of "objectivity of value"; the
second holds that Reality is to be equated with Con-

sciousness; the third suggests that "self" or "per-
sonhood" is the ultimate fact; the forth defends the
coherence of a single System as the only true fact.
Criticisms of idealism fail to account for this diversity, and thus are not helpful. Brightman documents
a growing sympathy and compromise among some
realists and idealists, such as R. B. Perry and
Bosanquet. He concludes by anticipating Whitehead's
criteria of philosophy: "Does it interpret life as a
whole? Does it envisage all the facts? Does it
make all the facts intelligible?"

437.   _____. "The Present Outlook in Philosophy of Religion: From the Standpoint of an Idealist." American Philosophies of Religion. Eds. Weiman and Meland. Chicago: Willett, Clark & Co., 1936. Pp.
318-325.

438.   Brinkley, Alan B. "Time in Hegel's Phenomenology."
Tulane Studies in Philosophy, 9 (1960), 3-15.
        Argues against the thesis that Hegel failed to rec-
ognize the importance of time, and criticizes Samuel
Alexander for abandoning Hegel and popularizing the
notion that Bergson was the first to "take time seriously." With reference to interpreters who have
seen the importance of time in Hegel, Brinkley argues
that time is the reality of the Concept, and thus the
"keystone of Hegel's system."

439.   Burbridge, John. "Concept and Time in Hegel." Dialogue, 12 (1973), 403-422.
        Burbridge argues that a philosophical-conceptual
system and a dynamic character of time can indeed
be reconciled. Time is the conceptual structure of
becoming; whence, time is congruent with Hegel's
"Concept," and represents a process of Concepts.

440.   Burton, Robert Glenn. Time, Determinism and Creativity. Diss. Northwestern University, 1969.

441.   Collingwood, Robin G. "Croce's Philosophy of History."
Hibbert Journal, 19 (1921).

442. * _____. The Idea of Nature. Oxford: The Clarendon Press, 1945. [Intro, no. 11]

443.   DeGennaro, Angelo A. "Croce and Marx." Personalist, 43 (Autumn 1962), 466-472.

444. _____. "Croce and Hegel." Personalist, 44 (Summer 1963), 302-308.

445. _____. "Croce and Collingwood." Personalist, 46 (Spring 1965), 193-202.
     In comparison with these other figures, the author criticizes Croce's metaphysics, while lauding his concept of liberty.

446. DiGiovanni, Giorgio. Contingency: Its Foundation in Hegel's Logic of Becoming. Diss. University of Toronto, 1970.
     Though critics charge that there is no room for contingency in absolute idealism, this thesis defends Hegel's description of contingency in the Logic, especially the dialectic of "reflection and activity." The "Absolute" is the source of contingency as well as of necessity.

447. Earle, William. "Inter-Subjective Time." Process and Divinity. Eds. Reese and Freeman. LaSalle, Ill.: Open Court, 1964. Pp. 285-297.
     Discusses the centrality of time in contemporary philosophy, especially in Croce, Whitehead, Bergson, Hartshorne and others, dating "the conspicuous turning point with Hegel." Discusses the difference of the present concept of time as a non-ultimate category--a product of existence or activity--from "time" in the philosophia perennis (Newton's abstract receptacle, Kant's sensuous a priori), in which time resembles eternity. Contemporary time is a real process with duration.

448. Englehardt, Dietrich V. "Das Chemische System der Stuffe, Krafte und Prozesse in Hegels Naturphilosophie und der Wissenschaft seiner Zeit." Hegel-Studien: Beiheft, 11 (1974), 125-139.

449. Ewing, A. C. Idealism: A Critical Survey. New York: Humanities Press, 1934.
     A penetrating, critical study by a non-idealist. A typology of idealism is given together with a review of the central problems and issues in idealist thought. The usual sense of "internal relations" is found to be unsupportable; nonetheless, since "causality" does imply "logical entailment," it does seem to be the case that the "world has something of the character of an intelligible system." Relations are,

in some modified sense, constitutive. Only if "coherence" implies "comprehensiveness" can one make
sense of "degrees of truth." Objections to theism
and panpsychism are noted.

450. _____. The Idealist Tradition, from Berkeley to
Blanshard. Glencoe, Ill.: Free Press, 1957.
Philosophers included in this discussion are Berkeley, Kant, Hegel, Schopenhauer, Green, Bradley,
Bosanquet, Royce, Rashdall, Howison, McTaggart,
Croce, and Blanshard, although the author briefly
acknowledges the contributions of Lotze, Perry,
Brightman and others to the tradition. He distinguishes between Berkeleyan esse est percipi, Kantian
phenomenalism-dualism, and absolute idealism. The
latter tradition does not argue for the mind-depend-
ence of the physical world; rather, it advocates coherence, internal relatedness and monism.

451. Findlay, J. N. Hegel: A Re-examination. Oxford:
Oxford University Press, 1958.

452. _____. "The Contemporary Relevance of Hegel."
Language, Mind, and Value. London: George Allen
and Unwin, 1963. Pp. 217-231. Reprinted in Alasdair MacIntyre (ed), Hegel: A Collection of Critical
Essays. Garden City, N.Y.: Doubleday and Co.,
1972. Pp. 1-20.
Argues that Hegel's idealism is less monistic than
Bradley's "absolute idealism and mysticism." Hegel's
is rather a dynamic organic teleology. Hegel also
does not stress holism or "wholes" as strongly as
does Bradley.

453. _____. "Hegel's Use of Teleology." The Monist,
48/1, (January 1964), 1-17.
Whereas other idealists, especially the later Bradley, are axiomatic, Findlay argues that Hegel is more
to be compared with Aristotle. Hegel's Begriff parallels the teleological Form of Aristotle: in both cases
one has a description of final cause, full actuality
and the achieved goodness of any entity. Findlay
discusses Hegel's criticism of natural science, suggesting that he anticipated Whitehead's "fallacy of
misplaced concreteness."

454. Goetzmann, William H., ed. The American Hegelians.
New York: Alfred A. Knopf, 1973.

Lively and entertaining account of the early American Hegelian movement in St. Louis, and of the development of the Journal of Speculative Philosophy, which carried articles by Peirce, James, and Dewey. Goetzmann suggests that John Dewey owed his sense of philosophy as process, his social conscience, and his theory of collective individualism to his early mentor, Hegel.

455. Harris, Errol E. "The Philosophy of Nature in Hegel's System." Review of Metaphysics, 3 (1949), 213-228.

456. _____. "Hegel's Theory of Feelings." New Studies in Hegel's Philosophy. Ed. Warren Steinkraus. New York: Holt, Rinehart and Winston, 1971. Pp. 71-91.
Discusses Hegel's theory of the body as an activity and a process of "feelings," and consciousness as an awareness, a reflexive examination and retention of that process or activity.

457. _____. "Hegel and the Natural Sciences." Beyond Epistemology. Ed. F. G. Weiss. The Hague: Martinus Nijhoff, 1974. Pp. 129-153.
Refutes decisively the charge that Hegel was contemptuous of natural science. Rather, his contempt was directed toward popular "philosophies" of science, as well as the form of scientific method then predominant.

458. _____. "Science and Objectivity." Contemporary Studies in Philosophical Idealism. Eds. Howie and Buford. Cape Cod, Mass.: Claude Stark, 1975. Pp. 81-94.
Supports the objectivity of scientific knowledge of the natural world against detractors, such as Popper, Husserl, and Heidegger, whose views tend to relativize and subjectivize science. "Science" is a coherent organization of actual experience, thus accounting for realism, and allowing for evolutionary development in understanding. "Truth" is thus an objective attainable by degrees.

459. Hashimoto, Rentaro. Process and Finality in Hegel. Diss. Fordham University, 1963.
"Process" is described by Hegel in terms of pairs of opposites. The Absolute Idea processively unfolds as an atemporal matrix, while the Phenomenology

and the Philosophy of Religion describe the temporal
aspirations of the finite and infinite toward a self-
transcendent unity.

460.   Henrich, Dieter. "Hegel's Theorie über den Zufall."
Kant-Studien, 50 (1958-59), 131-148.
Discusses the importance of chance and contingency
in Hegel's metaphysics and the dialectical relation-
ship of contingency and determinism in the Logic and
Philosophy of Nature.

461.   Hocking, William E. "Theses Establishing an Idealistic Metaphysics by a New Route." Journal of Philosophy, 38 (December 1941), 688-689.
A stunning, terse outline of an event-metaphysics,
based upon relativity and field theory. Events define space-time; persons are "fields of events."

462.   _____. Science and the Idea of God. Chapel Hill:
University of North Carolina Press, 1944.

463.   _____. "On Royce's Empiricism." Journal of Philosophy, 53/3 (February 2, 1956), 57-63.

464.   Hook, Sydney. "The Contemporary Significance of
Hegel's Philosophy." The Philosophical Review, 41
(1932), 237-260.
"Although Hegel officially denies the reality of
time, he recognizes its existence whenever he uses
the words 'finite' and 'appearance.' Under the aspect of time the world confronts man as an ever-
enduring process. Under the aspect of eternity the
world is a completed system. But to the process
belongs metaphysical primacy" (p. 249).

465.   Howie, John, and Buford, Thomas O., eds. Contem-
porary Studies in Philosophical Idealism. Cape Cod,
Mass.: Claude Stark, 1975.
Identifies a variety of contemporary schools: Ab-
solute (Bradley, Royce); panpsychistic (Leibnitz,
Whitehead, Hartshorne); personalistic (Hocking,
Brightman).

466.   Iwabuchi, Tsuyoshi. "The Concept of Nature in Hegel's
Philosophy of Spirit." Meijo-Shogaku, 25 (1976),
1-20.
An attempt to explore the relation of "mind" (sense-
perception) and spirit in Hegel's concept of nature.

An examination of passages in the Encyclopedia on
Nature and Spirit makes it clear that Hegel's Naturphilosophie is an attempt to comprehend, in a unified
(as opposed to a dualistic) manner, the process of
development of Nature and of the perceiving subject;
and that his Philosophy of History is also such an
attempt, in reference to the history of humankind
and of the knowing, perceiving subject.

467. Kayser, Ulrich. Das Problem der Zeit in der Ge-
schichts-philosophie Hegels. Diss. Berlin, 1930.

468. Kobligk, Helmut. Denken und Zeit. Beiträge zu einer
Interpretation des Hegelschen Zeitbegriffes. Diss.
Kiel, 1952.

469. Kroner, Richard. "Mure and Other English Hegelians."
Review of Metaphysics 7/1 (September 1953), 64-
73.
A brief summary of major English Hegelians,
from J. H. Stirling (The Secret of Hegel) to R. G.
Collingwood. In discussing Mure's contemporary
Hegelianism, Kroner shows the influence on Mure
of Collingwood and Pringle-Pattison.

470. Lutzow, Thomas. Hegel's Concept of Science. Diss.
Marquette University, 1977.

471. McCarthy, G. "Temporality and Science in Hegel's
'Logic'." Studies in Soviet Philosophy, 16 (1976),
251-266.
A discussion of the role of possibility and the
future in Marx's Capital, as compared with Hegel's
Science of Logic, suggesting implications for social
science. "Every attempt to understand the histori-
city of the objective world requires the comprehen-
sion of the structure of temporality, since the 'is'
exists only as 'having been' and the 'will' already
'is'."

472. Masuda, Ryohei. "Hegel's Concept of Nature." Re-
port of the Faculty of Liberal Arts of Gunma University, 10 (1976), 1-22.

473. Mays, W. "Temporality and Time in Hegel and Marx."
Study of Time II: Proceedings of the Second Conference of the International Society for the Study of
Time. Berlin; Heidelberg; New York: 1975. Pp.
98-113.

Discusses the relation of time to Hegel's dialectic, and his view of history.

474. Moore, G. E. "The Refutation of Idealism." Philosophical Studies. London: Routledge and Kegan Paul, 1922. Pp. 1-30.

475. Mure, G. R. G. An Introduction to Hegel. Oxford: Clarendon Press, 1940.

476. _____. A Study of Hegel's Logic. Oxford: Clarendon Press, 1950.

477. O'Hare, Joseph Aloysius. The Meaning of Action in the Phenomenology and Logic of Hegel. Diss. Fordham University, 1968.
O'Hare argues that Hegel's Logic is a "progressive revelation of a metaphysics of process, an ontology of dialectical being, which places a creative negativity at the heart of finite being." Hegel's ontology is conditioned by a teleology which is imminent and emergent through process.

478. Querner, Hans. "Die Stuffenfolge der Organismen in Hegels Philosophie der Natur." Hegel-Studien; Beiheft, 11 (1974), 153-163.
Amplifies Nietzsche's remark, "Denn ohne Hegel kein Darwin." For Hegel, Nature was the second stage in the development of the Idea, further subdivided into "Mechanism-Material," "Physics-Individuality," "Organic-Subjectivity." The philosophy of nature is thus primarily concerned with narrating the dialectical process of development of the Begriff. The representation of a real historical process of development, by contrast, was explicitly rejected by Hegel.

479. Reck, Andrew J. "Substance, Subject and Dialectic." Tulane Studies in Philosophy, 9 (1960), 109-133.
Hegel is presented as a critic of Spinozist "substance" philosophy, which represented a reversion to "Eleatic-Parmenidean monism." Such thought ignores the dynamic quality of substance as subject. "Substance is not an inert principle.... It is not a concealed substrate; it is rather a vital principle."

480. _____. "Idealism in American Philosophy Since 1900." Contemporary Studies in Philosophical Idealism. Eds. Howie and Buford. Cape Cod, Mass.:

Claude Stark and Company, 1975. Pp. 17-52.
Essentially the story of Royce's influence in America, especially on W. E. Hocking and Brand Bland-
shard.

481. Swift, Morrison Isaac. The Ethics of Idealism, As
      Represented by Aristotle and Hegel. Diss. Johns
      Hopkins University, 1885.

482. Wattles, Jeffrey Hamilton. Hegel's Philosophy of Or-
      ganic Nature. Diss. Northwestern University, 1973.

483. Webb, Thomas Remson. Hegelian Science and the
      Problem of Nature. Diss. University of Toronto,
      1977.

484. Whittemore, Robert C. "Hegel as Panentheist." Tu-
      lane Studies in Philosophy, 9 (1960), 134-164.
      "Panentheism" is presented as a term coined by
      Hegel's contemporary, K. C. F. Krause; as a con-
      cept in the Vedas; and in hymns to the Egyptian
      Aton. Whittemore argues that Hegel was a panen-
      theist, for whom the universe was included in God,
      who transcends the Universe as the Whole transcend-
      ing the sum of its parts. The universe, for Hegel,
      is seen as God's body. Compares Hegel's theism
      especially with Whitehead; also Bergson, Smuts,
      Morgan, and Lloyd.

485. Williams, M. E. "Time in Hegel's Philosophy." Dia-
      logue, 9 (1970), 154-167.

III. 1.   HEGELIAN IDEALISM AND PROCESS
          RATIONALISM: BIBLIOGRAPHY

---

486. Allan, George. "Croce and Whitehead on Concres-
      cence." Process Studies, 2/2 (Summer 1972), 95-
      111.

487. *Alston, William P. "Internal Relatedness and Plural-
      ism in Whitehead." Review of Metaphysics, 5 (1952),
      535-558. [I, no. 50]

488. Barnhart, J. E. "Bradley's Monism and Whitehead's
      Neo-Pluralism." Southern Journal of Philosophy,
      7/4 (Winter 1969-70), 395-400.
        Contrasts Bradley's monism and doctrine of the
      Absolute (of which pluralism is a mere appearance)
      with Whitehead's unyielding pluralism. For Bradley,
      monism follows, since no finite entity is self-con-
      tained. Whitehead reverses this conclusion, arguing
      from mutual immanence to plurality.

489. Brightman, Edgar S. "The Definition of Idealism."
      Journal of Philosophy, 30/16 (August 3, 1933), 429-
      435.
        Response to Barrett's reply to Pratt's criticisms
      of his anthology ("Is Idealism Realism?" 421-429;
      no. 432 above). Brightman reviews the four varia-
      tions of idealism: 1) Platonic, stressing the objec-
      tivity of value; 2) Berkeleyan "mentalism" (esse est
      percipi); 3) Hegelian, stressing the organic or holis-
      tic properties of reality (the whole has properties
      not accounted for by any part alone); and 4) the ideal-
      ism of Leibniz and Lotze, which stresses that only
      "selves" are real (reality is personal). Variation (3)
      is the only necessary condition for philosophical
      idealism. Thus, personalism embraces all four
      categories, while Samuel Alexander's "nisus toward
      totality" is an idealistic strain in a realistic system.
      Whitehead is a partial idealist. Idealism, like Real-
      ism, may have monistic and dualistic forms, es-
      pecially as regards epistemology and the concept of
      truth.

490. Butler, Clark. G. W. F. Hegel. "Twayne's World
      Author Series." Boston: Twayne Publishers, 1977.
        Discussing oriental roots and affinities of Hegel,
      Butler observes that Hegel's definition of "Absolute"
      is panpsychist in nature, and--in marked contrast
      to Charles Taylor's dismissal of its modernity--is
      advocated in the contemporary period by Teilhard,
      Whitehead, Hartshorne, and in the anti-materialistic
      event-metaphysics of Buddhism. Butler claims that
      many of these contemporary traditions have yet to
      discover their Hegelian vocation and destiny. Butler
      further notes Hegel's anticipation of evolution, and
      argues that Hegel's system of objective idealism is
      pluralistic.

491. Donagan, Alan. "A Contradiction in Collingwood's Phi-

losophy of Natural Science." The Later Philosophy
of R. G. Collingwood. Oxford: Oxford University
Press, 1962. Pp. 154-156.
    Collingwood praises Hegel for having anticipated
Whitehead's rejection of simple location and material
substance. Donagan charges Collingwood with "so-
phistry," and rejects the idea that "pure philosophical speculation itself often did and always could have
led to scientific advances."

492. *Eddington, Sir Arthur S. The Nature of the Physical
    World. "Gifford Lectures, 1927." Cambridge:
    Cambridge University Press, 1929. [I, no. 74]

493. *_____. The Philosophy of Physical Science. "Tar-
    ner Lectures, 1938." Cambridge: Cambridge Uni-
    versity Press, 1939. [I, no. 76]

494. Fever, Lewis S. "What Is Philosophy of History?"
    Journal of Philosophy, 49 (1952), 329-340.
        Whitehead, Marx, and Toynbee are discussed to
    illustrate the thesis that speculative philosophies of
    history are in fact projective value systems: as
    such they represent defensive psychological measures
    against "historical anxiety."

495. Haldane, R. B. "The Function of Metaphysics in
    Scientific Method." Contemporary British Philosophy,
    I. Ed. J. H. Muirhead. London: G. Allen and
    Unwin, 1924. Pp. 127-148.
        "On the whole, I think that Hegel has come nearer
    to the ultimately true view than anyone since the an-
    cient Greeks." Haldane offers a holistic analysis
    of the scientific enterprise. He compares Hegel and
    Goethe with Whitehead in contemporary thought, but
    is critical of Bradley. Each science has its own
    essential language--the language of biology is that
    of "organism," not physical reductionism.

496. *Harris, Errol E. Nature, Mind and Modern Science.
    London: George Allen and Unwin, 1954. [Intro, no.
    17]

497. *_____. Foundations of Metaphysics in Modern Sci-
    ence. London: G. Allen and Unwin, 1965. [Intro,
    no. 18]

498. _____. Hypothesis and Perception: The Roots of

Scientific Method. London: G. Allen and Unwin, 1970.
Argues that the role of a variable a priori in perception affects scientific theory. Compares in this vein the work of Thomas Kuhn, as well as Whitehead's discussion of the influence on science of the "prevailing climate of opinion." Hegel and Collingwood prefigure this modern acknowledgment of the formative role of ideas in science. Collingwood's "scale of forms" describes the logical and categorical structure of all "systems," whether natural or theoretical. The Hegelian "concrete universal" is thus an adequate model to interpret scientific discovery, advancement, and the role of the conscious mind.

499. Hartshorne, Charles. "Ideal Knowledge Defines Reality: What Was True in 'Idealism'." Journal of Philosophy, 43/21 (October 10, 1946), 573-582.
Hartshorne defends five premises: 1) In contrast to Royce, perfect knowledge of reality is not timeless, but only relatively complete; 2) ideal knowledge is not to be equated with the actualization of all desires; 3) truth is not merely coherence, but also conceptual clarity, and the correspondence of ideas (content) with events; likewise 4) truth is not passive or pure actuality, but self-activity; and 5) the object of knowledge is not just pure identity with, but also participation in what is known.

500. _____. "Royce's Mistake--and Achievement." Journal of Philosophy, 53/3 (February 2, 1956), 123-130.
Royce's "mistake" was his belief in antecedent, factual truth, despite Aristotle's warning and alternative. This view entails that all events are real eternally, once and for all. Hence, there can be no genuine novelty, and Royce consequently is led to a denial of real, alternative possibilities. Royce's "achievement" (which he mistakenly believed to follow from the preceding view, but which is in fact logically distinct from it) was his doctrine of the fundamental interrelatedness of all experiencing. Royce's lasting influence, then, is the view that finally all events must be data for an Ideal Experience.

501. _____. "The Case for Idealism." Philosophical Forum, 1/1 (Fall 1968), 7-23.

502. *Heipcke, Klaus. Die Philosophie des Ereignisses bei
     Alfred North Whitehead. Habilitationsschrift. Würz-
     burg: Julius-Maximilians Universität, 1964. [I,
     no. 107]

503. *Heisenberg, Warner. Across the Frontiers. Trans.
     Peter Heath. "World Perspective, Vol. 48." Ed.
     R. N. Anshen. New York: Harper & Row, 1974.
     [I, no. 112]

504. *Hélal, Georges. "La cosmologie: un nouvel examen
     de sa nature et de sa raison d'être." Dialogue,
     8/2 (1969). [II, no. 399]

505. Hocking, Richard. "The Polarity of Dialectical History
     and Process Cosmology." Christian Scholar, 50
     (1967), 177-183.
          Process cosmology and dialectical history are
     each based upon experience. They are polar op-
     posites, but complementary. Whitehead's philosophy
     sustains possibly both positions.

506. Hocking, William E. "Whitehead as I Knew Him."
     Journal of Philosophy, 58 (1961), 505-516.
          Casts interesting historical light on Whitehead's
     knowledge of Hegel, on the growing influence on
     Whitehead of American Hegelians such as Josiah
     Royce, as well as on Whitehead's increasing acknow-
     ledgment of F. H. Bradley.

507. Hoernlé, R. F. A. "The Revival of Idealism." Con-
     temporary Idealism in America. Ed. Clifford Bar-
     rett. New York: Macmillan, 1932. Pp. 297-326.
          Author identifies Whitehead as an idealist based
     upon his rejection of the principle of vacuous actu-
     ality, and his claim that every actual existent is an
     experience, or feeling. Article also documents the
     idealist influence on Dewey, labeling him an idealist
     as well.

508. Kambartel, Friedrich. "The Universe Is More Various,
     More Hegelian. Zum Weltverständnis bei Hegel und
     Whitehead." Collegium Philosophicum. "Studien
     für Joachim Ritter zum 60. Geburtstag." Stuttgart,
     1965. Pp. 72-98.
          Whitehead's view that universal conceptual theories
     are generally unable to capture the myriad manifesta-
     tions of concrete reality, parallels Hegel's similar

view that reality consists in a "growing together" of
the General and Particular, the Universal and Individual. Whitehead's view that the world consists of
experiencing subjects parallels Hegel's thought that
the opposition and antithesis between knowledge and
its object is overcome in self-consciousness. The
subsequent orientation of philosophy after Whitehead
toward a methodological ideal of mathematics (a
trend paralleled in post-Hegelian philosophy) fails
to recognize this feature of reality as process.

509. Kline, George L., ed. Alfred North Whitehead: Es-
     says on His Philosophy. Englewood Cliffs, N.J.:
     Prentice-Hall, Inc., 1963.
     Editor's introduction urges further Whitehead-
     Hegel study and suggests some possible areas of
     similarity. It also engages, by way of example,
     in a linguistic analysis of the Whiteheadian and the
     Hegelian uses of "abstract" and "concrete."

510. _____. "Whitehead in the Non-English Speaking
     World." Process and Divinity. Eds. Reese and
     Freeman. LaSalle, Ill.: Open Court, 1964. Pp.
     235-268.
     Calls for a moratorium on use of the vague, am-
     biguous, and misleading phrase "Philosophy of Or-
     ganism" to describe Whitehead's philosophy. White-
     head notes his own closeness to Aristotle and Hegel
     and the latter suggestion needs further exploration.
     Traces Continental (non-English) views of Whitehead,
     many of which appropriate him as a Hegelian.

511. _____. "Some Recent Reinterpretations of Hegel's
     Philosophy." The Monist, 47/1 (January 1964), 34-75.
     Comments on the similar difficulties encountered
     in Whitehead's and Hegel's vocabulary, both of which
     have been "more often deplored than analyzed."
     Presents a useful clarification of Hegelian termin-
     ology, distinguishing between systematic and non-
     systematic use of key terms. Claims that the sys-
     tematic use of key Hegelian terms closely parallels
     systematic Whiteheadian vocabulary.

512. _____. "Form, Concrescence and Concretum: A
     Neo-Whiteheadian Analysis." Southern Journal of
     Philosophy, 7/4 (Winter 1969-1970), 351-360.
     Includes a comparative analysis of the language of
     "concreteness" in both Hegel and Whitehead.

513. _____. "Life as Ontological Category: A White-
headian Note on Hegel." Hegel's Aesthetics and
Logic. Eds. Kenneth L. Schmitz and Warren E.
Steinkraus. New York: Humanities Press, 1980.
Pp. 158-162.
    Hegel's discussion of "das logische Leben" in the
Logic suggests properties of the "Concept" virtually
identical to those of Whitehead's "concrescences."

514. Knox, T. M. "Hegel in English-speaking Countries
Since 1919." Hegel-Studien, 1 (1961), 315-318.
    Discusses the strong Hegelian influence on Col-
lingwood, and praises Errol E. Harris's Nature,
Mind and Modern Science. Decries the negative influence on the English-speaking world of Karl Popper's "ignorant and unscholarly diatribe" against
Hegel (The Open Society and Its Enemies, 1945).

515. Kuehl, James Robert. Actuality as Spirit: A Study
in Hegel and Whitehead. Master's Thesis, Northwestern University, 1964.
    Kuehl proposes to examine Whitehead's alleged
"transformation of idealism onto a realistic basis"
with respect to the problem of God. Argues that
Whitehead's "primordial Nature" approximates Hegel's
"God the Father" (transcendent universal); the "Consequent Nature" approximates Hegel's "God the Son"
(particularity of God in the world); and God in his
totality as a concrete synthesis of the Primordial
and Consequent Natures approximates Hegel's God
as Spirit--an ongoing process of living active synthesis.

516. *Lucas, George R., Jr. Two Views of Freedom in
Process Thought. Chico, Cal.: Scholars Press,
1979. [Intro, no. 30]

517. Megill, Kenneth. "On Marx's Method." Southern
Journal of Philosophy, 9/1 (Spring 1971), 61-66.
    Uses the Whiteheadian notions of an "isolated
system" and the "fallacy of misplaced concreteness"
to discuss Marx as an empirical analyst of social
systems.

518. *Muirhead, John H. The Platonic Tradition in Anglo-
Saxon Philosophy. London: G. Allen and Unwin,
1931. [I, no. 133]

519. Norman, Ralph Vernon, Jr. Theodicy and the Form
     of Redemption: An Essay in the Christian Under-
     standing of Evil with an Examination of the Notion
     of Redemptive Order in Josiah Royce and A. N.
     Whitehead. Diss. Yale University, 1961.

520. O'Meara, Thomas F. "Process and God in Schelling's
     Early Thought." Listening, 14/3 (Fall 1979), 223-
     236.
     Discusses God as process in Schelling's System of
     Transcendental Idealism (1800): a theory of organism,
     polar dialectic, and history as real evolutionary
     novelty (the dialectic of freedom and necessity). Dif-
     fers from modern process theologies in that, for
     Schelling, human consciousness, in its history, is
     a finite projection of God, instead of projecting finite
     human characteristics into the nature of God Itself.
     His influence on Hegel is obvious.

521. Omeljanowski, M. E. "Hegel und die Dialektik in der
     modernen Physik." Hegel-Jahrbuch, 1975. Cologne,
     1976. Pp. 533-543.
     A polemic against Heisenberg's views, arguing
     that modern physics allies itself more closely with
     the "materialistic dialectic," which originated with
     and grew out of the rational core of Hegel's philos-
     ophy.

522. Parsons, Howard L. "History as Viewed by Marx and
     Whitehead." Christian Scholar, 50 (1967), 273-289.
     "The philosophy of history of Marx and Whitehead
     are complementary, and in dialectical tension. Each
     is inadequate for theory and practice without the
     other." Parsons sees their positions intersecting
     at several points. Whitehead was an activist who
     appreciated economics and the need for revolution.
     Marx was a scholar who favored the use of reason.
     Both recognized the dialectical role of thought and
     praxis in history, as well as the interdependence of
     man with ecology.

523. Pixley, Goerge V. "Whitehead y Marx sobre la di-
     námica de la historia." Dialogos, 7/2 (April-June
     1970), 83-107.
     Pixley discusses some similarities in Whitehead's
     speculative philosophy and Marx's "scientific" inter-
     pretation of history. He views process philosophy as

tending toward an evolutionary rather than a dialectical interpretation of history.

524. _____. "Justice and the Class Struggle: A Challenge for Process Theology." Process Studies, 4/3
(Fall 1974), 159-175.
Pixley contends that a revolutionary process theology is possible. Whitehead's own discussion of
culture and civilization, however, is available to
counterrevolutionaries. A need exists for further
consideration of justice in process terms.

525. Pratt, James B. "Is Idealism Realism?" Journal of
Philosophy, 30/7 (March 30, 1933), 169-178.
Review of anthology on idealism by Clifford Barrett
(no. 431; cf. 432). Idealism involves "esse est percipi." Redefinitions in Barrett's book hopelessly con-
fuse "idealism" and render it impossible to define or
distinguish.

526. Saintillau, Daniel. "Hegel et Héraclite au le Logos
qui n'a pas de contraire." Hegel et la pensée grecque.
"Publié sous la direction de J. D'Handt." Paris,
1974. Pp. 27-84.

527. Smith, James Leroy. "On Whitehead, Marx and the
Nature of Political Philosophy." Tulane Studies in
Philosophy, 24 (1975), 101-112.
The difference between Whitehead and Marx is
the difference between philosophy and "slipshod science." Offers Whitehead as a middle way between
a Marxist glorification of the empirical, and the
pure adulation of ahistorical ideals. Whitehead's
way alone is fruitful for political philosophy.

528. Smith, John E. "The Critique of Abstractions and the
Scope of Reason." Process and Divinity. Eds.
Reese and Freeman. LaSalle, Ill.: Open Court,
1964. Pp. 19-35.
Contributions of Hegel and Dewey cited in discussing the use and critique of reason--especially of
theoretical abstractions or categorial schemes. Suggests that Whitehead synthesized and surpassed these
traditional modes of abstraction.

529. Straton, George Douglas. Theistic Faith for Our Time:
An Introduction to the Process Philosophies of Royce
and Whitehead. Washington, D.C.: University Press
of America, 1979.

Through a modification of Whitehead in the direction of a personal idealism, and re-interpretation of
Royce's doctrine of time (to claim that Royce intended
to say that God is identical with time, or that time
is the ultimate expression of God's being), the author
attempts to illustrate affinities and exhibit Royce as
a "process" philosopher.

530. Vlastos, Gregory. "Organic Categories in Whitehead."
      Journal of Philosophy, 34 (May 1937), 253-263.
      Vlastos outlines two notions of becoming: a) con-
      crete synthesis, the development of an Idea, or
      Spirit (Hegel); b) concrete synthesis of diverse "feel-
      ings" as an actual entity (Whitehead). Whitehead's
      is a "heterogeneous" dialectic in terms of actual
      entities and eternal objects. Hegel's is a "homogen-
      eous" dialectic, in terms of Spirit. Whitehead's is
      a unique variation of Hegel's dialectic.

531. Wahl, Jean. "La Philosophie speculative de White-
      head." Revue Philosophique, 91 (1931), 341-378;
      92 (1931), 108-143.
      Sees Hegelian affinities in Whitehead's theory of
      perception. All perception is negative in that it in-
      volves discerning relations of "this" which is not
      "that" or another, as well as a contrast of the pos-
      sible (identifications) with the given (obejct). "As
      Plato and Hegel saw, (this) presupposes the idea of
      the other ... For Whitehead as for Hegel there is
      no strictly private term; whatever exists is linked
      to all the rest." Whitehead's connection of actuality
      with value represents a variation of Hegelianism.

532. Whitehead, Alfred North. Process and Reality. "Gif-
      ford Lectures, 1927-28." New York: Macmillan,
      1929.
      In this his seminal work, Whitehead claims to
      "transform the doctrines of absolute idealism onto
      a realistic basis." In Part II of the work, he con-
      cludes his description of actual entities and the proc-
      ess of concrescence by suggesting that concrescence
      represents nothing less than the Hegelian develop-
      ment of an Idea (Begriff).

533. Whittemore, Robert C. Panpsychism and the Function
      of God. Diss. Yale University, 1953.
      Whitehead's philosophy represents the first clear
      expression of panentheism and panpsychism as a way

to overcome divisions between science and religion.
Concern for this solution predates Whitehead, however, as seen especially in Lotze and Hegel.

534.   . "Whitehead's Process and Bradley's Reality."
The Modern Schoolman, 32 (November 1954), 56-74.
Traces the acknowledged influence of Bradley on
Whitehead, and the convergence of certain conclusions
of process philosophy's "realism" with idealism. In-
vestigates Bernard Bosanquet's charge of "panpsychism," leveled against Bradley's decidedly non-
Parmenidean view of the Absolute, concluding that
"monism" for Bradley is really panpsychism.

535.   . "Hegel's 'Science' and Whitehead's 'Modern
World'." Philosophy, 31/116 (January 1956), 36-54.
One of the earliest specific explorations of
Hegel-Whitehead affinities, stimulated by Collingwood
and Errol Harris. Presents a special comparison
of "dialectic" with "process."

536. *   . "Hegel as Panentheist." Tulane Studies in
Philosophy, 9 (1960), 134-164. [III, no. 484]

537. Williams, Daniel Day. "Philosophy and Faith: A
Study in Hegel and Whitehead." Our Common His-
tory as Christians: Essays in Honor of Albert C.
Outler. Eds. J. Drescher, L. T. Howe, and K.
Penzel. New York: Oxford University Press, 1975.
Pp. 157-175.
Compares Hegel's attempt to justify Christianity
as the Absolute Religion with Whitehead's similar
attempt to show that the essential truth of Christianity can be exhibited via a philosophical critique.
Both involve rationalistic faith via philosophy. For
Hegel, "Spirit" is equivalent to "community," a
union of God and Man. For Whitehead, incarnation
is the victory of persuasion over force. Discerning
the universal structure of religion is never, for
Hegel or Whitehead, done in abstraction from experience. Whitehead is more open to the problem of
evil as "brute fact" and "surd" than is Hegel.

538. Williamson, Clark M. "Whitehead as Counterrevolu-
tionary? Toward Christian-Marxist Dialogue." Process Studies, 4/3 (Fall 1974), 176-186.
Marxism and process thought both view metaphysics as a "social requirement." Both accept "relativ-

ism" with regard to established social order; both
advocate a "negative anthropology." Transcendence
as a basic dimension of reality is affirmed by both,
leading to a dialectical approach to religion.

III. 2. HEGELIAN IDEALISM AND EVOLUTIONARY
         COSMOLOGY: BIBLIOGRAPHY

---

539. Auersperg, Alfred von. Poesie und Forschung: Goethe,
     Weizsäcker, Teilhard de Chardin. Stuttgart: Enke,
     1965.

540. Barthelemy-Madaule, Madeleine. "Teilhard de Char-
     din, Marxism, Existentialism: A Confrontation."
     International Philosophical Quarterly, 1/4 (December
     1961), 648-667.
         Compares Teilhard with Marx, whose materialism
     became a "substitute Absolute." Examining Teil-
     hard's criticism of Marxism, the author contends
     that Teilhard's vision attempts to incorporate the
     exigencies and concerns of Marx regarding the legiti-
     mate needs of modern man.

541. Borne, Etienne. "Les communistes et le P. Teilhard."
     France-forum, 34 (1960).

542. Bravo Vivar, Noe. "La conception de l'homme chez
     Karl Marx et Teilhard de Chardin." Typescript.
     Paris: Faculté de lettres et sciences humaines de
     l'Université de Paris, 1969.

543. Brown, A. Barratt. "Intuition." International Journal
     of Ethics, 24/3 (1913-1914), 282-293.
         Compares Bradley's and Bergson's concept of in-
     tuition.

544. Bubner, Rüdiger. Hegel und Goethe. Heidelberg:
     Carl Winter Universitätsverlag, 1978.
         While mainly concerned to trace the growing dif-
     ferences in the interpretation of art by Goethe and
     Hegel, the monograph briefly traces the "three per-
     iods" of the personal relationships and influences:
     at Jena (c. 1801); approximately 1816-1818, while

Hegel was at Heidelberg; and, finally, during the
last years of Hegel's and Goethe's lives, in Berlin.

545. *Butler, Clark. G. W. F. Hegel. "Twayne's World
Author Series." Boston: Twayne Publishers, 1977.
[III, no. 490]

546. Capek, Milic. "Time and Eternity in Royce and Bergson." Revue Internationale de Philosophie, 79-80/1-
2 (1967), 22-45.
Many comparisons of Royce and Bergson are made.
"In spite of an honest and sincere effort to take time
seriously," Royce moved finally toward the view of
Bradley and McTaggart: ultimately, time is unreal.

547. Carr, Herbert Wildon. "Time" and "History" in Contemporary Philosophy: With Special Reference to
Bergson and Croce. London: Proceedings of the
British Academy VIII (March 20, 1918). Oxford University Press.
From different standpoints Bergson and Croce
reach a similar dynamic conception of reality.

548. _____. The Problem of Truth. London and Edinburgh: T. C. and E. C. Jack, 1913.
Chapter 7 compares Bradley's and Croce's concepts of truth.

549. Carter, G. S. A Hundred Years of Evolution. London: Sidgwick and Jackson, 1957.
Along with the common contrast of the "analytic"
method of Kant and Hegel with the method of evolutionary biology, Carter quotes Sir William Dampier
to suggest that philosophy's resistance to 19th-century
materialism drew the wedge between experimental
science and philosophy.

550. Chaix-ruy, Jules. "Vitalité et élan vital: Bergson
et Croce." Etudes Bergsoniennes, 5 (1960), 143-
167.

551. Cornu, August. "Bergsonianism and Existentialism."
Philosophic Thought in France and the United States.
Ed. Marvin Faber. Albany, N. Y.: State University
of New York Press, 1968. Pp. 151-168.
A marxist interpretation of Bergson.

552. Croce, Benedetto. "Note Concerning Bergson's Philosophy." Critica, (July 27, 1929), 276.

Bergson's critique of theoretical reasoning was
undertaken earlier by Hegel, who did not end with
intuition, but proceeded to the concrete "concept of
the Concept."

553. Dalle Nogare, Pedro. "Teilhard e. Marx." A tarde,
December 13, 1966.

554. Evolution, Marxism and Christianity: Studies in the
Teilhardian Synthesis. "The Teilhard Study Library,
Vol. II," London: Garnstone, 1967.

555. Fries, Carl. "Hegel und der Neo-Vitalismus." Ver-
handlungen des Dritten Hegel Kongresses. Ed. B.
Wigersma. Tübingen: J. C. B. Mohr, 1934.
Hints at certain similarities and dependencies of
"vitalist" evolutionary cosmologists on Hegel's thought.

556. Garaudy, Roger. "The Meaning of Life and History
in Marx and Teilhard de Chardin: Teilhard's Contribution to the Dialogue Between Christians and
Marxists." Evolution, Marxism and Christianity:
Studies in the Teilhardian Synthesis. London: Garnstone, 1967. Pp. 58-72.

557. _____. "Freedom and Creativity: Marxist and
Christian." The Teilhard Review, 2 (1968-69), 42-
49.
A distinguished French Marxist intellectual comments sympathetically but critically on Teilhard's
views.

558. *Glass, Bentley; Temkin, Owsei; Strauss, W. L., Jr.;
Eds. Forerunners of Darwin: 1745-1859. Baltimore: Johns Hopkins University Press, 1959. (II,
no. 253]

559. Hoernlé, R. F. A. "Idealism and Evolutionary Naturalism." Monist 36/3 (October 1926), 561-576.
Author charges that there is more of "naturalism"
than "evolution" in the "evolutionary naturalism" of
behaviorism, instrumentalism and realism.   These
theories have resisted subsequent developments in
evolutionary theory, such as the necessity not only
of accounting for past and present actuality as products of evolution, but also of allowing for future
evolution.   In this sense, Alexander is the only philosopher to take evolution seriously; by contrast,

Lloyd Morgan's universe appears as a final, finished product.

560. James, William. "Bradley or Bergson?" Journal of Philosophy, 7/2 (January 20, 1910), 29-33. A response to an article by Bradley in the October 1919 issue of Mind. Compares Bradley's and Bergson's strong similarities and sharp divergence. Ripostes Bradley's insistence on the sharp difference of the philosopher's knowledge and concerns from those of "common life," and praises Bergson's empiricism.

561. Joussain, Andre. "Bergsonisme et marxisme." Ecrits de Paris, 137 (April, 1956), 50-55. Contrasts Bergson with Sartre and with "reactionary metaphysics." Bergson is a believer in conservatism and traditions, but is not reactionary, since he believes in creativity and an "open future."

562. Kachama-Nkoy, Stephane. "De Karl Marx à Pierre Teilhard de Chardin dans la pensée de L. S. Senghor et Mamadou Dia." Journées africaines--Louvain 1963. Voies africaines du socialisme. Leopoldville: Bibliothèque de l'Etoile, 1963. Pp. 63-83.

563. Kahane, Ernest, and Garaudy, Roger. Teilhard de Chardin. Budapest: Kossuth Könyvkiado, 1967.

564. Kronenberg, Moritz. "Bergson und Hegel." Das Literarische Echo, 16/13 (1914), 877-881.

565. Kuhn, Wolfgang. "Teilhard de Chardin y el materialismo dialéctico. Ciencia o metafísica?" Estudios Centroamericanos, 19 (1964), 4-8.

566. Le Roy, Edouard. L'exigence idealiste et le fait de l'evolution. Essai d'une philosophie première. Paris: Presses universitaires de France, 1956.

567. Ligneul, Andre. "Dialectique et convergence chez Teilhard de Chardin et Marx." Univers, 1 (1964), 29-42.

568. Lischer, Richard. Marx and Teilhard: Two Ways to a New Humanity. Maryknoll, N.Y.: Orbis, 1979.

569. Lovejoy, Arthur O. "Kant and Evolution." Forerun-

ners of Darwin: 1745-1859. Eds. Glass, Temkin,
Strauss. Baltimore: Johns Hopkins University
Press, 1959. Pp. 173-206.

570. _____. "Schopenhauer as an Evolutionist." Forerunners of Darwin: 1745-1859. Eds. Glass, Temkin, Strauss. Baltimore: Johns Hopkins University
Press, 1959. Pp. 415-437.

571. Lukacs, Jozsef. "'Tremtö egyesüles.' A teilhardi
'union creatrice' es a törtenelem tendenciaja."
["Creative Union." The "Creative Union" of Teilhard and the Tendency of History.] Vigilia, 38
(1973), 583-585.

572. Macaskill, John. "Intellect and Intuition: A Footnote
to Bergson and Bradley." Contemporary Review,
108/7 (July 1915), 91-99.
Cites parallels between Bergson and Bradley.

573. McCarthy, Joseph M. Pierre Teilhard de Chardin:
A Comprehensive Bibliography. New York: Garland, 1981.
Cites 59 books and articles comparing Teilhard
and Marx or Marxism.

574. McMullin, Ernan. "Teilhard, China and Neo-Marxism."
The Month, 1221 (1969), 274-285.

575. Morris, Charles William. Six Theories of Mind.
Chicago: University of Chicago Press, 1931.
Chapter One, entitled "Mind as Process," com-
pares Hegel, Bradley, Bosanquet, and Bergson.

576. Osborn, Henry F. From the Greeks to Darwin. New
York: Scribners, 1894.
A prominent American biologist and natural historian discusses philosophical interpretations of evolution. He suggests that many of the causal mechan-
isms in Darwin and Lamarck were anticipated in
Aristotle. One of the greatest precursors of Darwin was Goethe, who, in 1790, became the first to
suggest the Man-Ape lineage. "It is not an exagger-
ation to say that Goethe was the first to conceive
Evolution in the modern sense of the term, and that
his transfer from science to literature retarded the
demonstration of the evolutionary law by half a century." [These sorts of sweeping claims in Osborn's

work have been disputed, however, by subsequent
intellectual historians.]

577.   Pluzanski, Tadeusz. "Marksizm e teilhardyzm."
       [Marxism and Teilhardism.] Studia Filozoficzne,
       3 (1966), 101-134; 4 (1970), 159-176.

578.   _____ . Marksizm a fenomen Teilharda. [Marxism
       and the Teilhardian Phenomenon.] Warszawa: Ksi-
       aski a Wiedza, 1967.

579.   _____ . "Teilhardyzm miedzy Pascalem a Heglem."
       [Teilhardism Between Pascal and Hegel.] Euhemer,
       4 (1969), 107-113.

580.   Polikarov, Azarja. "Die Dialektik der Stationären
       Prozesse." Hegel-Jahrbuch, 1974. Cologne: 1975.
       Pp. 343-346.
       Details Hegel's discussion of distinct concepts of
       development in relation to different versions of the
       dialectic--especially the difference between dialecti-
       cal and so-called "evolutionary conceptions" of de-
       velopment.

581.   Ritchie, David G. Darwin and Hegel, with other Phil-
       osophical Essays. London: Swan Sonnenschein and
       Co. , 1893. [Relevant essay from the Proceedings
       of the Aristotelian Society, 1 (1891), 55-74].
       A reconciliation of Idealism and Materialism.
       Treats the problem of Hegel's preference for "eman-
       ationism" over evolution, and develops a possible
       reconciliation of the "Philosophy of Nature" with Dar-
       win's principle of "natural selection." Discusses
       Alexander's dependence on both Darwin and Hegel.
       Discusses Hegel as an "evolutionary ethicist," and
       the subsequent development of naturalism in ethics.

582.   *Rust, Eric. Evolutionary Philosophies and Contempor-
       ary Theology. Philadelphia: Westminster, 1969.
       [II, no. 416]

583.   Shastri, Prablu Datta. The Conception of Freedom in
       Hegel, Bergson, and Indian Philosophy. Calcutta:
       Albion Press, 1914.

584.   Taylor, Charles. Hegel and Modern Society. Cam-
       bridge: Cambridge University Press, 1979.

Hegel "missed a trick in not espousing a theory
of evolution a half-century before Darwin." Human
culture, according to Hegel, has a sequential (temporal) development; nature does not. The ascending
order of forms in nature is not temporal; only "Spirit"
can have a history. But evolution would have been
consistent with his thought--the transitions in nature
could have been temporal. This deficiency, according to the author, provides another example of how
Hegel's Naturphilosophie was dependent upon his understanding of then-contemporary science (as was
Schelling's), while in the study of history and man
he broke new ground on his own.

585. Waelhens, Alphonse de. "Notes on Some Trends of
Contemporary Philosophy." Diogenes, 5 (Winter
1959), 39-56.
Mentions certain similarities between Bergson,
Hegel, and Marx.

586. Zaba, Zbigniew. "Hegel, Kierkegaard, Teilhard de
Chardin, Trzy interpretacje opozycji: Jednostka a
zbiorowosc." [Hegel, Kierkegaard, Teilhard de
Chardin. Three Interpretations of Opposition: The
Individual and the Collective.] Mysl O. Teilharda de
Chardin w Polsce. [The Thought of Father Teilhard
de Chardin in Poland.] Warszawa: Pax, 1973.
Pp. 192-213.

587. Zaehner, R. C. Matter and Spirit: Their Convergence
in Eastern Religions, Marx, and Teilhard de Chardin.
New York: Harper & Row, 1963.
Discusses the relationships between Marx, marxism, and Teilhard's thought. All are examples of
particular types of "spirituality" which overcome the
dualism of mind and matter.

PART IV: PRAGMATISM AND REALISM

The resurgence of realism in contemporary philosophy is
formally dated with the publication of Moore's "refutation" of
idealism in 1903. The realist reaction to Hegelianism in
America, however, considerably antedates this event. Indeed the neo-realism with which William James, Ralph Barton Perry and their disciples opposed the brief dominance
in America of absolute idealism is itself largely a more so-
phisticated restatement of an enduring American philosophical
tradition. The origins of realism in America encompass the
Puritan heritage in American intellectual life, which in turn
owes much to Thomas Reid, Dugal Steward, and the Scottish
school of common-sense realism. In both Great Britain and
America, then, the development of neo-realism and subsequently "critical realism" (a movement with which Whitehead
strongly identified) in fact represents an attempt to restate
the philosophical problematic in a native idiom, after a relatively brief flirtation with a largely alien perspective.

Our present interests are less in chronicling this
longstanding cultural conflict than in recovering and analyzing
whatever process perspectives are developed in these comparatively recent schools. Here again one encounters the
residual confusion stemming from the casual historical ap-
propriations of the process tradition as a whole. The influence of James, Dewey, and Peirce on Whitehead and Hartshorne, for example, already has been cited. As these three
philosophers form the "primary triad" of American pragmatism, the conclusion seems naturally to follow that pragmatism is itself a precursor of contemporary process philosophy.

Such common inferences are highly misleading. The
formal concerns of pragmatism are not especially germane
to process philosophy, and the critical problems and weak-
nesses of pragmatism are largely irrelevant to the metaphysics of process itself. Once again, traditional historical as-

sociations obscure rather than clarify the intellectual heritage of modern process thought.

One source of difficulty in effecting a proper historical classification arises in assessing the dependence of pragmatism as a tradition on evolution and on evolutionary cosmologies. Although pragmatism does not hold a place directly in the mainstream of the development of evolutionary cosmology, it is nonetheless distinctly post-evolutionary, involving essential ideas and concepts which were inconceivable prior to the rise of evolutionary theories.

> Pragmatism is unmistakably a post-Darwinian philosophy. Its empiricism is a biologically oriented empiricism: "experience" itself progressively comes to be interpreted as involving a living organism and its world. [1a]

The characteristic emphasis of pragmatists such as C. S. Peirce and William James on change and emergent novelty illustrate this evolutionist influence, together with the unique insistence that even change and emergent novelty are bounded by laws or principles which themselves evolve. [1b] As noted earlier, however, the themes of change and novelty occur in virtually all post-Hegelian and post-Darwinian speculative metaphysics, and do not uniquely specify process philosophy.

Pragmatism, to be sure, extended the implications of the evolutionary doctrine on a tangent that leads far from the original ideas of Darwin. Examples of this can be found in discussions of the evolution of value systems, the changing nature of truth, and the evolution of social systems. It is important to recognize that the basic idea of biological evolution led to the formation of pragmatism; however, the tradition as a whole is not primarily an evolutionary cosmology in the style of Bergson, Morgan, or Teilhard. It remains to be seen, then, whether pragmatism and all pragmatists (apart from the common manifestation of this modest evolutionist influence) are properly subsumed as a school of process thought.

A second major difficulty stems from the systematic ambiguity in the use of the term "pragmatism" itself by many commentators. The term has a systematic and a non-systematic usage. "Pragmatism" in the systematic sense is primarily a doctrine of meaning, function, and "significance" (Peirce), or a criterion of truth (James). In either case,

pragmatism in the systematic sense is perfectly consistent
(or can be rendered consistently) with the metaphysical claims
of subjective idealism, absolute idealism or Hume's variety
of epistemological and metaphysical skepticism, as many early
pragmatists themselves insisted.[1c] While historically pragmatism is a cognate intellectual development with realism
in America, pragmatism in this systematic sense is neither
itself primarily a metaphysical doctrine, nor is it the property
of any particular metaphysical doctrine.[2] Indeed, pragmatism
deliberately begs the question of metaphysical validity in holding that function (fortunately) is not normally contingent upon
metaphysical certitude. That one can, must, and in fact does
discern a functional meaning and act in the absence of metaphysical certainty tells us nothing about the relative merit of
different metaphysical systems.[3]

    The non-systematic use of the term is more difficult
to specify. "Pragmatism" is sometimes used loosely as a
label for certain variations of action theory, or simply to
call attention to the primary emphasis on praxis in a certain
argument or position. The term is sometimes employed, in
a manner similar to "positivism," as a non-specific disa-
vowal of any explicit metaphysical position (albeit by the different route of ignoring, rather than denouncing, the metaphysical enterprise). Pragmatism is occasionally used as
a synonym for practicality, efficacy, or--as often as
not--as a term interchangeable with "common sense" or
realism.[3a]

    In contrast to pragmatism in the systematic sense,
realism in any of its historical phases is an explicitly metaphysical doctrine. In Perry's words, realism tends toward
"identifying reality with the elements, processes and systems
of experience. But it maintains that these elements, processes and systems are independent of being experienced."[4]

    There is more the character of historical accident
than logical necessity or connection in the twin influence of
William James on the formation of American pragmatism and
American realism. Such dual influence in this case is more
than a bit confusing. John Dewey, for example, suggests
that James's precursor in pragmatism, C. S. Peirce, was
also a realist.[5] But, as Victor Harlow notes, "James's
realism was established before he became an admirer of
Peirce. None of the realists suggest indebtedness to Peirce,
directly or indirectly."[6]

    Thus, it is my impression that pragmatists such as

Peirce and Fiske have proved influential in the process
tradition not because of their pragmatism, but because of
of their more explicit development of evolutionary cosmologies. [7] Pragmatists such as James and Dewey who are not
evolutionary cosmologists, are properly subsumed as process
philosophers--not because of their pragmatism or instrumentalism, but due to their advocacy of varieties of metaphysical
realism. [8] Reference to pragmatism in the historical development of the process tradition thus masks the contributions of
two distinct schools, neither bearing any necessary systematic
relationship to pragmatism.

This suggestion yields several interesting results in
historical perspective. Whitehead's explicit acknowledgment
of James, Bergson, and Alexander (with some qualifications
regarding the last),[9] can be reduced to the dual influence of
evolutionary cosmology and neo-realism. Pragmatism need
not be cited at all. In the case of neo-realism (as noted in
Part I), Whitehead's Platonism originates in the assumptions
regarding universals held by virtually all realists in the
early twentieth century.

Hartshorne's claim, furthermore, to have arrived at
a process doctrine prior to his acquaintance with Whitehead (with the exception of Whitehead's novel analysis of
causality in the doctrine of "prehensions"[10]) becomes perfectly intelligible. As a Harvard graduate student and teach-
ing fellow during this exciting period, Hartshorne's intellectual development occurred under precisely the same two distinctive influences which Whitehead himself acknowledged:
evolutionary cosmology and neo-realism, together with Peirce's
early Platonic realism. Whitehead's neo-realist antecedents
in James and in English realism, however, did not include
the strong explicit component of panpsychism. [10a] The latter
doctrine, based upon the philosophical psychology of Fechner,
was evident primarily in the deliberations of several influential American realists in the early 20th century whom
Whitehead does not acknowledge, such as C. A. Strong and
Durant Drake. [11] Thus, one can simultaneously account for
the strong emphasis by Hartshorne of a doctrine scarcely
mentioned by Whitehead.

The substitution of realism and evolutionary cosmology
for pragmatism in the historical development of process philosophy permits analysis of figures otherwise arbitrarily excluded
from the tradition. R. B. Perry's views are primarily realist rather than pragmatist, but are important for the development of process philosophy. [12] Bertrand Russell rejected out-

right the epistemological skepticism of pragmatism--but in
doing so fell prey to the confusion I have just discussed.
His early criticisms of James's metaphysics proceeded in
large part on the assumption that these were the metaphysical underpinnings of pragmatism. As Russell's subsequent
long and circuitous journey to a metaphysical position strongly
similar to the event metaphysics of James and Whitehead
reveals, [13] however, James's process views are a logical
extension of the realist assumptions they shared, rather than
of the pragmatism over which they differed. Likewise, the
process metaphysics of C. I. Lewis is a result of his realism, rather than his pragmatism. [14]

     A more striking historical revelation, however, is
the remarkable correlation of later "critical realism" with
idealism. A careful study of the historical evolution of realism reveals, ironically, that the ongoing revision of untenable
positions in realism gradually led to the re-admission of
many of the idealist doctrines that realists intended initially
to deny. [15] Just as Hume's skepticism develops inevitably
from the commonsense empiricist assumptions of Locke, so
analogously does the final phase of critical realism--culmin-
ating in the "objective relativism" of Whitehead and the explicit rationalism and idealism of Northrop, Hartshorne, and
others of his disciples--develop inevitably from sustained
correctives to the metaphysical assumptions of commonsense
representationism and later neo-realism. [16]

     That such is the case can be seen in the dissolution
of the realist movement itself in the 1930's. Indeed, the
strong affinities of all phases of realism with certain tenets
of idealism is a cause of much of the confusion and con-
sternation among critics of realism, as well as among its
advocates. [17] Why this should be the case involves an examination of the basic metaphysical tenets of realism, which
I consider in conclusion. The effect of this historical irony
is to explain the strong similarities of process rationalism
and Hegelian idealism, despite the lack of direct, mutual
influence.

                         *   *   *

The resurgence of neo-realism in America and Great Britain
originates in a reaction to the view prevailing in both countries at the end of the 19th century:

          to be real, or even barely to exist, is to fall
          within sentience; sentient experience, in short, is

reality, and what is not this is not real. There
is no being or fact outside of that which is commonly called psychical experience. [18]

While such idealistic views passed for "Hegelianism,"
it is at once evident to those with a firsthand acquaintance
with Hegel how far English idealism had strayed from Hegel
on such points. Bradley's views, if anything, bear a closer
resemblance to Berkeley than to Hegel. Indeed, the failure
to distinguish types of idealism, and the apparent confusion
of subjective for objective idealism, are characteristic of
many influential realists in this early period, including James,
Perry, Russell, and G. E. Moore. [19]

Setting aside the polemical aspects of the realist movement, the metaphysical assertions of the school include the
following: 1) a rejection of "mystical monism" in favor of
pluralism; 2) a rejection of internal relatedness in favor of
the view that perceived objects are themselves undisturbed
by their inclusion in a relation with a knower; 3) that knower
and known are part of a homogeneous environment. To these
is added a remarkable and finally fatal tenet of neo-realism;
viz. , 4) a commitment to Platonic realism. [20]

The third "thesis" of neo-realism represents a de
facto commitment to epistemological monism, which was, of
course, the cornerstone of Hegel's philosophy--the spearhead
of his reaction against the epistemological dualism of Des-
cartes and Kant. Ironically, the attack upon Bradley and
Berkeley embodied in assertion (2) makes it impossible to
defend either (3) or (4). The denial of internal relations
re-introduces a dualism between knower and known, subject
and object, which (3) denies--and, as Russell later realized,
it is impossible to explain the ingredience of universals in
particulars apart from some doctrine of real relatedness.
In addition, the failure to distinguish between epistemological
and ontological monism led to a great deal of confused debate
among realists themselves. [21]

These conflicts led to the dissolution of neo-realism
and the rise of critical realism in Great Britain and America.
This movement retains a commitment to ontological pluralism
and epistemological monism by postulating a logical entity--
an intermediary "object"--between knower and known: an
"essence" (Santayana) or sense-datum (Moore, Broad, Russell,
and others). While accounting for illusion and perceptual differences, this theory replaced the question of the relations
between objects and knowers with the questions of the relations

between objects and their logical "essences," and with
the question of the ontological status of the latter. Outside
of a theory of internal relatedness, this dilemma could only
be solved by postulating an ontological plethora of entities
where relatively few had previously existed. Alternatively,
C. A. Strong's advocacy of Santayana's views, and his explanation of them via a theory of panpsychism, appeared to
re-introduce the criteria of universal sentience and internal
relatedness which realists had sought to refute. [22] In either
case, the idealist leanings of critical realism came to be of
sufficient embarrassment to force the abandonment of the
theory by the 1930's. Some realists, such as Spaulding,
Montague, Morgan, Strong, and Drake turned increasingly to
emergent evolutionism to account simultaneously for epistemological monism and ontological pluralism. Other developments included what A. E. Murphy described as "objective
relativism," of which Victor Harlow gave a revealing account
in 1931:

> This is an attempt to turn the at present dominant
> physical theory of relativity into a philosophical
> system of relativity. It asserts the reality of a
> pluralistic world, yet asserts with it a relativity
> of characters which would make relations the es-
> sential elements of that reality. It takes two forms.
> The first ... is that presented by Alfred North
> Whitehead, which though pluralistic is essentially
> a philosophy of an organic world--and immediately
> suggests memories of Hegel--and which he admits
> to be very similar to the conclusions of Bradley.
> Murphy, who holds essentially the same position,
> includes Dewey among the "objective relativists."
> The other, which is presented by F. S. C. Nor-
> throp, a pupil of Whitehead, and supported by F. E.
> Hoskyn, presents a type of atomism or monadism
> that is strongly reminiscent of Leibniz.... Both
> ... might be considered types of neo-realism in
> their assertion of epistemological monism, their
> pluralism and their denial of traditional substance. [23]

Finally, recalcitrant realists such as Lovejoy, unable
to give a consistent formulation of their own views but un-
happy with this decidedly-idealist turn of events, were forced
to content themselves with attacking these newer views. [24]

* * *

In summary, it is surely the case that William James

and his pragmatist colleagues stressed, in a variety of ways, themes such as time, change, pluralism, freedom, potentiality, and novelty. [25] This alleged "metaphysics of pragmatism," however, turns out to be a conglomeration of views drawn either from evolutionary cosmology or from the neorealist resurgence against idealism. Pragmatism itself turns out to be compatible with realism (James, Dewey, Mead, Lewis), with idealism (Royce, W. E. Hocking), and with evolutionary cosmology (Peirce, Fiske, Morgan, Montague).

The metaphysical foundations of commonsense realism do not include specific commitments to process and change so much as to ontological pluralism, epistemological monism, Platonism or "ontological realism" and a denial of internal relatedness. Finally, the historical development and demise of realism illustrate the conceptual incoherence of these views.

It is instructive to note that Whitehead's philosophy attempts to encompass all but the last view on internal relatedness. Indeed, Whitehead's philosophical development can be portrayed in part as an attempt to restate the fundamental metaphysical commitments of realism on a more coherent basis. In order to do this, however, Whitehead was forced to readmit a doctrine of "organism" or interconnectedness to account simultaneously for causality and freedom, actuality and potentiality, actual entities and non-discrete forms of definiteness. This was accomplished, as Hartshorne notes, [26] through the doctrine of prehension, which solved the dilemma of internal relations, freedom and causality by exhibiting such relations as temporally asymmetric. The solution to these complex realist issues is completed finally in the doctrine of a principle of limitation or "concretion," necessary to account for finite, determinate actuality in the face of indefinite or pure possibility.

Ironically, these doctrines of holism, real (although asymmetrical) internal relatedness, and teleological process are precisely the views reminiscent of Bradley. Whitehead's proposed "antecedent limitation of pure possibility" (his early term for the Primordial Nature of God) is strongly reminiscent of Hegel's Begriff or Absolute Idea, against which James had so strongly rebelled. To be sure, Whitehead attempts to recast these views in a manner more consistent with the presumed "realism" of relativity physics.

The immediate efficient causes of contemporary process philosophy--especially process rationalism--can be seen

as an attempt to develop the doctrines of evolutionary cosmology in a manner consistent with critical realism, and
integrated with relativistic (and, to a lesser extent, quantum)
physics. Realism--either in its commonsense, or in its
older Platonic mode--ends up asserting the primacy of un-
observables (sense-data, actual occasions, eternal objects,
or the elementary particles of physics)--thereby ultimately
denying the primacy of commonsense experience in favor of
views with a decidedly idealistic slant. What begins as a
rejection of idealism thus ends as a synthesis of the main
points of idealism on a realistic basis, or as a re-assertion
(by Whitehead, Perry, Lewis, and others) of many of the
most significant doctrines of idealism under the guise of
process. [27]

NOTES

(1a) Charles Morris. The Pragmatic Movement in American
      Philosophy. (New York: Braziller Press, 1970), 7-8.

(1b) C. S. Peirce, criticizing and rejecting what he found
      to be the "mechanical evolution" of Herbert Spencer,
      commented: "law ought more than anything else to
      be supposed a result of evolution ... philosophy re-
      quires thorough-going evolutionism or none." Cf.
      Collected Papers of Charles Sanders Peirce, ed.
      Charles Hartshorne and Paul Weiss (Cambridge, Mass. :
      Harvard University Press, 1965), VI, 15-16, § 2,
      14. Justus Buchler quotes Peirce as claiming that
      evolution "means nothing but growth in the widest sense
      of that word. All laws are the result of evolution
      and continue to evolve. Thus no laws are absolute.
      The tendency of everything is to take on habit." The
      Philosophy of Peirce. (London: Harcourt, Brace,
      1950), 360.

(1c) An early 20th-century dissertation, for example, dis-
      cusses elements of pragmatism in Hegel's philosophy,
      while a recent manuscript discusses the pragmatic
      element in Royce's idealism. Cf. Sidney S. Rubins,
      Hegel's Pragmatism (Diss. Harvard University, 1910);
      Mary B. Mahowald, An Idealistic Pragmatism (The
      Hague: Martinus Nijhoff, 1972). Despite the essen-
      tially post-Darwinian character of this school, some
      early pragmatists themselves insisted on the universal
      character of the movement, claiming that Socrates,
      Aristotle, Bacon, Spinoza, Hume, and Kant were all
      pragmatists. Cf. Charles Morris, op. cit. , p. 7.

(2)   This point was argued early on by John E. Boodin and
      reaffirmed more recently by John E. Smith. Boodin
      argues that even though pragmatism is most compatible
      with realism, pragmatism is not itself a metaphysical
      doctrine. Rather, it is a useful test for relative
      adequacy among competing doctrines. Cf. "What Prag-
      matism Is and Is Not," Journal of Philosophy, 6/23
      (November 11, 1909), 627-635; and "Pragmatic Real-
      ism," The Monist, 20/4 (October 1910), 602-614. See
      also John E. Smith, "Purpose in American Philosophy,"
      International Philosophical Quarterly, 1 (1961), 390-
      406, discussing the interplay of pragmatism and pur-
      pose in American philosophy.

(3)   That pragmatism is historically an epistemological per-
      spective rather than a metaphysical system is further
      exhibited in its earliest American formulation in Puri-
      tan Calvinist theology. The "natural reason" systems
      of Cotton Mather and Thomas Hooker, for example,
      develop and advocate a pragmatic test for doctrinal
      authenticity within a theological framework closely
      resembling the metaphysics of absolute or objective
      idealism.

(3a) A. O. Lovejoy delineates most of these difficulties in
      terminology in his helpful attempt at clarification of
      pragmatism: "Thirteen Pragmatisms," Journal of
      Philosophy, 5 (1908), 1-12; 29-39.

(4)   "A Realistic Theory of Independence," in Holt, Marrin,
      Montague, Perry, Pitkin, and Spaulding: The New
      Realism (New York: Macmillan, 1912), p. 103.

(5)   John Dewey, "The Pragmatism of Peirce," Journal of
      Philosophy, 13/26 (December 21, 1916), 709-715.

(6)   Bibliography and Genetic Study of American Realism
      (Oklahoma City, 1931), p. 17f., n.4. Peirce, early
      on, for example, can be considered a realist in the
      scholastic sense, by virtue of his belief in the auton-
      omous ontological status of concepts. James, by
      contrast, is a nominalist in this sense. E.g., cf.
      Peirce's essay, "What Pragmatism Is," The Monist,
      51/2 (April 1905), 161-181, where he distinguishes
      his theory of meaning from James's criterion of truth,
      including his (Peirce's) belief in "scholastic realism."

(7)   Cf. Philip P. Wiener, Evolution and the Founders of
      Pragmatism (Cambridge, Mass.: Harvard University

Press, 1949), also James Collins, "Darwin's Impact
on Philosophy," Thought, 34 (June 1959), 185-248;
Josiah Royce, "Peirce as a Philosopher," Journal of
Philosophy, 13/26 (December 21, 1916), 701-709; and
a whole series of studies by John Dewey on the influence of evolutionary cosmology on pragmatism, listed
in Part IV:2 of the bibliography following.

(8)   Cf. John Dewey, "The Realism of Pragmatism," Journal
      of Philosophy, 2/12 (June 8, 1905), 324-327. Dewey
      seems, at this phase of his career, wedded to the
      idea of the identity of pragmatism and realism. Though
      none of his contemporaries appear to take this view
      seriously, his considerable subsequent influence could
      be in part responsible for perpetrating this false con-
      junction.

(9)   Alexander is hard to classify, given his affinities with
      process rationalism and evolutionary cosmology, as
      well as with idealism. See Part V(B) below.

(10) Charles Hartshorne, "Whitehead's Revolutionary Con-
      cept of Prehension," International Philosophical Quar-
      terly, 19/3 (September 1979), 253-263.

(10a) I do not, of course, intend to deny that James's philos-
      ophy was implicitly panpsychist; only that this element
      would not have been as explicit in Whitehead's influ-
      ences as in Hartshorne's. Cf. Marcus Ford, "William
      James: Panpsychist and Metaphysical Realist," Trans-
      actions of the C. S. Peirce Society, 17/2 (Spring
      1981), 158-170.

(11) C. A. Strong, Why the Mind Has a Body (New York:
      Macmillan, 1903); and The Origin of Consciousness:
      An Attempt to Conceive the Mind as a Product of
      Evolution (New York: Macmillan, 1918). Durant
      Drake, "Panpsychism Again," Journal of Philosophy,
      16/16 (July 31, 1919), 433-439.

(12) For example, note the evolution of Perry's realism and
      his advocacy of Whitehead's views in the late 1930's:
      "American Philosophy in the First Decade of the Twen-
      tieth Century," Revue Internationale de Philosophie,
      3 (April 15, 1939), 423-443.

(13) E. g., Bertrand Russell, My Philosophical Development
      (New York: Simon and Schuster, 1959), 16-27.

(14) So it seems the case, for example, that customary treatments of the "metaphysics of pragmatism" usually intend, in fact, a metaphysics of realism: Sandra B.
Rosenthal, "C. I. Lewis: Toward Categories of Process and a Metaphysics of Pragmatism," Journal of the
History of Philosophy, 15/2 (April 1977), 195-201.
That pragmatism need not entail a uniquely realist
metaphysics, however, is illustrated partially in n. 1c
and n. 3 above.

(15) In Harlow's work (op. cit.), note especially pp. 101-
132.

(16) Harlow, op. cit., pp. 103ff. The term "objective relativism" was coined by A. E. Murphy in part to describe Whitehead's early metaphysical views in The
Concept of Nature and Science and the Modern World.
Harlow notes the affinities of Whitehead's later development of his position with Bradley and Hegel.

(17) Here the complaints of confusion are almost too numerous to document. As a representative sample of the
frustrated dialogue between realists (or "pragmatists")
and idealists, consider: Bernard Bosanquet, "Realism
and Metaphysics," Philosophical Review, 26/1 (January 1917), 4-15; F. H. Bradley, "Appearance and
Contradiction," Mind, 18/72 (October 1909), 489-508;
William Caldwell, Pragmatism and Idealism (London:
Adam and Charles Black, 1913); C. I. Lewis, "Realism and Subjectivism," Journal of Philosophy, 10/2
(January 16, 1913), 43-49; Charles M. Perry, "A
New Herakleiteanism," Journal of Philosophy, 25/9
(April 26, 1928), 225-233; and J. E. Turner, A Theory
of Direct Realism, and the Relation of Realism to
Idealism (New York: Macmillan, 1925).

(18) A. O. Lovejoy's citation of F. H. Bradley's position,
in Adams and Montague, eds., Contemporary American
Philosophy, vol. II (1930), p. 85.

(19) J. E. Turner, writing during this period, is cognizant
of this prevailing distortion in his development of a
theory of "direct realism." Relying on exhaustive
documentation, he notes that Hegel himself parted
company with Fichte and Schelling over their advocacy
of just those views which subsequent neo-realists accused Hegel of promulgating. Cf. A Theory of Direct
Realism. New York: Macmillan, 1925.

(20) Harlow, op. cit., pp. 54-56.

(21) To Dewey's claim to be a pluralist (ontologically), A. O.
Lovejoy charges (falsely) that pluralism is a species
of dualism, which realism denies. This prompts a
series of sharp exchanges between the two philosophers.
In the Journal of Philosophy, see Dewey's "Realism
Without Monism or Dualism," 19/12 (June 8, 1922),
309-317; 19/13 (June 22, 1922), 351-361; Lovejoy's
rejoinders, 19/19 (September 14, 1922), 505-515;
19/20 (September 28, 1922), 533-541; and Dewey's
surrejoinders, 21/8 (April 10, 1924), 197-204; 21/22
(October 23, 1924), 601-611. To this rather vacuous
foolishness, juxtapose C. Lloyd Morgan's sensible
clarification: "Three Aspects of Monism," The Monist, 4/3 (April 1894), 321-332. There are clearly
occasions when philosophers would profit from greater
attentiveness and less publication.

(22) In addition to C. A. Strong's Origin of Consciousness
(loc. cit.), note also his articles on "Idealism and
Realism," arguing for the congruence of realism and
panpsychism: Journal of Philosophy 1/19 (September
15, 1904), 519-526; 1/20 (September 29, 1904), 543-
551. Cf. also William P. Montague's sharp dissocia-
tion of panpsychism from realism: "Panpsychism and
Monism," Journal of Philosophy 2/23 (November 9,
1905), 626-629.

(23) Harlow, op. cit., pp. 103ff. The term "objective relativism" is applied to both Whitehead and Dewey by
A. E. Murphy, "Objective Relativism in Whitehead
and Dewey," The Philosophical Review, 36 (1927),
121-144. John Dewey puts the matter somewhat dif-
ferently in discussing the relative distinction between
"subjects" and "objects": "The Objectivism--Subjec-
tivism of Modern Philosophy," Journal of Philosophy,
38/20 (September 25, 1941), 533-542.

(24) Such polemic is central to Lovejoy's major works,
which succeed more in dismantling positions than in
posing alternatives. See his Revolt Against Dualism
(LaSalle, Ill.: Open Court, 1930); The Great Chain
of Being (Cambridge, Mass.: Harvard University
Press, 1942). His early essay on "The Place of
Time in Contemporary Philosophy" [Journal of Philosophy, 7/25 (December 8, 1910), 683-693] reveals this
tendency. Lovejoy is equally critical of idealist and

pragmatist treatments of time. One is left wondering, despite the cogency of his criticisms, what view Lovejoy himself held.

(25) A complete list of James's central principles of "pragmatism" (realism), suggesting their affinity with process philosophy, is offered by Andrew J. Reck, Introduction to William James (Bloomington: Indiana University Press, 1967).

(26) Hartshorne, "Whitehead's Revolutionary Concept of Prehension," loc. cit.

(27) Such summary commentary on the results of the realist discussion are offered by Charles M. Perry, "Back to Dialectic," The Monist, 11/3 (July 1930), 381-393; and Ralph Barton Perry, "American Philosophy in the First Decade of the Twentieth Century," loc. cit. Indeed, it is ironic to note that James himself, in praising Bergson, called attention to the idealistic flavor of process thought--recognizing (in his own words) Bergson's "process philosophy as a verification of Hegel's Logic." See James's A Pluralistic Universe (New York: Longmans, Green, 1909), pp. 270-274.

IV.   PRAGMATISM AND REALISM: BIBLIOGRAPHY

---

588. Bode, B. H. "Realism and Pragmatism." Journal of Philosophy, 3/15 (July 19, 1906), 393-401.
      The problem of realism is its implicit ego-centrism. It is difficult to state what things are (e. g., sounds, tastes, secondary qualities) apart from some reference to physiological states associated with "consciousness." Pragmatism comes to the aid of realism here, by suggesting that the "truth" of realism is to be found in the relational nature of consciousness itself: consciousness presupposes "real" external objects to which it is related.

589. Boodin, John E. "What Pragmatism Is and Is Not." Journal of Philosophy, 6/23 (November 11, 1909), 627-635.

Pragmatism is a method and a theory of truth.
It is not a metaphysical doctrine; rather, it provides
a means of testing the relative adequacy of competing
metaphysical claims. Pragmatism is "realistic"
only "insofar as it intends a world beyond our finite,
cognitive purposes."

590. _____. "Pragmatic Realism." The Monist, 20/4
(October 1910), 602-614.
Defines realism in contrast to the doctrine that
"all reality is sentience" (subjective idealism). Suggests that the method of explanation most appropriate
to epistemological realism is pragmatism: the "scientific method" of James and Peirce.

591. _____. A Realistic Universe: An Introduction to
Metaphysics. New York: Macmillan, 1916.

592. _____. "Fictions in Science and Philosophy."
Journal of Philosophy, 40 (December 1943), 673-682;
701-716.

593. Boutroux, E. The Contingency of the Laws of Nature. Trans. F. Rothwell. Chicago: Open
Court, 1920.

594. Brightman, Edgar S. "The Versatile James." Religion in Life, 12 (1942-43), 9-19.

595. Buchler, Justus. The Philosophy of Peirce. London:
Harcourt & Brace, 1950.

596. Dewey, John. "The Realism of Pragmatism." Journal of Philosophy, 2/12 (June 8, 1905), 324-327.
Argues that pragmatism, in contrast to skepticism,
relativism, or idealism, provides a way through
which philosophy can once again enter into a discussion of the "really real."

597. _____. "The Pragmatism of Peirce." Journal of
Philosophy, 13/26 (December 21, 1916), 709-715.
There is greater emphasis on the method of prag-
matism--testing, logic, experience, and their relation to human purpose--in Peirce than in James.
Dewey suggests, however, that both are equally realists. For Peirce, "reality" is that which is ascer-
tained by its consequences, the knowledge of which
is built up by dependable repetition and habit. Finally,

this is the way out of the "ego-centric predicament."

598.   _____. "The Scientific Factor in Reconstruction of
Philosophy." Reconstruction in Philosophy, ch. 3.
New York: Henry Holt, 1920.

599.   _____. "Realism Without Monism or Dualism," I.
Journal of Philosophy, 19/12 (June 8, 1922), 309-
317.
Against Lovejoy, Dewey argues that pragmatism
is not dualistic, and need not imply dualism. It
intends, rather, to highlight the exact nature of the
temporal distinction between past, present and future,
as well as their mutual interrelatedness and inter-
penetration. In particular, pragmatism focuses on
the need to assume knowledge without absolute certitude in order to devise working hypotheses for practical action. (Note that Dewey here uses pragmatism
interchangeably with realism.)

600.   _____. "Realism Without Monism or Dualism," II.
Journal of Philosophy, 19/13 (June 22, 1922), 351-
361.
For Lovejoy, one's possibilities seem limited
either to monism (idealism), or dualism. Dewey
claims he is clearly not a monistic idealist, but objects to his resultant classification as a "dualist."
Lovejoy's rejoinders: Journal of Philosophy, 19/19
(September 14, 1922), 505-515; and 19/20 (September,
28, 1922), 533-541; stress that pluralism is a species of dualism, whence Dewey is in fact a dualist.
Dewey's surrejoinders: Journal of Philosophy, 21/8
(April 10, 1924), 197-204; and 21/22 (October 23,
1924), 601-611.

601.   _____. "The Development of American Pragmatism,"
in The Philosophy of John Dewey. Ed. John J. Mc-
Dermott. Chicago: University of Chicago Press,
1981.
This article includes Dewey's assessment of the
importance of biology and evolutionist theory for
philosophy in general, and for pragmatism in particular.

602.   Fauser, John Joseph. The Theory of Freedom in
William James. Diss. St. Louis University, 1967.
Provides an excellent illustration of the "process"
affinities of James. According to James, moral ex-

perience of freedom supports the metaphysical concepts of indeterminism, creativity, and novel possibilities. Man is a "novelty-producing agent." In a
pluralistic universe, the past entails but does not
determine the present. James's view of the hope
and promise of freedon leads finally to his "melior-
ism doctrine": the world can improve through the
actions of persons.

603.   Flournoy, T. The Philosophy of William James. New
       York: Henry Holt, 1917.

604.   *Harlow, Victor Emmanuel. Bibliography and Genetic
       Study of American Realism. Oklahoma City, 1931.
       [Intro, no. 16]

605.   Hartshorne, Charles, and Weiss, Paul, eds. Collected
       Papers of Charles Sanders Peirce. Cambridge,
       Mass. : Harvard University Press, 1965.

606.   Hicks, G. Daws. Critical Realism. London: Mac-
       millan, 1938.

607.   Hocking, William Ernest. "Dewey's Concepts of Ex-
       perience and Nature." The Philosophical Review, 49
       (March 1940), 228-243.

608.   James, William. "The Dilemma of Determinism."
       Unitarian Review, (September 1884).
           Discusses the origins of determinist doctrines in
       a mistaken fear of "chance and randomness" which
       would render events inexplicable. The "dilemma"
       of determinism is the resulting incoherence of the
       notion of choice and moral responsibility as well as
       the denial of the real constitutive nature of temporal
       passage. The essay highlights the importance of
       the concepts of chance, freedom and possibility in
       James's philosophy.

609.   _____. The Principles of Psychology. 2 Vols.
       New York: Henry Holt, 1890.

610.   _____. "The Pragmatic Method." Journal of Phi-
       losophy, 1/25 (December 1904), 673-687.

611.   _____. Pragmatism: A New Name for Some Old
       Ways of Thinking. New York: Longmans & Green,
       1907.

612. _____. The Meaning of Truth: A Sequel to "Pragmatism." New York: Longmans & Green, 1909.

613. _____. A Pluralistic Universe. New York: Longmans & Green, 1909.

614. _____. Some Problems of Philosophy: A Beginning of an Introduction to Philosophy. New York: Longmans & Green, 1911.

615. _____. Essays in Radical Empiricism. New York: Longmans & Green, 1912.

616. Krikorian, Yerrant H. Recent Perspectives in American Philosophy. The Hague: Martinus Nijhoff, 1973. Introductory chapter situates the process philosophy of Alexander, Bergson, James, Mead, Whitehead, and Roy Wood Sellars with respect to American empiricism, understood as "experimentalism."

617. Lewis, C. I. "Realism and Subjectivism." Journal of Philosophy, 10 (1913), 43-49.

618. Lovejoy, Arthur O. "The Place of Time in Contemporary Philosophy." Journal of Philosophy, 7/25 (December 8, 1910), 683-693. Especially critical of "eternalist idealists" (Royce and Bradley), but almost as critical of the discussion of time by pragmatists. "Real time is affirmed as an aspect of reality in pragmatism."

619. _____. "Realism Versus Epistemological Monism." Journal of Philosophy, 10 (1913), 561-572.

620. Mead, George Herbert. The Philosophy of the Act. Chicago: University of Chicago Press, 1938.

621. Montague, W. P. "The New Realism and the Old." Journal of Philosophy, 9 (1912), 39-46.

622. Morgan, C. Lloyd. "The Realities of Experience." The Monist, 8/1 (October 1897), 1-18. In criticism of Thomas Huxley's acceptance of Berkeley's views, Morgan asserts a bold realism and naturalism--"a system of knowledge founded on experience in its widest and most comprehensive sense."

623. _____. "Causation, Physical and Metaphysical."
The Monist, 8/2 (January 1898), 230-249.
Physical causation involves an explanation of phenomena in terms of the necessary and sufficient antecedent events for their occurrence. Metaphysical
causation provides, in contrast, explanations of phenomena in terms of their raison d'être, purpose, or
teleological pattern. Hume's attack on physical causation fails if connectedness, uniformity, and regu-
larity (holism) are assumed, rather than derived
from experience. But in this case, physical causation presupposes metaphysical causation. This pre-
supposition is rendered explicit in pragmatism, as
a "conviction without which the search for knowledge
is a vain and illusory dream-quest."

624. Morris, Charles. The Pragmatic Movement in American Philosophy. New York: Braziller Press, 1970.

625. Mortland, Thomas R. The Metaphysics of William
James and John Dewey: Process and Structure in
Philosophy and Religion. New York: Philosophical
Library, 1963.

626. Muehler, Walter G. "William James and the Problem
of Religious Empiricism." The Personalist, 23
(April 1942), 159-171.

627. *Muirhead, John H. The Platonic Tradition in Anglo-
Saxon Philosophy. London: George Allen and Unwin, 1931. [I, no. 133]

627a. The New Realism. Eds. Edwin B. Holt, Walter T.
Marvin, et al. New York: Macmillan, 1912.

628. Pannill, H. Burnell. The Religious Faith of John
Fiske. Durham, N.C.: Duke University Press, 1957.
Details the life and work of John Fiske in America
as a synthesizer of pragmatism with evolutionary
cosmology, and as a popularizer of the views of
Herbert Spencer.

629. Peirce, C. S. "What Pragmatism Is." The Monist,
51/2 (April 1905), 161-181.
In this famous essay, Peirce distinguishes his
"pragmaticism" (a theory of meaning) from James's
pragmatism as a test of truth. Pragmaticism affirms
science, habits, instincts, and scholastic realism.
Correct meaning is thus a function of purpose, in-

tention, and future results which, in the present,
may not be fully determinate.

630. Perry, Charles M. "A New Herakleiteanism." Journal of Philosophy, 25/9 (April 26, 1928), 225-233.
In a sense, this article marks the transition from
realism to the rise of process rationalism. Personalism, Hegelianism, realism, pragmatism and
empiricism are all discussed as half-truths. "Becoming"--opposition and strife--represents that principle which takes seriously both objects and their
mutual relations. The New Herakleiteanism accounts
for novelty, creativity, freedom, identity, and reciprocity. Thus, both realism and idealism are
true--and both are equally inadequate.

631. _____. "Back to Dialectic." The Monist, 11/3
(July 1930), 381-393.
The central point of idealism is that relations
are internal to their terms. A self-sufficient Ding-
an-sich is denied in favor of organic holism. In
Hegel and Bradley, dialectical process (rather than
identity-in-the-Absolute) is stressed, in which the
problem both of having and knowing real, discrete
individuals, and of acknowledging relations between
them, can be solved.

632. Perry, Ralph Barton. "The Ego-Centric Predicament."
Journal of Philosophy, 7/1 (1910), 5-14.

633. _____. Present Philosophical Tendencies. New
York: Longmans, Green, 1916.

634. _____. The Thought and Character of William
James. 2 Vols. Boston: Little, Brown, 1935.

635- Roth, Robert J. "Is Peirce's Pragmatism Anti-Jame-
6. sian?" International Philosophical Quarterly, 5 (December 1965), 541-563.
Cautioning against overstating the differences between Peirce and James, the author notes strong
similarities, especially as regards empiricism, and
the right to hold views (such as theism) when evidence
does not decide the issue.

637. Woodbridge, Frederick J. E. "The Problem of Time
in Modern Philosophy." Journal of Philosophy, 7/15
(July 21, 1910), 410-416.
This essay establishes the centrality of a doctrine

of "real time" in realism, and attacks idealism for
its failure to take account of real, evolutionary change
(which requires a concept of temporalism).

IV. 1. PRAGMATISM, REALISM, AND PROCESS
        RATIONALISM: BIBLIOGRAPHY

---

638. Alexander, Samuel. The Basis of Realism. Oxford:
      Oxford University Press, 1914.

639. *_____. Space, Time and Deity. 2 Vols. "Gifford
      Lectures, 1916-1918." London: Macmillan, 1920.
      [I, no. 49]

640. Brotherston, Bruce W. "The Wider Setting of 'Felt
      Transition'." Journal of Philosophy, 39 (1942), 97-
      104.
           Limits the comparison of Whitehead and pragma-
      tism by suggesting that William James's analysis of
      "conjunctive experience" does not provide sufficient
      ground in itself to justify Whitehead's atomic plural-
      ism.

641. Brown, Patricia B. An Analysis of the Theories of
      John Dewey and Alfred North Whitehead on the Quali-
      tative Aspects of Experience and the Relation of these
      Theories to Education. Diss. New York University,
      1962.

642. Bubser, Eberhard. "Sprache und Metaphysik in White-
      heads Philosophie." Archiv für Philosophie, 10/1-2
      (1960).
           Whitehead's philosophy of language is a blending
      of three diverse trends: the rationalistic optimism
      of mathematical logicians; the anti-rationalism of
      Bergson; and American pragmatism. In the final
      analysis, however, Whitehead is much closer to
      Bradley than to any of these three trends.

643. *Cesselin, Felix. La Philosophie organique de White-
      head. Paris: Presses Universitaires de France,
      1950. [II, no. 383]

644. Dewey, John. "Whitehead's Philosophy." The Philosophical Review, 46 (1937), 170-177.
While Dewey agrees with Whitehead's comprehensive approach to metaphysics, he suggests a choice
must be made between a "genetic functional" (i. e.,
naturalistic) and a "mathematical formal" interpretation of first principles. As illustrated by the doctrine of "eternal objects," Dewey fears that Whitehead's mathematical formalism (which is static) will
take precedence over the naturalism and empiricism
to which Whitehead himself is committed. Whitehead's rejoinder (pp. 176-78) praises both James
and Dewey, and suggests that his own relation to
Hegel's thought is made plain in this exchange with
Dewey.

645. _____. "The Objectivism-Subjectivism of Modern
Philosophy." Journal of Philosophy, 38/20 (September 25, 1941), 533-542.
Discusses the Whiteheadian meaning of "subjective,"
concerning what can be experienced rather than what
has been experienced. What can be experienced are
"objects," and Dewey discusses Whitehead's Platonic
definition of "objects," as opposed to that of physics
and commonsense.

646. _____. "The Philosophy of Whitehead." The Philosophy of Alfred North Whitehead. "Library of
Living Philosophers, vol. III." Ed. Paul Arthur
Schilpp. Evanston, Ill. : Northwestern University
Press, 1941. Pp. 641-661.
A negative criticism, highlighting growing contrasts between his own philosophy and Whitehead's,
which is no longer a philosophy of "concrete experience" (as is pragmatism), but a mathematical
and speculative set of abstractions.

647. Dilworth, David A. The Platonism-Pragmatism Polarity
of Whitehead's Thought. Diss. Fordham University,
1963.
Argues that Whitehead synthesized pragmatism
and Platonism to develop his unique viewpoint.

648. Dordick, Webb. An Examination of Whitehead's Doc-
trine of Causal Efficacy. Diss. State University of
New York (Buffalo), 1972.
Examines Whitehead's doctrine of causal efficacy

from the standpoint of his theory of perception, trac-
ing the critical influence on these theories of James,
Alexander, and Bradley.

649. Eisendrath, Craig R. The Unifying Moment: The Psy-
chological Philosophy of William James and Alfred
North Whitehead. Cambridge, Mass.: Harvard Uni-
versity Press, 1971.
Integrates Whitehead's theory of concrescence with
James's theory of the Will.

650. Feibleman, James K. An Introduction to Peirce's Philosophy Interpreted as a System. New York: Harper
and Bros. , 1946.
Includes a provocative discussion of the "astound-
ing" similarities between the philosophies of Whitehead and Peirce.

651. _____. "Realism from Plato to Peirce." An Introduction to Peirce's Philosophy. London: George
Allen and Unwin, 1961. Pp. 459-463.
A brief but significant discussion of the parallels
between Whitehead and Peirce, both of whom serve
to "demonstrate how two philosophers who have been
subjected to similar influences and environments may,
without knowledge of each other, come to strikingly
similar conclusions."

652. Fontinell, Eugene. "Transcendent Divinity and Process
Philosophy." New Theology, vol. 7. Eds. Dean
Peerman and Martin G. Marty. New York: Macmillan, 1970. Pp. 173-189.
Discusses pragmatism's distinctive doctrines as
"one expression of a multiplicity of process philosophies," including Bergson, Whitehead, Teilhard,
and Hartshorne.

653. _____. "Pragmatism, Process and Religious Education." Religious Education, 68 (1973), 322-331.
Suggests an "open educational approach" based
upon a synthesized metaphysics of pragmatism and
process.

654. _____. "Process Theology: A Pragmatic Version."
Religious Experience and Process Theology. Eds.
Harry J. Cargas and Bernard Lee. New York:
Paulist Press, 1976. Pp. 23-39.

655. Ford, Marcus P. "William James: Panpsychist and
      Metaphysical Realist." Transactions of the C. S.
      Peirce Society, 17/2 (Spring 1981), 158-170.
          James is both a realist and a panpsychist. The
      basic units of reality are (at least partially) centers
      of self-experience.

656. Forderhase, Earl Duane. A Study of the Concepts of
      a Finite God in the Philosophies of William James
      and Alfred North Whitehead. Diss. University of
      Oklahoma, 1973.
          Suggests similarities in the concept of the world-
      dependence of a finite God in James and Whitehead.

657. Frye, Robert E. Pragmatism in Recent Non-Pragmatic
      Systems: Santayana, Bergson, and Whitehead. Diss.
      Indiana University, 1956.

658. Green, Thomas H. S. J. The Idea of Novelty in Peirce
      and Whitehead. Diss. University of Notre Dame,
      1968.

659. *Harlow, Victor Emmanuel. Bibliography and Genetic
      Study of American Realism. Oklahoma City, 1931.
      [Intro, no. 16]

660. Hartshorne, Charles. "A Critique of Peirce's Idea
      of God." Philosophical Review, 50 (Summer 1941),
      516-522.

661. _____. "The Idea of Creativity in American Philos-
      ophy." Journal of Karnatak University--Social Sci-
      ences, 2 (1966), 1-13.
          Discusses competition of the themes of self-
      creativity and logical determinism in American
      process philosophy, from the origins of modern prag-
      matism to the present.

662. *_____. "Whitehead's Revolutionary Concept of Pre-
      hension." International Philosophical Quarterly,
      19/3 (September 1979), 253-263. [I, no. 105]

663. Helm, Bertrand P. "William James on the Nature of
      Time." Tulane Studies in Philosophy, 24 (1975),
      33-47.
          This discussion of James's philosophy of time
      suggests implicitly a number of striking parallels
      to Whitehead's treatment of time.

664. Kennick, William E. A Methodological Approach to
     Metaphysics with Special Reference to the Philoso-
     phies of Aristotle, Hume, Dewey and Whitehead.
     Diss. Cornell University, 1952.

665. Kultgen, J. H. "The 'Future-Metaphysics' of Peirce
     and Whitehead." Kant-Studien, 51 (1959-60), 285-
     293.
     Contrasts the basic metaphysical presuppositions
     of Peirce and Whitehead with Kant.

666. Lee, Harold N. "Process and Pragmatism." Tulane
     Studies in Philosophy, 13 (1964), 87-97.
     Theories of object, truth and meaning in pragma-
     tism are compared with process philosophy (using
     Bergson as example), showing how the pragmatist's
     stress on action is given a proper context by process
     philosophy, which emphasizes the flux of changing
     events.

667. Limper, Peter Frederick. Value and the Individual
     in the Philosophies of Whitehead and Peirce. Diss.
     Yale University, 1975.
     Suggests contrasts in the analysis of "individuals"
     by both philosophers, who agree that the "human
     self" is not an individual. Theology is immanent
     in Whiteheadian "individuals" (actual entities), while
     purpose is external and more generalized for Peirce.
     "Value" is equated with individual intensity of ex-
     perience, coupled with diversity and pluralism for
     Whitehead, while for Peirce, "value" is equated with
     a generalized and unified concept of "reasonableness."

668. Lowe, Victor. "William James and Whitehead's Doc-
     trine of Prehensions." Journal of Philosophy, 38
     (1941), 113-126.
     Whitehead's doctrine that the experient or "feeler"
     emerges in the process of feeling is not unique; it
     is also the view of James, whose description of "ex-
     perience in transition" in the Principles of Psychology
     is an early description of the theory later perfected
     by Whitehead as the doctrine of prehension.

669. _____. "William James' Pluralistic Metaphysics of
     Experience." In Commemoration of William James:
     1842-1942. New York: Columbia University Press,
     1942.
     What is the nature of the "plurality" in James's

"pluralistic universe"? This is not clearly specified,
since pluralism was primarily for James a polemic
against monistic idealism and determinism. "Persons" are rejected as the ultimate units, as is the
"pure atomic experience" of Hume. James's note-
books of 1905-1907 suggest that he came very close
to affirming events (moments or "pulses" of experience) as ultimate, as Whitehead later did.

670. *_____. "The Influence of Bergson, James and
Alexander on Whitehead." Journal of the History of
Ideas, 10 (1949), 267-296. [I, no. 127]

671. _____. "Peirce and Whitehead as Metaphysicians."
Studies in the Philosophy of C. S. Peirce. Eds.
E. C. Moore and R. S. Robin. Amherst: University of Massachusetts Press, 1964. Pp. 430-454.
For Peirce, metaphysical concepts mirror logical
concepts, while for Whitehead, logic is but one part
of the larger task of metaphysics, which consists in
the imaginative generalization of experience. Connectedness and synthesis are thus more important
for Whitehead than for Peirce.

672. Mack, Robert D. The Appeal to Immediate Experience:
Philosophic Method in Bradley, Whitehead and Dewey.
New York: King's Crown Press, 1945.
Whitehead differs from Bradley and Dewey in the
more active role given to mind in his later philos-
ophy: immediate experience is inherently cognitive.

673. Mead, George H. "The Nature of the Past." Essays
in Honor of John Dewey. New York: Holt, Rinehart, & Winston, 1929. Pp. 235-242.
Mead is critical both of Whitehead's concept of
the specious present and Bergson's theory of the
past as a massive accumulation of images. Both
fail to distinguish adequately present from past,
which "consists of the relations of an earlier world
to an emergent affair--relations which have therefore emerged with the affair."

674. Meland, Bernard E. Higher Education and the Human
Spirit. Chicago: University of Chicago Press, 1953.
Whitehead's analysis of concrescence exhibits ap-
parent similarities with the work of William James.

675. *_____. "The New Realism in Religious Inquiry."
Encounter, 31/4 (Autumn 1970), 311-324. [II, no. 408]

676. Minor, William S. , ed. Charles Hartshorne and Henry
      Nelson Weiman: Critically Analyzed. Carbondale,
      Ill. : Foundation for Creative Philosophy, 1968.
      Notes that both Weiman and Hartshorne, followers
      of Whitehead, are also "bridges" to American prag-
      matism and empiricism via James, Peirce, Dewey,
      and the "Chicago School. "

677. Murphy, Arthur E. "Objective Relativism in Dewey
      and Whitehead. " Philosophical Review, 36 (1927),
      121-144.
      Analyzes the similar attempts of both Whitehead
      and Dewey to render realism and objectivity con-
      sistently with the physical theory of relativity.

678. Murphy, Frances. The Place of Moral Responsibility
      in the Philosophies of Whitehead and Peirce. Diss.
      Brown University, 1940.
      Whitehead and Peirce shared the belief that in-
      determinism accounts for moral responsibility better
      than determinism.

679. Perry, Ralph Barton. "American Philosophy in the
      First Decade of the Twentieth Century. " Revue In-
      ternationale de Philosophie, 3 (April 15, 1939), 423-
      443.
      Pragmatism replaces Kant with Darwin, down-
      playing the constitutive role of mind in experience
      by substituting organic adaptation to livability and
      practicality for a priori cognitive structures. Amer-
      ican realists stress pluralism, moral "dualism,"
      theological finitism, organism, and "neutral monism"
      --the homegeneity of mental and physical reality.
      Organism is similar to idealism, but emphasizes
      biology, physics, and the continuity of experience.
      Perry cites Whitehead, James, Peirce, Mead, Berg-
      son, and Alexander as leaders of this intellectual
      revolution.

680. Platt, David. "Transcendence of Subjectivity in Peirce
      and Whitehead. " Personalist, 49 (1968), 238-255.
      Discusses the similarities of Whitehead and Peirce
      on the issue of subjectivity.

681. Pols, Edward. Meditation on a Prisoner: Towards
      Understanding Action and Mind. Carbondale: South-
      ern Illinois University Press, 1975.

Suggests that James inadvertently provided the
necessary background for Whitehead's subsequent
development of the epochal theory of time.

682. Reck, Andrew J. "The Philosophy of Charles Hartshorne." Tulane Studies in Philosophy, 10 (1961),
89-108.
Demonstrates that Hartshorne's dependence on
Peirce--especially regarding theism--is as great
as on Whitehead.

683. _____. Introduction to William James. Bloomington: Indiana University Press, 1967.
James's pluralism was derived primarily from
Renouvier, Bergson, and Peirce. In turn, the concepts he chose to emphasize--creative becoming,
freedom, indeterminacy, objective change, continuity,
evolutionary love, God as finite and struggling--are
central to contemporary philosophical cosmologies,
such as Whitehead's.

684. Reese, William L. Philosophic Realism: A Study of
the Modality of Being in Peirce and Whitehead. Diss.
Harvard University, 1952.

685. Rosenthal, Sandra B. "C. I. Lewis: Toward Categories of Process and a Metaphysics of Pragmatism."
Journal of the History of Philosophy, 15/2 (April
1977), 195-201.
Widely considered the least metaphysical of the
pragmatists, Lewis nonetheless articulates a metaphysical stance similar to that of Peirce, James,
Dewey, Mead, and proponents of process philosophy.
Lewis emphasizes potentiality or "lawfulness," possibility as a real feature of metaphysical reality,
and actuality, the stubborn, irreducible facticity of
experience. He rejects the category of substance
as a description of enduring objects, in favor of a
"type of lawfulness embodied in process." An object is, finally, "an event; some continuous volume
in space-time comprising a history of enduring."

686. Schrag, Calvin O. "Struktur der Erfahrung in der
Philosophie von James und Whitehead." Zeitschrift
für Philosophische Forschung, 23 (1969), 479-494.

687. Smith, John E. "Purpose in American Philosophy."

International Philosophical Quarterly, 1 (1961), 390-
406.
 Pragmatism is not merely concerned with the
external, the mechanical, or with the manipulation
of objects. The position is unintelligible apart from
a notion of immanent purposiveness. Royce, James,
Dewey, Peirce and Whitehead agree in emphasizing
the importance of purpose.

688. *_____. "The Critique of Abstractions and the Scope
of Reason." Process and Divinity. Eds. Reese and
Freeman. LaSalle, Ill.: Open Court, 1964. Pp.
19-35. [III, no. 528]

689. Strong, C. A. Why the Mind Has a Body. New York:
Macmillan, 1903.
 Citing the influence of Fechner, the author defends
panpsychism as a fourth alternative to interactionism,
parallelism, and Thomas Huxley's theory of the "conscious automation" to account for the mind-body relation.

690. _____. The Origin of Consciousness: An Attempt
to Conceive the Mind as a Product of Evolution.
New York, Macmillan, 1918.
 Mind-body dualism is overcome by postulating
rudimentary psychic properties of all physical entities. The doctrine of emergent evolution, coupled
with panpsychism, accounts for the advent of human
consciousness.

691. Todd, Quinton Robert. James, Whitehead and Radical
Empiricism. Diss. Pennsylvania State University,
1969.
 Treats similarities and differences in the parallel
attempts by James and Whitehead to develop a completely immanent account of the order and structure
of experience.

692. Virtue, Charles F. Sawhill. "General Philosophy and
Philosophy of Education: A Word from an Academic
Philosopher." Educational Theory, 8 (1958), 203-
212.
 Whitehead and Dewey are offered as illustrations
of the need to root philosophy of education within
the larger context of a wide philosophical commitment.

693. Vitali, Theodore R. "The Peirceian Influence on
      Hartshorne's Subjectivism." Process Studies, 7/4
      (Winter 1977), 238-249.

694. Whitehead, Alfred North. "John Dewey and His Influ-
      ence." The Philosophy of John Dewey. "Library
      of Living Philosophers, vol. I." Ed. Paul Arthur
      Schilpp. Evanston, Ill.: Northwestern University
      Press, 1939.
      Dewey shares with the author, and embodies in
      his philosophy, the need to temper dogmatism with
      the concepts of creative advance, adventure, and
      novelty.

IV. 2. PRAGMATISM, REALISM, AND EVOLUTIONARY
COSMOLOGY: BIBLIOGRAPHY

---

695. Bergson, Henri. "Lettre à W. James: 6 janvier
      1903." Revue des Deux Mondes, 17/20 (October 15,
      1933), 793f.
      A portion of the larger correspondence between
      Bergson and James, published in this same issue
      by Ralph Barton Perry (pp. 783-823). In this letter,
      Bergson draws comparisons between his concept of
      "duration" and James's "stream of consciousness."
      Despite such extensive correspondence, however,
      Bergson persistently denied any direct or major in-
      fluence from James.

696. Boodin, John E. Cosmic Evolution. New York: Mac-
      millan, 1925.
      A noted pragmatist outlines a theistic evolution-
      ary cosmology.

697. _____. "The Universe as a Living Whole." Hibbert
      Journal, 28 (1930), 583-600.

698. _____. "Analysis and Wholism." Philosophy of
      Science, 10 (1943), 213-229.

699. Capek, Milic. "Stream of Consciousness and 'Dureé
      Reélle'." Philosophy and Phenomenological Research,
      10/3 (March 1950), 331-353.

There are much stronger affinities between James's
and Bergson's views of the inner perception of time
than the latter would acknowledge. The differences
are also noted: 1) Bergson generalized from psychological introspection to a general metaphysical
view of time, while James embraced initially only
a psychological view; 2) Bergson insisted on the
"immortality of the past," which James initially rejected; 3) in James's final "process philosophy,"
set forth in A Pluralistic Universe (1909), he came
much closer to Bergson under the latter's influence.

700. _____. "La Signification actuelle de la philosophie
de James." Revue de Metaphysique et de Morale,
67/3 (1962), 291-321.
      Sec. V of this article discusses the reciprocal
influence of James and Bergson.

701. *Collins, James. "Darwin's Impact on Philosophy."
Thought, 34 (June 1959), 185-248. [II, no. 206]

702. Culliton, Joseph T. The Cosmic Visions of John Dewey
and Teilhard de Chardin: A Comparative Study. Diss.
Fordham University, 1972.
      Teilhard and Dewey share an interest in natural-
istic values, respect for the "material" world, a
wholehearted commitment to progress and full evolutionary development.

703. _____. A Processive World View for Pragmatic
Christians. New York: Philosophical Library, 1975.

704. _____. "Dewey and Teilhard." The Teilhard Review, 11 (1976), 42-47.

705. Delaney, C. F. "Bergson on Science and Philosophy."
Process Studies, 2/1 (Spring 1972), 29-43.
      Discusses Bergson's view of the relationship of
science and philosophy, and possible criticisms from
the perspective of C. S. Peirce's critique of intuition.

706. Dewey, John. "Evolution and Ethics." The Monist,
8/3 (April 1898), 321-341.

707. _____. "The Evolutionary Method As Applied to
Morality: Its Scientific Necessity." Philosophical
Review, 11/2 (March 1902), 107f.

708. _____. "The Philosophical Work of Spencer."
      Philosophical Review, 13/2 (March 1904), 159f.

709. *_____. The Influence of Darwin on Philosophy and
      Other Essays in Contemporary Thought. New York:
      Henry Holt, 1910. [II, no. 222]

710. *_____. "Spencer and Bergson." Edited with French
      trans. by Gérard Deledalle. Revue de Metaphysique
      et de Morale, 70/3 (1965), 325-333. [II, no. 223]

711. Drake, Durant. "Panpsychism Again." Journal of
      Philosophy, 16/16 (July 31, 1919), 433-439.
      A review of C. A. Strong's Origin of Conscious-
      ness. Gives realist support to emergent evolution
      and the panpsychist doctrine of mind, relating the
      latter to neo-realist philosophies of mind, especially
      in regard to sense-data theory.

712. _____. Mind and Its Place in Nature. New York:
      Macmillan, 1925.
      Advocates a thoroughgoing realism as regards
      scientific description, in opposition to the Platonism
      and strange ontological in-economy of neo-realist
      "sense-data" theorists. While disturbed at his mys-
      ticism, the author proclaims his allegiance to Henri
      Bergson, as well as to C. A. Strong, in advocating
      a critical, monistic realism: the world consists of
      one substance and a single spatio-temporal realm.
      Mind and body are not distinct, but manifestations
      of the total experience and consciousness of a unified
      organism. Organic consciousness emerges gradually
      in the evolutionary process.

713. Elliot, Richard Lee. The Hypothesis of Creative Evo-
      lution in the Philosophy of Charles Sanders Peirce.
      Diss. University of New Mexico, 1974.
      Discusses Peirce's "agapism" as the goal of cre-
      ative evolution in demonstrating the "common inquiry"
      of science and theology.

714. Fairbanks, Matthew J. "A Note Concerning Peirce's
      Debt to Hegel." New Scholasticism, 36 (1962), 219-
      224.

715. *Fontinell, Eugene. "Transcendent Divinity and Process
      Philosophy." The New Theology, vol. 7. Eds. Marty

and Peerman. New York: Macmillan, 1970. Pp.
173-189. [IV, no. 652]

716. Frye, Robert E. Pragmatism in Recent Non-Pragmatic
Systems: Santayana, Bergson, Whitehead. Diss.
Indiana University, 1956.

717. Gibson, A. Boyce. "Mystic or Pragmatist?" Aus-
tralasian Journal of Psychology and Philosophy,
25/1 (1947), 81-103.
Suggests strong affinities between Bergson and
pragmatism.

718. *Gunter, P. A. Y., ed. Bergson and the Evolution of
Physics. Knoxville: University of Tennessee Press,
1969. [II, no. 393, 394]

719. *Harlow, Victor Emmanuel. Bibliography and Genetic
Study of American Realism. Oklahoma City, 1931.
[Intro, no. 16]

720. Hausman, Carl R. "Eros and Agape in Creative Evolution: A Peircean Insight." Process Studies, 4/1
(Spring 1974), 11-25.

721. Heintz, Joseph-Walter. La Notion de conscience chez
William James et Henri Bergson. Diss. University
of Paris, 1950.

722. *Hoernlé, R. F. A. "Idealism and Evolutionary Naturalism." The Monist, 36/3 (October 1926), 561-
576. [III, no. 559]
Rejoinder: R. W. Sellars, The Monist, 37/1
(January 1927), 150-155. Surrejoinder: Hoernlé,
pp. 156-160.

723. Hook, Sidney. The Metaphysics of Pragmatism. Intro.
by John Dewey. Chicago: Open Court Publishing
Co., 1927.
Traces the evolutionary development of pragmatism
from the "personal and consolatory pragmatism of
Schiller" and the "mystical and nominalistic pragmatism of James" to the contemporary "social and scientific pragmatism of Peirce and Dewey." Traces
some affinities of pragmatism and Bergson's thought
through themes such as evolution, freedom, and possibility.

724. Jacoby, Gunther. "Bergson, Pragmatism and Schopen-
      hauer." The Monist, 20/3 (October 1912), 593-611.

725. James, William. "Remarks on Spencer's Definition
      of Mind as Correspondence." Journal of Speculative
      Philosophy, 12/1 (January 1878), 1-18.
      Spencer's theory of "mental evolution" according
      to the formula of the "adjustment of inner to outer
      relations" appears overwhelming in detail. Yet, it
      is simplistic and selective, ignoring sentiment, aes-
      thetic impulses, religion, and personal emotions.
      "Correspondence," upon examination, turns out to
      be a vacuous concept.

726. _____. "Necessary Truths and the Effects of Ex-
      perience." The Principles of Psychology. 2 Vols.
      New York: Henry Holt, 1890. Ch. 28.

727. _____. "Great Men and Their Environment." The
      Will to Believe and Other Essays in Popular Philos-
      ophy. New York: Longmans, Green, 1897. Pp.
      216-254.
      Attacks the mechanism and environmental behavior-
      ism of Herbert Spencer's philosophy of cultural evo-
      lution. James argues that indeterminism is more
      to be noticed in social evolution than determinism.
      Historical development results from the "interaction
      of two wholly distinct factors," the individual "great
      man" with his peculiar creative gifts, and the social
      environment, "with its power of adopting or rejecting
      both him and his gifts."

728. _____. A Pluralistic Universe. New York: Long-
      mans, Green, 1909.
      Traditional rationalism suggests a static universe,
      thus mandating, to a certain degree, an anti-rational
      "intuitionist" approach to account for change and
      process, the "Manyness in Oneness," and "things in
      the making." James praises Bergson, suggesting
      that his "process philosophy" constitutes a verifica-
      tion of Hegel's Logic.

729. _____. Le Pragmatisme. Forward by Henri Berg-
      son. Trans. by E. LeBrun. Paris: Flammarion,
      1968.
      A French translation of the author's Pragmatism.
      Bergson's foreword provides further evidence of the

strong affinities and mutual influence of the two
philosophers.

730. Kallen, Horace M. "James, Bergson and Dr. Pitkin."
Journal of Philosophy, 7 (June 25, 1910), 353-357.
Defends William James's interpretation of Bergson
against the attack by Pitkin (see no. 745 below).

731. _____. "James, Bergson and Traditional Metaphysics." Mind, 23/90 (April 1914), 207-239.
Criticizes Bergsonian metaphysics as "traditional
and compensatory" in contrast to James.

732. _____. William James and Henri Bergson: A Study
in Contrasting Theories of Life. Chicago: University
of Chicago Press, 1914.

733. _____. "La Méthode de l'intuition et la méthode
pragmatiste. Revue de Metaphysique et de Morale,
29/1 (January-March 1922), 35-62.
Bergson's philosophy makes appeal to "direct intuition" in contrast to pragmatism, which is only
marginally intuitionist.

734. Lovejoy, Arthur O. "A Note on Peirce's Evolutionism." Journal of the History of Ideas, 7 (June
1946), 351-354.

735. MacDonald, Matthew Anita. Epistemological Dimensions
of Process Philosophy in John Dewey and Pierre
Teilhard de Chardin. Diss. University of Pennsylvania, 1973.

736. *Mead, George H. "The Nature of the Past." Essays
in Honor of John Dewey. New York: Holt, Rinehart and Winston, 1929. Pp. 235-242. [IV, no. 673]

737. *Meland, Bernard E. "The New Realism in Religious
Inquiry." Encounter 31/4 (Autumn 1970), 311-324.
[II, no. 408]

738. *Montague, William P. "A Materialistic Theory of Emergent Evolutionism." Essays in Honor of John Dewey.
New York: Holt, Rinehart and Winston, 1929. Pp.
257-273. [II, no. 301]

739. Moore, A. W. "Bergson and Pragmatism." The Philosophical Review, 21/4 (July 1912), 397-414.

Denies that Bergson is a pragmatist, and offers
several criticisms of his views from the perspective
of pragmatism.

740. *Morgan, C. Lloyd. "Three Aspects of Monism." The
Monist, 4/3 (April 1894), 321-332. [II, no. 303]

741. Neve, Paul. Le Pragmatism et la philosophie de M.
Bergson. Louvain: Institut supérieur de philosophie,
1912.

742. Peirce, Charles Sanders. "Synechism, Fallibilism,
and Evolution." Philosophical Writings of Peirce.
Ed. Justus Buchler. New York: Dover Publications,
1955.

743. _____. "Evolutionary Love." The Collected Papers
of Charles Sanders Peirce. Eds. Charles Hartshorne
and Paul Weiss. Cambridge, Mass.: Harvard University Press, 1965. VI: 287-317.
Peirce discusses three possible modes of evolution: by fortuitous variation ("tychasm"); by mechanical necessity ("anancasm"); and by creative love
("agapasm"). Certain features of the evolutionary
process, especially human cultural evolution, suggest the third hypothesis.

744. *Perry, Ralph Barton. "American Philosophy in the
First Decade of the Twentieth Century." Revue Internationale de Philosophie, 3 (April 15, 1939), 423-
443. [IV, no. 679]

745. Pitkin, Walter B. "James and Bergson: Or, Who is
Against the Intellect?" Journal of Philosophy, 7/9
(April 28, 1910), 225-231.
While both James and Bergson manifest a certain
anti-intellectual posture, Bergson does not reject
conceptual thought. Response by Bergson: Journal
of Philosophy, 7/14 (July 7, 1910), 385-388.

746. *Reck, Andrew J. Introduction to William James.
Bloomington: Indiana University Press, 1967. [IV,
no. 683]

747. Royce, Josiah, and Kernan, Fergus. "Peirce as a
Philosopher." Journal of Philosophy, 13/26 (Decem-
ber 21, 1916), 701-709.
Distinguishes Peirce's evolutionism from that of

Darwin, Spencer, and Fiske. As a logician, Peirce
was interested in the possibility of evolution in the
"laws" of nature themselves--a viewpoint highly influential with James. Laws are approximate, and
those of the greatest generality are the most stable.
The assumption of the randomness of evolution demands logically an empirical account of the present
order.

748. *Sellars, Roy Wood. "Emergent Evolution: The New
Philosophy of Nature." Scribner's Magazine, 87
(January-June 1930), 316-325. [II, no. 329]

749. *Strong, C. A. Why the Mind Has a Body. New York:
Macmillan, 1903. [IV, no. 689]

750. *_____. The Origin of Consciousness: An Attempt
to Conceive the Mind as a Product of Evolution. New
York: Macmillan, 1918. [IV, no. 690]

751. Thayer, Horace S. "Dewey: Continuity--Hegel and
Darwin." Appendix; Meaning and Action: A Critical
History of Pragmatism. Indianapolis, Ind. : Bobbs-
Merrill, 1968. Pp. 460-487.

752. Wiener, Philip P. Evolution and the Founders of Pragmatism. Cambridge, Mass. : Harvard University
Press, 1949.
        Traces the differing degrees of influence of evolu-
tionary doctrines on Chauncey Wright, C. S. Peirce,
William James, John Fiske, and other members of
the Cambridge Metaphysical Club.

753. Wilson, Alexander P. The Concept of Human Freedom
in Bergson and James. Diss. University of Washington, Seattle, 1950.

754. Woodbridge, Frederick James Eugene. The Purpose
of History: Reflections on Bergson, Dewey and Santayana. New York: Columbia University Press,
1916.

IV. 3.   PRAGMATISM, REALISM, AND HEGELIAN
         IDEALISM: BIBLIOGRAPHY

755.   Ackerman, Phyllis. "Some Aspects of Pragmatism
       and Hegel." Journal of Philosophy, 15/13 (June 20,
       1918), 337-356.
            According to Dewey's version of pragmatism,
       there is an active relation between the process of
       knowing and the object known: "the life of the mind
       is the history of a process that is a series of little
       processes." Author argues that Hegel anticipates
       Dewey on most of these points. Even the alleged
       differences regarding temporalism disappear upon
       careful treatment of Hegel's thought.

756.   *Bosanquet, Bernard. "Realism and Metaphysics."
       Philosophical Review, 26/1 (January 1917), 4-15.
       [III, no. 434]

757.   Bradley, F. H. "Appearance and Contradiction."
       Mind, 18/72 (October 1909), 489-508.
            Bradley assesses James's Pluralistic Universe,
       suggesting the views there expressed are entirely com-
       patible with his own. He questions the thesis of pure ex-
       ternal relations, suspects monism is lurking in the
       alleged "pluralism," and fails to find any differences
       between pragmatic doctrines of free will and "that
       which I, for instance, have advocated since 1876...."

758.   *Brightman, Edgar S. "Modern Idealism." Journal of
       Philosophy, 17/20 (September 23, 1920), 533-550.
       [III, no. 436]

759.   _____. A Philosophy of Ideals. New York: Holt,
       1928.
            Argues for the objectivity of value and obligation,
       whether or not one believes in God. Ideals, then,
       are properly considered a part of ultimate reality.
       Claims that, despite other differences, realism and
       pragmatism agree with idealism on the utility of
       ideals in experience.

760.   Caldwell, William. Pragmatism and Idealism. Lon-
       don: Adam and Charles Block, 1913.

Discusses British neo-Hegelianism (especially
Bosanquet) and Bergson in relation to pragmatism,
arguing for the continuity of certain emphases, as
well as the historic roots of British and American
pragmatism in earlier Hegelian idealism.

761. Cook, Daniel J. "James's 'Ether Mysticism' and
Hegel." Journal of the History of Philosophy, 15/3
(July 1977), 309-319.
Based on his own experience with nitrous oxide,
James sometimes claimed that certain mystical insights had influenced Hegel's own thinking. Cook
argues that James's nitrous oxide insights should
be taken seriously, and that these reveal clearly that
James's actual understanding of Hegel was seriously
deficient. Thus, these states are not simply light-
hearted drug euphoria, but serious, and seriously-
deficient, philosophy.

762. Dewey, John. "Pragmatism's Debt to Hegel" (c. 1884).
The American Hegelians. Ed. William H. Goetzmann. New York: Alfred A. Knopf, 1973. Pp.
149-153.
Analyzes Hegel's improvement upon Kantian dualism, and discusses dialectic as the rational principle
of real process and change in the world. "The only
conception adequate to experience as a whole is organism."

763. _____. "My Pedagogic Creed" (c. 1897). The
American Hegelians. Ed. William H. Goetzmann.
New York: Alfred A. Knopf, 1973. Pp. 310-320.
Dewey acknowledges Hegel's influence on his own
understanding of evolution.

764. _____. "From Absolutism to Experimentalism" (c.
1930). The American Hegelians. Ed. William H.
Goetzmann. New York: Alfred A. Knopf, 1973.
Pp. 380-392.
Dewey retraces his philosophical development from
Transcendentalism, Kant, and Hegel to his final views
regarding Experimentalism and Instrumentalism--
perspectives that are more actor than spectator-
oriented. Acknowledges his debt to Hegel throughout. Hegel's schematism seems now "artificial,"
but there is "greater richness and variety of insight
in Hegel than any other speculative philosopher."
Dewey discusses James's revision of the Hegelian

category of "organism" in light of his interests in
psychology and biology, rendering the category more
dynamic, temporal, and pluralistic.

765. Elton, William. "Peirce's Marginalia in W. T. Har-
      ris's Hegel's Logic." Journal of the History of
      Philosophy, 2 (1964), 82-84.
          Peirce's marginal notes in his personal copy of
      his friend, W. T. Harris's, book, Hegel's Logic:
      On the Genesis of the Categories of the Mind (Chi-
      cago, 1890), "confirm his complex attitude toward
      Hegel, crucial for the development of his philosophy."
      Peirce's ambivalence toward Hegel is evident, as he
      notes in 1890, "I reject his philosophy in toto," but
      then again in 1903, "Hegel is the greatest philosopher
      who ever lived." Peirce's marginalia also reveal
      his frustration over the mathematical imprecision of
      Hegel's Logic, as well as over the absence of "exact
      sciences" in the Encyclopedia, but also reveal his
      appreciation for Hegel's realism and refutation of
      skepticism.

766. Fisch, Max H. "Hegel and Peirce." Hegel and the
      History of Philosophy. Eds. Joseph O'Malley, et al.
      The Hague: Martinus Nijhoff, 1974.
          Author considers "the two principal occasions
      when Peirce developed his philosophy at length in
      relation to Hegel's": viz., his "New List of Cate-
      gories" (1867), and his "proof of pragmatism" (1903-
      11). Also traces Peirce's relations to two leading
      American Hegelians, Josiah Royce and W. T. Harris.

767. Flay, Joseph Charles. Hegel and Dewey and the Prob-
      lem of Freedom. Diss. University of Southern Cali-
      fornia, 1965.

768. *Goetzmann, William H., ed. The American Hegelians.
      New York: Alfred A. Knopf, 1973. [III, no. 454]

769. *Harlow, Victor Emmanuel. Bibliography and Genetic
      Study of American Realism. Oklahoma City, 1931.
      (New York: Kraus Reprints, 1972.) [Intro, no. 16]

770. Hartshorne, Charles. "Santayana's Defiant Eclecticism."
      Journal of Philosophy, 61 (January 1964), 35-43.
          Santayana's philosophy is a sharp rejection of
      idealism, and Hartshorne's review is a devastating
      indictment of this: Santayana is accused of having

overlooked the "more sensible form of idealism represented by Peirce."

771.   Hocking, William Ernest. Science and the Idea of God.
        Chapel Hill: University of North Carolina Press,
        1944.

771a.   _____. "On Royce's Empiricism." Journal of Phil-
        osophy, 53/3 (February 2, 1956), 57-63.

772.   James, William. A Pluralistic Universe. New York:
        Longmans, Green, 1909.
            Quarrels with Bradley's "Absolute," and Lotze's
        "Monism." James accuses these philosophers,
        together with Royce, of "vicious intellectualism":
        an attitude toward universals that, by definition, they
        exclude what their name does not specifically include.
        In a manner reminiscent of Hegel's similar complaint
        about formal logic, James accuses logicians of ex-
        cessive classification and narrowness of view. James
        offers a positive view of Hegel by contrast, suggest-
        ing that pluralism involves Hegel's concept of "con-
        tradictions," and that Hegel was himself an anti-
        rationalist. Discusses the difference of the terms
        "absolute" and "God," and claims that Hegel was
        guilty of "vicious intellectualism" here, and at sev-
        eral other points in his philosophy.

773.   Lewis, C. I. "Realism and Subjectivism." Journal
        of Philosophy, 10/2 (January 16, 1913), 43-49.
            This essay is a balanced critique of the realist
        attacks upon idealism. Lewis reminds his audience
        that idealism intends a way out of the ego-centric
        predicament posed by earlier empiricism; not vice-
        versa. Furthermore, there are different types of
        idealism, many of which assert, not that reality is
        known, but that it is knowable. The proper approach
        of the realist is to assert that the idealism argument
        against subjectivism is false: namely, that an "in-
        dependent reality" is unknowable, whence reality is
        not independent. Realism, by contrast, defends the
        subjectivist assumptions, but not its solipsistic con-
        clusions. Finally, all such discussions merely con-
        stitute assertions. The realist has not disproven
        idealism as a legitimate dogma, but has undermined
        its claim to empirical and logical authority.

774.   Lovejoy, Arthur O. "A Temporalistic Realism." Con-

temporary American Philosophy, vol. II. Eds. Adams
and Montague. New York: Russell and Russell,
1930. Pp. 85-104.
    The problem of idealism is temporalism. How
can a timeless absolute of "eternal truths" be made
up of parts which are actual and temporal? Nonetheless, this seemed to be the claim jointly of Bradley and Royce. The nature of finite, discrete, individual experience, by contrast, is that it is transi-
tory, but seems final. This experience thus cannot
be part of a timeless absolute. The temporal, pluralistic aspect of experience leads away from idealism to realism.

775. *Mack, Robert D. The Appeal to Immediate Experience:
Philosophic Method in Bradley, Whitehead and Dewey.
New York: King's Crown Press, 1945. [IV, no.
672]

776. Mahowald, Mary Briody. An Idealistic Pragmatism:
The Development of the Pragmatic Element in the
Philosophy of Josiah Royce. The Hague: Martinus
Nijhoff, 1972.
    Contrary to popular opinion, pragmatism is not
opposed to idealism, but only to monism. Josiah
Royce provides an example of the compatibility of
idealism and pragmatism. Pragmatism is a way of
philosophizing which is action-oriented toward the
future--asking "what difference would this idea make
to us" (Peirce), or "to me as an individual" (James).
No other philosophy claims this method as its defining characteristic. All process philosophy, especially
that of Whitehead, involves such an emphasis, but
this emphasis alone does not define the content of
that philosophy. Indeed, "evolutionary thought in
general represents a context which accents future
experience," whereas pragmatism is itself only a
way of philosophizing, a method of future-orientation.

777. Montague, William P. "Panpsychism and Monism."
Journal of Philosophy, 2/23 (November 9, 1905),
626-629.
    Attacks the monism inherent in panpsychism, which
is not a form of realism, but rather "the Darwini-
zation of Berkeley." The appeal to evolution, however, is irrelevant to the categorial relation of mind
and body.

778. Nisbet, Arthur Lee. A Comparative Analysis of Her-
      bert Marcuse's and John Dewey's Conceptions of
      Freedom. Diss. State University of New York, (Buf-
      falo), 1974.
         Offers a summary of Marcuse's views of libera-
      tion, freedom, and dialectical logic, comparing these
      with Hegel. Accuses both of a "fallacious a prior-
      ism," as for example in the open advocacy of politi-
      cal repression and deception. Freedom in Marcuse's
      system is merely "conformity" to the absolute con-
      clusions of the Marxist-dialectical logic. This is
      a marked contrast to Dewey, for whom freedom rep-
      resented the ongoing development of individual capaci-
      ties.

779. Perry, Ralph Barton. "Professor Royce's Refutation
      of Realism and Pluralism." The Monist, 12/3 (April
      1902), 446-458.
         Objects to the unassailable arrogance of "logical
      necessity" in Royce's "constructive idealism." Royce's
      concern for realism is not "what is real?" but rather,
      "what is it to be real?" But this is personalism,
      not realism. By contrast, "things" and "thoughts
      about things" are distinct; objects are mind-independ-
      ent. These are the conclusions of pluralism, which
      Perry defends against Royce's monistic attack.

780. *_____. "American Philosophy in the First Decade
      of the Twentieth Century." Revue Internationale de
      Philosophie, 3 (April 15, 1939), 423-443. [IV, no.
      679]

781. Royce, Josiah. "William James and the Philosophy of
      Life." "Phi Beta Kappa Oration: Harvard Univer-
      sity, June, 1911." William James and Other Essays
      on the Philosophy of Life. New York: Macmillan,
      1911.
         Discusses James's importance in American phi-
      losophy, and his use of ideals in his philosophy of
      life. Attempts to draw some parallels between his
      (Royce's) views and those of James and the "evolu-
      tionary movement" of Darwin, Spencer and Huxley.
      Other essays in this volume oppose pragmatism's
      doctrine of truth vis-à-vis Royce's doctrine of Ab-
      solute Truth.

782. *_____, and Kernan, Fergus. "Peirce as a Philos-
      opher." Journal of Philosophy, 13/26 (December 21,
      1916), 701-709. [IV, no. 747]

783. Rubins, Sidney Swaim. Hegel's Pragmatism. Diss.
     Harvard University, 1910.

784. Rucker, Darnell. The Chicago Pragmatists. Minne-
     apolis: University of Minnesota Press, 1969.
        Details the formation of the first actual "school"
     of pragmatism under Dewey's influence at the Uni-
     versity of Chicago, combining James's practical ori-
     entation with Peirce's belief in the broad, applicable
     character of natural science. A chapter on psychol-
     ogy argues that the pragmatic method which Mead
     and Dewey helped to shape is a "physiological psy-
     chology," in which "Hegel's view of process within
     a wholeness has not been so much rejected as ex-
     panded upon and brought up to date."

785. Santucci, Antonio. "Peirce, Hegel e la dottrina delle
     categorie." Incidenza di Hegel. Ed. Fulvio Tes-
     sitore. Naples: Morano, 1970. Pp. 963-984.

786. *Smith, John E. "Purpose in American Philosophy."
     International Philosophical Quarterly, 1 (1961), 390-
     406. [IV, no. 687]

787. Strong, C. A. "Idealism and Realism, Pts. I & II."
     Journal of Philosophy, 1/19 (September 15, 1904),
     519-526; and 1/20 (September 29, 1904), 543-551.
        Argues that naive realism, insofar as it is accep-
     table, is not wholly dissimilar to panpsychism in
     psychology.

788. Thayer, Horace S. Meaning and Action: A Critical
     History of Pragmatism. Indianapolis, Ind.: Bobbs-
     Merrill, 1968.
        While the author does not treat the nineteenth
     century in any detail, he includes an appendix dis-
     cussing Dewey's continuity with Hegel and Darwin,
     as well as a second appendix treating the theme of
     "possibility" in pragmatism.

789. Townsend, H. G. "The Pragmatism of Peirce and
     Hegel." The Philosophical Review, 37 (1928), 297-
     303.

790. Turner, J. E. A Theory of Direct Realism, and the
     Relation of Realism to Idealism. New York: Mac-
     millan, 1925.
        Citing Whitehead's colleague, Haldane, Turner
     offers the argument that idealism is not only con-

sistent with, but also the "logical corollary" of realism. Cites R. B. Perry's false conjunction of Berkeley and Hegel as proof of the serious misunderstanding of idealism by realists. Offers a careful
documentation of this sytematic realist blunder, and
carefully cites Hegel's texts to illustrate his affinity
with realist doctrines. Argues that Hegel and the
English Hegelians are themselves realists, rather
than subjectivists. Concludes by outlining a theory
of sense-perception which is held to be similar to
that of Samuel Alexander.

791. Ward, L. R. "John Dewey in Search of Himself."
Review of Politics, 19 (1957), 205-213.
       Discusses the Hegelian roots of Dewey's philos-
ophy.

792. White, Morton G. The Origin of Dewey's Instrumentalism. New York: Columbia University Press, 1943.
       Relates Dewey's intellectual pilgrimage from un-
critical Hegelianism to Instrumentalism, showing the
elements of Hegelian idealism which persisted nonetheless in Dewey's later categories.

793. Wilkins, Burleigh Taylor. "James, Dewey and Hegelian Idealism." Journal of the History of Ideas, 17
(June 1956), 332-346.

PART V: BRIDGE MOVEMENTS

There remain a number of philosophers and lesser philosophical movements which escape neat classification within the historical schema I have elaborated. These include such names as Royce, Alexander, W. E. Hocking, and E. S. Brightman, and movements such as so-called "English" Hegelianism. Royce and Alexander serve to illustrate the problem.

Royce, especially in light of his German training and Hegelian background, is generally considered an idealist. Yet he is, on occasion, also classified as a pragmatist, a realist, or a personalist. [1] When one considers the diversity of opinions labeled "idealistic," this confusion seems less problematic. Royce certainly reflects, in a unique way, the ongoing interpretation of the Hegelian tradition discussed in Part III. Some of that ongoing interpretation resulted in "personal idealism" or personalism, which we shall consider momentarily. In addition, as an American philosopher, Royce tended to incorporate the native pragmatist tendency in his philosophizing--a method, as noted, which is entirely compatible with a number of metaphysical perspectives. Finally, as a Harvard faculty member at the turn of the twentieth century, he was hardly immune from--indeed, he was frequently the focus of--the realist revolt against idealism. [2] It is, then, hardly surprising to find these motifs reflected in his thought in a way which prompts his classification by different scholars under a number of otherwise distinct and diverse philosophical movements.

Alexander presents a slightly different problem Once again, his principal training under the "prevailing climate of opinion" was in the variety of idealism represented by Bradley and McTaggart. On the basis of his own self-understanding, he is widely perceived to have broken ranks with the idealists over issues such as evolutionary change, temporal-

181

ism, pluralism, and theological finitism. As a result, he
is sometimes classified as a precursor of Whitehead, although I argue that he is more properly assimilated with
Bergson and other evolutionary cosmologists.

Pluralism and theological finitism are, of course,
integral to realism and pragmatism, as Perry noted.[3] The
themes are likewise stressed by a number of idealists, especially those in the personalist tradition, such as Lotze and
Brightman. While temporalism and evolutionary change are
admittedly de-emphasized by the major English and American
idealists Bradley, Royce, and McTaggart, these themes are
nonetheless stressed by the personalists, as well as yet other
idealists, including Bosanquet, Collingwood and (as we noted
in Part III), Hegel. Thus, it was hardly necessary for Alexander to announce a "break" with idealism to encompass such
themes. In addition, Alexander's "space-time nisus" can lay
no more claim to empirical verification than can Bergson's
élan vital or Whitehead's "category of the ultimate"--whence
the vestige of idealism and speculative intuitionism in the
Hegelian-Bradleyan mode remains to haunt his philosophy.[4]
As a result, Alexander likewise could be classified under
any of the headings heretofore proposed. A common heritage
in all such "problem" cases emerges: viz., the idealist
(or rather, Hegelian) legacy itself. These residual difficulties in historical and doctrinal classification result largely
from the continued evolution and development of the Hegelian
tradition, especially as that tradition attempted to respond
to, and incorporate subsequent developments in the understanding of nature attained through contemporary physical
and biological science. The major issue in the course of
this development was whether an individual trained initially
in the Hegelian tradition found anything worth salvaging, trans-
forming, or updating (as did Collingwood, Bosanquet, Croce,
Lotze, and Brightman), or whether instead felt the entire
tradition had to be set aside (as James, Perry, Russell,
and Moore evidently held).

It is important to stress that this is not an objective
question of doctrinal consistency or coherence (as the matter
is customarily represented). Surely we now recognize that
one can demonstrate the continued vitality and adaptability
of contemporary idealism in successfully grappling with issues
in modern science and the philosophy of nature.[5] Rather,
one witnesses here instead the further illustration of Fichte's
deceptively-simple maxim in the first introduction to his
Wissenschaftslehre: "Was für eine Philosophie man hat, das
hangt davor ab, was für ein Mensch man ist."

In general, most of those philosophers who are difficult to classify in the process tradition are those who found
something of enduring worth in the school of Hegelian idealism, and who proceeded in diverse ways (in Croce's famous
phrase) to separate what was living from what was dead in
that tradition. While opinions varied as to what lived and
what died, the major re-shuffling and re-structuring along
the lines of a process philosophy came from those who identified themselves (or who were subsequently identified) as either
personalists or English Hegelians.

A.   Personalism

It is tempting, after the fact, to label personalism
a purely theological movement, thus largely irrelevant to
the purposes of this investigation. The American legacy
of Lotze at Boston University in the first half of the twentieth century produced a movement which was primarily theological in orientation. Indeed, the "Boston personalism" of
Bowne, Knudson, Brightman, Bertocci, Muelder, and their
students represented perhaps the sole enduring contribution
to philosophical theology from the Methodist tradition. Other
forms of personalism--such as those of Royce, J. E. Turner,
W. E. Hocking, and Andrew Seth Pringle-Pattison--although
theistic in implication were not necessarily theological or
confessional in orientation.

In the main, personalism results from idealism's attempt to accommodate the prevailing fashion of pluralism
and empiricism. In so doing, the general claim that consciousness (or, at least sentience) is the primary datum is
replaced by the claim that personal experience finally constitutes the irreducible fact. This claim embodies a pluralist polemic against the perceived monism of Bradleyan and
absolute idealism. In contrast to what appears a simple re-
affirmation of the Cartesian "cogito," however, personal experience is interpreted more broadly than merely rational
consciousness. Personality entails feelings, creativity, community, and organic inter-relatedness or reciprocity with the
world and with other persons. [6] Furthermore, the term "person" refers to traits and experiences not limited to human
beings. Other non-human entities may be "persons"--God,
for example, is perceived as a person in the Boston school
(or, more correctly, we have in the experience of "persons"
our most revealing clue as to God's intrinsic nature). [7]

The modes in which such claims are presented are

diverse, ranging from the grand evolutionary cosmology of
Lotze[8] (similar in many respects to that of Alexander), to
the highly-technical vocabulary of Edgar Sheffield Brightman,
similar in many respects (and at some points indebted) to
Whitehead's complex categorial scheme.[9]

In their common affirmation of organism, pluralism,
creative evolutionary advance, and theological finitism, personalists as a group serve to bridge the gap between the
mainstream of Hegelian idealism and other schools of process
thought--especially evolutionary cosmology and process rationalism, but, through the marked influence on James of
the French personalist Renouvier, pragmatism and realism
as well.[10]

B. "English" Hegelianism

The label "English Hegelians" is rather arbitrary.
Richard Kroner[11] uses the term to designate the interpreters
of Hegel in England, from J. H. Stirling to G. R. G. Mure,
including the personalist A. S. Pringle-Pattison. This hardly
seems fair to Scotch and Irish Hegelians. The term "British"
Hegelians might be more appropriate. One must also include
the American Hegelians, from W. T. Harris, G. H. Howison,
and G. H. Palmer to W. H. Sheldon and Brand Blanshard.[12]
If one chooses to speak of English Hegelians or English idealists, then one is de facto committed to treating everyone in-
volved in the translation into the English language--and, in
the process, the transformation--of the ideas of Kant, Hegel
and Schelling, from Coleridge and Carlyle to the present
Hegelian revivalists in America.[13] Thus, while it is impossible to specify precisely any unique school of English
Hegelians, I shall intend by the term those English-speaking
philosophers acknowledging some indebtedness to Hegel. I
shall focus on those within that group for whom a "process"
interpretation of Hegelianism--stressing temporalism, evolutionary change, historical emergence of novelty, organism
and reciprocal interrelatedness, pluralism (as qualified by
a doctrine of real, constitutive relations), and theological
finitism--is primary.

In some sense, the earlier British Hegelians, such as
McTaggart and F. H. Bradley, are responsible for the "bad
odor" associated with idealism in English-language philosophy.
Our earlier discussions of idealism imply that, indeed, it was
the austere and mystical variation of monism and non-
temporal absolutism associated with thinkers like Bradley,

McTaggart, and Royce--rather than the qualified pluralism
and temporalistic doctrine of organic teleology characterizing
Hegel's philosophy--which was rejected by the majority of
twentieth-century philosophers. [14] We have had occasion,
however, also to note that some of the views of these absolute
idealists (e. g. , Royce and Bradley) survive and exert a profound influence on realism and evolutionary cosmology.

If one chooses to focus on the surviving vestiges of
Bradley and Royce, together with the contributions of Bosanquet, Collingwood, and Alexander--as interpreted more recently by vigorous exponents such as J. N. Findley and Errol
E. Harris--one finds in certain quarters of English Hegelianism views remarkably akin to those of the canonical process
schools. As in the case of personalism, such revitalized
idealisms are not merely a "throwback" to Hegel, but an attempt likewise to separate the "living" from the "dead," and
to render those idealist intuitions which survive realist and
analytic criticisms in acceptable contemporary forms. Especially in the case of Collingwood and Harris, this amounts
once again to the recasting of some of the main insights of
idealism onto a secure realist or empiricist footing in the
form of a process metaphysics. [15]

NOTES

(1) Jack William Jones claims to discern personalism in
     Royce's thought: Personalistic Tendencies in the
     Thought of Josiah Royce (Diss. Boston University,
     1968), while Mary Briody Mahowald discusses Royce's
     pragmatism: An Idealistic Pragmatism (The Hague:
     Martinus Nijhoff, 1972). William E. Hocking describes
     Royce as an empiricist: "On Royce's Empiricism,"
     Journal of Philosophy, 53/3 (February 2, 1956), 57-
     63; while Andrew Reck and George D. Straton claim
     to discern realist and process elements in Royce's
     thought. Cf. Reck, Recent American Philosophy (New
     York: Pantheon Books, 1962), p. xvi-xvii; and Stra-
     ton, Theistic Faith for Our Time: An Introduction to
     the Process Philosophies of Royce and Whitehead
     (Washington, D. C. : University Press of America,
     1979).

(2) E. g. , Ralph Barton Perry, "Prof. Royce's Refutation
     of Realism and Pluralism," The Monist, 12/3 (April
     1902), 446-458.

(3) "American Philosophy in the First Decade of the Twen-

tieth Century," Revue Internationale de Philosophie,
3 (April 15, 1939), 439.

(4) Bertram D. Brettschneider offers a devastating critique
of Alexander's claims of independence from idealism
and advocacy of realism and empiricism, backed with
a careful, point-by-point comparison of Alexander's
views with those of F. H. Bradley. Cf. The Philosophy of Samuel Alexander: Idealism in "Space, Time
and Deity" (New York: Humanities Press, 1964).

(5) See for example, R. G. Collingwood, The Idea of Nature
(Oxford: The Clarendon Press, 1945); and Errol E.
Harris, The Foundations of Metaphysics in Science
(London: G. Allen & Unwin, 1965); and Hypothesis
and Perception: the Roots of Scientific Method (Lon-
don: G. Allen & Unwin, 1970). The vigor of con-
temporary idealistic interpretations of modern science
is further revealed in two recent articles by Harris:
"Science and Objectivity," in Contemporary Studies in
Philosophical Idealism, eds. Howie and Buford (Cape
Cod, Mass.: Claude Stark & Co., 1975), pp. 81-94;
and "Nature, Man and Science: Their Changing Relations," International Philosophical Quarterly, 19/1
(March 1979), 1-14.

(6) A. C. Knudson lists six metaphysical categories for
personalism: pluralism, community, creativity, free-
dom, personality, and the "phenomenality of matter."
The Philosophy of Personalism (New York: Abingdon,
1927). Cf. also Borden Parker Bowne, Personalism
(New York: Houghton Mifflin, 1908), and H. C. Weld,
Some Types of Personalism in the United States (Diss.,
Boston University, 1944).

(7) A. S. Pringle-Pattison argues this position early on
against the impersonal, monistic absolute of then-
traditional idealism, in his Hegelianism and Personality
(London, 1887). Cf. also E. S. Brightman, "An Empirical Approach to God," The Philosophical Review,
46/2 (March 1937), 147-169; and "A Temporalist View
of God," Journal of Religion, 12 (1932), 545-555.

(8) See his Mikrokosmos, 3 vols. (Leipzig, 1856-1864).

(9) Cf. E. S. Brightman, The Problem of God (New York:
Abingdon Press, 1930); Nature and Values (New York:
Abingdon, 1945); and Person and Reality (posthumous),

ed. Peter Bertocci (New York: Ronald Press, 1958).
Also cf. his later essay, "Personalism," in A History
of Philosophical Systems, ed. V. Ferm (New York:
1950), pp. 340-352.

(10) As example of personalism's influence on pragmatism,
cf. Otto F. Kraushaar, "Lotze's Influence on Pragmatism and the Practical Philosophy of William
James," Journal of the History of Ideas, 1 (1940),
439-458; of personalism on evolutionary cosmology,
cf. Milic Capek, "Process and Personality in Bergson's Thought," Philosophical Forum, 17 (1959-60),
25-42; and Andre Ligneul, Teilhard and Personalism,
trans. P. J. Oligny and M. D. Meilach (Glen Rock,
N. J. : Paulist Press, 1968). The influence of personalism on realists and process rationalists is discussed by Paul Kuntz, in his introduction to George
Santayana's Lotze's System of Philosophy (Bloomington: Indiana University Press, 1971); as well as by
Philippe Devaux, Lotze et son Influence sur la Philosophie Anglo-Saxonne (Brussels, 1932); and by Paul
Kuntz again in a recent article, "Lotze as a Process
Philosopher," Idealistic Studies, 9/3 (September
1979), 229-241. Finally, Andrew J. Reck discusses
the work of Hocking and Brightman, pointing out their
similarities on many points to both Hegel and Whitehead: Recent American Philosophy (New York: Pan-
theon Books, 1962).

(11) "Mure and Other English Hegelians," Review of Metaphysics, 7/1 (September 1953), 64-73.

(12) A complete account of the major American figures is
presented in William H. Goetzmann, The American
Hegelians (New York: Alfred A. Knopf, 1973).

(13) Hegelianism, through the agency of such figures as
T. M. Knox, Mure, Findley, and others has always
retained a minority status in Great Britain. Recent
activities of the newly formed Harvester Press in
Britain provide evidence of an increasing interest
among younger scholars in Hegel. The American
revival of Hegel, stimulated by Findley, Harris and
other British Hegelians in America has been on the
increase since the mid-1960's.

(14) This phenomenon is treated briefly in my book, Two
Views of Freedom in Process Thought (Chico, Cal. :

Scholars Press, 1979), p. 2f. Cf. also J. N. Findlay, Hegel: A Re-examination (Oxford: Oxford
University Press, 1958), p. 21f.

(15) A possible third category of "bridge movement" might
be added here, treating certain affinities between
process philosophies and contemporary phenomenology.
The organic event-views of perception and knowledge
put forth by Husserl and Heidegger--but more especially by Maurice Merleau-Ponty (Phenomenologie de
la perception. Paris, 1945)--do indeed bear a striking resemblance in certain aspects to the epistemology
and psychology of the process rationalists Whitehead
and Hartshorne. Husserl's close similarity with
Bergson regarding such issues is a matter of historical record. Errol E. Harris's work in these areas,
especially as detailed in his book Hypothesis and
Perception (London, 1970), calls attention to these
similarities, and their common Hegelian roots. Cf.
also Charles Hartshorne's contribution to Philosophical Essays in Memory of Edmund Husserl (Cambridge, Mass.: Harvard University Press, 1940),
and Robert E. Doud, "Whitehead and Merleau-Ponty:
Commitment as a Context for Comparison," Process
Studies, 7/3 (Fall 1977), 145-160.

V. A.   PERSONALISM--ITS RELATION TO OTHER
          SCHOOLS OF PROCESS THOUGHT:
                    BIBLIOGRAPHY

---

794. Baker, Ronnie Bell. The Concept of a Limited God.
      Washington, D. C.: Shenandoah Publishing Co.,
      1934.
         The doctrine of the "limited God" in personalism
      is linked to the views of Fechner, James, Renouvier,
      and McTaggart. Author attacks the "irrational, de-
      rogatory" limitation on God in Brightman and Rash-
      dall, in favor of the view of a self-imposed limitation
      advocated by F. R. Tennant.

795. Bertocci, Peter. "William James' Psychology of Will:
      An Evaluation." Philosophical Forum, 4 (Spring
      1946), 2-13.

796. _____. "Brightman's View of the Self, the Person,
and the Body." Philosophical Forum, 8 (Spring
1950), 21-28.

797. _____. "Edgar Sheffield Brightman." The Personalist, 34 (Autumn 1953), 358f.

798. _____. Religion as Creative Insecurity. New York:
Association Press, 1958.
Religion is not an avenue to peace of mind, but
rather a state of creative insecurity, involving the
risk of freedom which leads to maturity. Love,
suffering and the experience of forgiveness constitute
true happiness in the completion of the self.

799. _____. "Edgar S. Brightman--Ten Years Later."
Philosophical Forum, 20 (1962-63), 3-10.

800. _____. "Toward a Metaphysics of Creation." Review of Metaphysics, 17 (1964), 493-510.
Argues against the traditional view that Being
must be perfect and unchanging, substituting the alternative model of personalism in terms of persons
as finite centers of creative activity. This process
view of persons is then utilized to develop a concept
of God and of the God-world relation, in comparison
with Hartshorne.

801. _____. "An Impasse in Philosophical Theology."
International Philosophical Quarterly, 5 (September
1965), 379-396.
Argues against the association of immutability
and flawlessness in God.

802. _____. The Goodness of God. Washington, D. C. :
University Press of America, 1981.
In this attempt to summarize his personalist phi-
losophy, the author argues that, after Brightman,
Whitehead was the principal influence in the develop-
ment of the author's process views.

803. _____, and Corea, M. Alicia. "Edgar Sheffield
Brightman: Through His Students' Eyes." Philosophical Forum, 12 (1954), 53-67.

804. Bowne, Borden Parker. Metaphysics. New York:
1898.

805. _____. Theism. New York: 1902.

806. _____. Personalism. New York: Houghton, Mifflin, 1908.
A theologically-oriented defense of "personal realism," the commonsense belief in personal experience, knowledge, and faith asserted in opposition to mechanism, positivism, and atheism.

807. *Brightman, Edgar Sheffield. "Modern Idealism."
Journal of Philosophy, 17/20 (September 23, 1920), 533-550. [III, no. 436]

808. *_____. A Philosophy of Ideals. New York: Holt, 1928. [IV, no. 759]

809. _____. "A Misunderstanding of Idealism." Journal of Philosophy, 26/22 (October 24, 1929), 605-607.
A defense of the author's Philosophy of Ideals. Properly understood, idealism is an interpretation of the metaphysical objectivity of ideals and values, which, in turn, are verifiable dimensions of actual experience.

810. _____. The Problem of God. New York: Abingdon Press, 1930.
At the time of its initial publication, this was an important and controversial work. In a manner analogous to Whitehead and H. N. Weiman, Brightman suggests that there are certain inherent limitations on the divine nature that qualify the concept of omnipotence, thus accounting for irrational, chaotic, or "surd" evil in the world. An early "process theodicy."

811. _____. "A Temporalist View of God." Journal of Religion, 12 (1932), 545-555.

812. _____. "The Finite Self." Contemporary Idealism in America. Ed. Clifford Barrett. New York: Macmillan, 1932. Pp. 169-195.
Different forms of idealism suggest varied and often contradictory views of the "self." There are four propositions common to virtually all forms of idealism: 1) the self is an organic system; 2) experience is primarily of a self-existent unity (monadic); 3) the self enjoys conscious experience; 4) the self is active. The first is Hegel's view, while Leibniz, Lotze, and Bowne primarily emphasize form (2).

813. *_____. "The Definition of Idealism." Journal of
Philosophy, 30/16 (August 3, 1933), 429-435. [III,
no. 489]

814. _____. "The Present Outlook in Philosophy of Religion: From the Standpoint of an Idealist." American Philosophies of Religion. Eds. Weiman and
Meland. Chicago: Willett, Clark, 1936. Pp. 318-
325.

815. _____. "An Empirical Approach to God." Philosophical Review, 46/2 (March 1937), 147-169.
Text of the presidential address for the Eastern
Division of the American Philosophical Association.
Author argues that the empirical approach to theology
supports the doctrine of a limited God. The most
relevant evidence is found in the record of evolutionary change in the physical order, the psychological
order, and the ideal or axiological order. The idea
of God provides a sense of unity and coherence among
the interrelated data of these three orders of human
experience.

816. _____. Nature and Values. New York: Abingdon,
1945.
Nature is the realm of transcendent values which
are nonetheless objective.

817. _____. "Bowne: Eternalist or Temporalist?" The
Personalist, 28 (1947), 257-265.

818. _____. "Personalism." A History of Philosophical
Systems. Ed. V. Ferm. New York: 1950. Pp.
340-352.

819. _____. Person and Reality: An Introduction to
Metaphysics. New York: Ronald Press, 1958.
A posthumous publication, edited by Peter Bertocci and others, which sets forth in a systematic
way some of the major themes of Brightman's version of personalism. Personalism resolves the tension between naturalism and theism. All primary
data are immediate, conscious experiences (the "shin-
ing present"), conditioned or rendered intelligible by
the orientation from a past and toward a future (the
"illuminating absent"). Reality consists of a society
of persons, including the ultimate, uncreated Person
and finite persons, whose primary experience is expressed historically, rather than in nature. The

order of nature represents the being and, in a sense, the "behavior" of the ultimate Person.

820.   Capek, Milic. "Process and Personality in Bergson's Thought." Philosophical Forum, 17 (1959-60), 25-42.

821.   Devaux, Philippe. Lotze et son Influence sur la Philosophie Anglo-Saxonne: Contribution a l'étude historique et critique de la Notion de Valeur. Brussels, 1932.
       Whitehead's philosophy is discussed at several points, and the author claims that a special kind of inference--viz., the argument by analogy--is central to the philosophical method of Whitehead and Alexander. Suggests without documentation that this approach might have been derived from Lotze.

822.   Flewelling, Ralph Tyler. Personalism and the Problems of Philosophy. Introduction by Rudolph Eucken. New York: Methodist Book Concern, 1915.
       The principal "problems" discussed are freedom and evil. This is largely an exposition of Bowne's positions on idealism and pragmatism, in contrast to other formulations of these positions. Author is especially critical of Bergson.

823.   _____. Bergson and Personal Realism. New York: Abingdon, 1920.
       A polemical treatment of Bergson's concepts of intuition (a "false guide"), duration and vitalism as mechanistic and overly intellectualistic. Freedom belongs to personality. Bergson's indeterminism and immaterialism are of little real value in examining the question of freedom. Author attacks Bergson's "amoral, incomplete" God, whose "personality" becomes "a matter of degree." Poses "personal realism" as a better standpoint from which to examine these questions.

824.   _____. "James, Schiller and Personalism." The Personalist, 23 (Spring 1942), 172-181.

825.   Hartshorne, Charles. "Philosophy of Religion in the United States." Philosophy and Phenomenological Research, 11 (1951), 406-410.
       Discusses the concepts of religious experience found in Brightman, Whitehead, and in process thought generally.

826. Hocking, William E. "Some Second Principles." Con-
      temporary American Philosophy, vol. I. Eds. G. P.
      Adams and W. P. Montague. New York: Russell
      and Russell, Inc., 1930. Pp. 385-400.
          Hocking recalls his early fascination and subse-
      quent disillusionment with Herbert Spencer. He ex-
      presses an affinity for both James and Royce without
      total discipleship. Claims to perceive Royce's "ab-
      solute" behind James's discussion of mysticism in
      Varieties of Religious Experience. Nature as known
      primarily through experience is provisional and con-
      tingent. Reason is not all, but it is the last word.
      There is no telos without nous. Hocking advocates
      a mysticism similar to that of Bradley, Spinoza,
      and Bergson, but on other grounds. Thought is
      never fully adequate to its total object. Monism and
      Pluralism thus may be true simultaneously, without
      contradition or paradox.

827. *_____. "Theses Establishing an Idealistic Metaphys-
      ics by a New Route." Journal of Philosophy, 38
      (December 1941), 688f. [III, no. 461]

828. _____. Science and the Idea of God. Chapel Hill:
      University of North Carolina Press, 1944.

829. _____. "Brightman: Colleague and Friend." The
      Personalist, 34 (Autumn 1953), 363f.

830. *Howie, John, and Buford, Thomas O., eds. Contem-
      porary Studies in Philosophical Idealism. Cape Cod,
      Mass.: Claude Stark, 1975. [III, no. 465]

831. Hutchinson, John A. "The Philosophy of Religion:
      Retrospect and Prospects." Journal of Bible and
      Religion, 30 (1962), 12-17.
          Positivism has been replaced by a renewed in-
      terest in the philosophy of religion, especially proc-
      ess philosophy and personalism.

832. Jones, Jack William. Personalistic Tendencies in the
      Thought of Josiah Royce. Diss. Boston University,
      1968.

833. Knudson, Albert C. The Philosophy of Personalism.
      New York: Abingdon, 1927.
          The metaphysics of personalism is characterized
      by six categories: individuality (pluralism); unity
      (community); activity (creativity); volitional causality

(freedom); phenomenality of matter (panpsychism);
and Personality.

834. Kraushaar, Otto F. "Lotze's Influence on Pragmatism
      and the Practical Philosophy of William James."
      Journal of the History of Ideas, 1 (1940), 439-458.

835. Kuntz, Paul G. "Lotze as a Process Philosopher."
      Idealistic Studies, 9/3 (September 1979), 229-241.
      Lotze rejected idealism, materialism and mecha-
      nism on the grounds of "incomplete disjunction" and
      reductionism. Being is compared rather to a musi-
      cal melody--a whole consisting of, but transcending
      its parts. Change is fundamental, but order (as in
      the pattern of a melody) underlies all change. Lotze
      emphasizes (as does Whitehead) real process, plural-
      ism, self-induced change, a cosmic order, and God.

836. Ligneul, Andre. Teilhard and Personalism. Trans.
      P. J. Oligny and M. D. Meilach. Glen Rock, N. J. :
      Paulist Press, 1968.

837. Lotze, Rudolf Hermann. Mikrokosmus. 3 Vols. Leip-
      zig: 1856-1864. Trans. E. Hamilton and E. E. C.
      Jones. 2 Vols. Edinburgh: Clark, 1885-86.
      Lotze defends the reality of God and of values,
      holding that these operate through the causal nexus
      discovered in the natural sciences. Mechanism, as
      here advocated, is not to be equated with materialism,
      and does not entail the denial of psychic forces or
      the rule of purpose in the world. Facts, laws, and
      values finally are inseparable. Monism is rejected
      in favor of the direct experience of a multiplicity of
      entities (primarily conscious entities, or "persons")
      in a state of flux or change.

838. _____. Logik. Leipzig, 1874.

839. _____. Metaphysik. Leipzig, 1879.

840. *Meland, Bernard Eugene. "From Darwin to Whitehead:
      A Study in the Shift in Ethos and Perspective Under-
      lying Religious Thought." Journal of Religion, 40
      (1960), 229-245. [II, no. 407]

841. Muelder, Walter G. "Personalism, Theology and the
      Natural Law." Philosophical Forum, 14 (1956), 3-
      20.

842.   Mullen, Wilbur H.   A Comparison of the Value Theories
       of E. S. Brightman and A. N. Whitehead.   Diss.
       Boston University, 1955.
           Author proposes grounds for a useful synthesis of
       the value theories of personalism and Whiteheadian
       "panpsychism," leading to a greater emphasis on or-
       ganic relatedness in the former, and a clarification
       of the doctrine of God in the latter.

843.   Pringle-Pattison, Andrew Seth.   Hegelianism and Per-
       sonality.   Edinburgh, 1887.
           This work represents the beginnings of an internal
       idealist revolt against Hegel, Bradley, and Bosan-
       quet.   The individual is not merged in the universal,
       but is unique.   God, too, is a distinct and self-
       conscious Person, although we cannot know God or
       the universe in their totality as we can know their
       constituent parts.

844.   _____.   Man's Place in the Cosmos.   Edinburgh,
       1892.

845.   _____.   The Idea of God in the Light of Recent
       Philosophy.   "Gifford Lectures, 1912-1913."   Oxford:
       Oxford University Press, 1917.

846.   Reck, Andrew J.   Recent American Philosophy.   New
       York: Pantheon Books, 1962.
           Author's introduction argues for the mutual and
       similar influence on the recent history of philosophy
       of Whitehead, James, Peirce, Hocking, Royce, and
       Brightman, all of whom are of "one school."   Chap-
       ters on Hocking and Brightman discuss their versions
       of personal idealism, and their similarities with
       Whitehead and Hegel.   Personalism, like process
       thought, represents an "empirical metaphysics."

847.   Renouvier, Charles Bernard.   Le personnalisme suivi
       d'une étude sur la perception exterue et sur la force.
       Paris: Felix Alcan, 1903.
           Renouvier, a French personalist philosopher who
       deeply influenced James, discusses the problems of
       perception from a personalist-pluralist perspective,
       with reference to James's theories of space, will,
       and perception.

848.   Sanburn, Herbert C.   "Hegelian Influences in Bright-
       man."   The Personalist, 34 (Autumn 1953), 369-371.

849.   Santayana, George. Lotze's System of Philosophy.
       Introduction and Bibliography by Paul Kuntz. Bloom-
       ington: Indiana University Press, 1971.
            In his introduction to this edition of Santayana's
       doctoral dissertation, Kuntz draws attention to the
       parallels between Whitehead and Lotze regarding
       the treatment of the many and the one, the relation
       of parts to wholes, and the problem of order. Lotze,
       like Whitehead, develops the "event" as the basic
       unit of existence. Like Whitehead, he stresses the
       interrelatedness and causal efficacy between temporal
       series of events.

850.   Shive, J. R. The Meaning of Individuality: A Com-
       parative Study of Alfred North Whitehead, Borden
       Parker Bowne, and Edgar S. Brightman. Diss.
       University of Chicago, 1961.

851.   Stahl, Roland, Jr. "Hegel and Dr. Brightman's Idea
       of Truth." Philosophical Forum, 8 (Spring 1950),
       15-20.

852.   Thompson, J. Arthur. Concerning Evolution. "Terry
       Lectures." New Haven, Conn. : Yale University
       Press, 1925.
            A professor of natural history at the University
       of Aberdeen argues that evolutionist descriptions are
       not at all inconsistent with religious worldviews.
       Cites Lloyd Morgan and Lotze in claiming that evolu-
       tion discloses a "sublime, cosmic process ... towards
       more dominance of mind." Paley's teleology is dis-
       carded for the wider view of holism and interdepend-
       ence.

853.   Thompson, Tyler. Lotze's Conception of the Self.
       Diss. Boston University, 1950.
            Although Lotze's formal relation to Hegel was
       "chiefly one of revolt," nonetheless Lotze took from
       Hegel "the idea that the world is a meaningful unity."
       Lotze cannot be classified (and refused classification)
       as either a monist or a pluralist. Rather, his view
       stressed "independence-in-dependence" and panentheism.

854.   Turner, J. E. Personality and Reality. New York:
       Macmillan, 1926.
            Having accepted both materialism and evolution,
       Turner wishes nonetheless to demonstrate the reality
       of the existence of "personality" and a "Supreme Per-

sonality." His is a "pluralist-monist" personalism
like Lotze's, allowing for some constitutive relations. Turner is suspicious of the reductionist-
holistic hypothesis of James, as well as of the social-
holism of Bradley. The "self" is discrete, particular, and real.

855. Weld, Hiram Chester. Some Types of Personalism in
the United States. Diss. Boston University, 1944.
Outlines a history of personalism in America
reaching back to Samuel Johnson and Jonathan Edwards, including W. T. Harris and Josiah Royce.
The three main types of personalism are "pluralistic,"
"absolutistic," and "Plural-Monistic". Bowne and
his students are cited as most influential to the
growth of personalism, stressing a limitation on the
nature of God, community and co-creativity, freedom, pluralism, but with an underlying divine-mon-
istic unity.

856. Werkmeister, W. H. "Some Aspects of Contemporary
Personalism." The Personalist, 32 (Autumn 1951),
349-357.

857. Zaba, Zbigniew. "Ewoluejonistyczny personalizm Teilharda de Chardin." (The Evolutionary Personalism
of Teilhard de Chardin.) Zycie i mysl, 5 (1965),
15-29.

V. B. "ENGLISH" HEGELIANISM--ITS RELATION TO
OTHER SCHOOLS OF PROCESS THOUGHT:
BIBLIOGRAPHY

---

858. Abbagno, Nicola. Sorgenti irrazionali del pensiero.
Naples: F. Perella, 1923.
Compares the views of Bradley, Royce and Berg-
son.

859. *Alexander, Samuel. "Hegel's Conception of Nature."
Mind, old series, 9/41 (1886). [Intro, no. 1]

860. _____. Moral Order and Progress: An Analysis
of Ethical Conceptions. London: Trubner, 1889.

861. _____. The Basis of Realism. Oxford: Oxford
     University Press, 1914.

862. *_____. Space, Time and Deity. "Gifford Lectures,
     1916-18." 2 Vols. London: Macmillan, 1920.
     [I, no. 49]

863. _____. "Some Explanations." Mind, 30 (1921),
     409-428.
     Author attempts to elaborate on his own position
     in response to criticisms from C. D. Broad. Alex-
     ander discusses his divergence from Whitehead.

864. *Barnhart, J. E. "Bradley's Monism and Whitehead's
     Neo-Pluralism." Southern Journal of Philosophy,
     7/4 (Winter 1969-70), 395-400. [III, no. 488]

865. *Barrett, Clifford, ed. Contemporary Idealism in Amer-
     ica. "Festschrift for Josiah Royce." New York:
     Macmillan, 1932. [III, no. 431]

866. Bedall, Gary. "Bradley's Monistic Idealism." The
     Thomist, 34/4 (October 1970), 581f.
     Hegel's insistence on the rational nature of the
     future, and the identity of the actual with the rational,
     sometimes led him to affirm necessary connections
     between events whose relation is only contingent.
     Bradley refused to follow this "foolish pseudo-demon-
     stration," but escapes only by asserting that some
     reality is inaccessible to thought. Agnosticism and
     a certain demotion in significance of actual experience
     and knowledge are the consequence.

867. _____. "Bradley and Hegel." Idealistic Studies,
     7/3 (Summer 1977), 262-290.
     A major re-assessment of Bradley's strengths
     and weaknesses, as distinct from Hegel, Green,
     Bosanquet, and Royce. Bradley's influences included
     not only Hegel but also the personalists Lotze and
     Herbart. Russell's reduction of Bradley's views to
     simple subject-predicate logic vis-à-vis Russell's
     own propositional logic is misleading, confusing the
     propositional with the intentional structure of language
     and thought. Hegel's appeal to Negation afforded a
     dialectic for which everything is accessible, in prin-
     ciple, to reason; while Bradley's method of "critical
     dialectic" implied that reality was more than merely
     thought (from whence comes his epistemic agnosti-

cism). In contrast to Hegel's Absolute as a "self-
revolving state of crisis," Bradley's is a peaceful
and harmonious whole in which "contradiction is
eliminated by virtue of each part being assigned its
proper place, where it no longer jostles the others."

868. Bosanquet, Bernard. Knowledge and Reality: A Criticism of Mr. Bradley's Principles of Logic. London:
1885.
Charges Bradley with a serious deviation from
Hegel, with his firm distinction between knowledge
and reality. This introduces a grave agnosticism
into the heart of idealist metaphysics.

869. _____. Logic, or the Morphology of Knowledge.
2 Vols. London: 1888.

870. _____. The Principle of Individuality and Value.
"Gifford Lectures." London: Macmillan, 1912.
Advocates a pluralistic personalism. Individuals
are examples of Hegel's "concrete universals," and
the Absolute is finally and supremely an "individual."
Mind is not independent of matter; rather, mind is
a perfection of an organism adapting to its world.

871. _____. The Value and Destiny of the Individual.
"Gifford Lectures." London: 1913.

872. * _____. "Realism and Metaphysics." Philosophical
Review, 26/1 (January 1917), 4-15. [III, no. 434]

873. _____. Science and Philosophy, and Other Essays.
London: 1927.

874. _____, trans. and ed. Lotze's System of Philosophy.
Oxford: Oxford University Press, 1884.
Translation by Bosanquet of Lotze's Logik (1874)
and Metaphysik (1879), the first two of three volumes
proposed by Lotze to elaborate his philosophical system.

875. Bradley, Francis Herbert. Appearance and Reality.
Oxford: The Clarendon Press, 1893.
Bradley's famous critique of relational thinking
in Part One implies that knowledge is necessarily
organic and holistic, whence incomplete for any finite
mind. Part Two implies that, while unknowable,
reality (the Absolute) must be a consistent, harmon-

ious, all-inclusive whole, whence plurality, temporalism, and external relatedness are all appearances
of an underlying, timeless Unity which itself trans-
cends thought.

876. *_____. "Appearance and Contradiction." Mind,
18/72 (October 1909), 489-508. [IV, no. 757]

877. _____. Essays on Truth and Reality. Oxford:
Oxford University Press, 1914.

878. Brandon, Melvin Joseph. F. H. Bradley's Ethics of
Self-Realization. Diss. St. Louis University, 1972.
The "Absolute" is merely Bradley's way of claim-
ing that there are no "self-contained facts"; whence
moral concepts such as pleasure or duty are utterly
meaningless and vacuous when treated apart from
some larger, specific moral context. The "self"
becomes "real" when it is united with, and thus becomes part of the whole of the universe. The moral
"ought" arises in this inner tension of the ideality
and reality of the "self."

879. Brettschneider, Bertram D. The Philosophy of Samuel
Alexander: Idealism in "Space, Time and Deity."
New York: Humanities Press, 1964.
A thorough, critical analysis of Alexander's views,
which repudiates his claim to have "broken" with
idealism in favor of realism, as demonstrated specifically through a point-by-point comparison of his
views with Bradley's. Both are objective idealists,
despite Alexander's denials. His "empirical" analysis and superficial realism purport to discover the
primordial "stuff" of space-time via a phenomenological analysis. In fact, "space-time" is a product of
intuitional methods, and corresponds to nothing in
our experience. His dependence on coherence and
internal relatedness as criteria of truth expose Alexander as an objective idealist.

880. *Brown, A. Barratt. "Intuition." International Journal
of Ethics, 24/3 (1913-1914), 282-293. [III, no. 543]

881. *Capek, Milic. "Time and Eternity in Royce and Bergson." Revue Internationale de Philosophie, 79-80/1-2
(1967), 22-45. [III, no. 546]

882. *Cesselin, Felix. La philosophie organique de White-

head.   Paris: Presses Universitaires de France,
1950. [II, no. 383]

883. Collingwood, Robin G. "Croce's Philosophy of History." Hibbert Journal, 19 (1921).

884. _____. An Essay on Philosophical Method. Oxford: Oxford University Press, 1933.
Discusses Collingwood's theory of relations, and
the concept of a "scale of forms," proceeding from
lesser to greater complexity, as an approach to
metaphysical classification and analysis.

885. _____. An Essay on Metaphysics. Oxford: The
Clarendon Press, 1941.
Defends the notion of metaphysics as a second-
order examination and critique of levels of complexity,
and of first principles or "hidden assumptions."

886. * _____. The Idea of Nature. Oxford: The Clarendon Press, 1945. [Intro, no. 11]

887. _____. The Idea of History. Oxford: The Clarendon Press, 1946.
Argues against the idea that nature can have a
history. Evolution is not equivalent to a "natural
history," since all history is the record of effects
whose causes are purposes, goals, or ideas enter-
tained in conscious, rational minds.

888. Donagan, Alan. The Later Philosophy of R. G. Collingwood. Oxford: The Clarendon Press, 1962.
A critical analysis of Collingwood's mature views
by an analytic philosopher. Collingwood's philosophy
of science is really a history of scientific ideas and
an account of that which science presupposes, without any clear explanation of how scientists come to
change their positions on these issues. Collingwood
seems to hold that science makes assumptions about
the world which are neither true nor false; yet the
Baconian method does seem to bring us nearer to
"scientific verification" of theories than any alternative. While Hegel did indeed seem to anticipate
some contemporary trends in science, he also made
numerous contradictory statements about the nature
of truth, thus compromising Collingwood's claim of
his "modernity." In any case, science has no room
for anticipation. Finally, Collingwood affirms that

our present concept of nature parallels the Greek
view, supplemented by the firm affirmation of the
reality of a world of events, change and process.
This "process" view shows marked similarities with
Bergson, Whitehead, and Hegel; it obviates any possibility of physico-chemical determinism or mechanism, without foreclosing on possible new discoveries
in the natural sciences.

889. *Dordick, Webb. An Examination of Whitehead's Doctrine of Causal Efficacy. Diss. State University of
New York (Buffalo), 1972. [IV, no. 648]

890. *Ewing, A. C. , ed. The Idealist Tradition, from Berkeley to Blanshard. Glencoe, Ill. : Free Press,
1957. [III, no. 450]

891. Gustafson, James W. Causality and Freedom in Jonathan Edwards, Samuel Alexander, and Brand Blanshard. Diss. Boston University, 1967.
In Alexander's discussion of the universe as a
continuity of spatio-temporal events, causality as
merely a continuity of events, and freedom as mind's
conscious awareness of its own causal determinism,
Alexander is himself too accepting of one mode of
causality. A personalist alternative offers a richer,
more varied explanation of modes of causality.

892. Habermehl, Lawrence LeRoy. Value in the Evolution-
ary World. Views of Samuel Alexander, C. Lloyd
Morgan, and Pierre Teilhard de Chardin. Diss.
Boston University, 1967.

893. *Haldane, R. B. "The Function of Metaphysics in Scientific Method." Contemporary British Philosophy,
vol. I. Ed. J. H. Muirhead. London: George
Allen and Unwin, 1924. Pp. 127-148. [III, no. 495]

894. *Harris, Errol E. Nature, Mind and Modern Science.
London: George Allen and Unwin, 1954. [Intro, no.
17]

895. *_____. Foundations of Metaphysics in Science.
London: George Allen and Unwin, 1965. [Intro, no.
18]

896. *_____. Hypothesis and Perception: the Roots of
Scientific Method. London: George Allen and Unwin,
1970. [III, no. 498]

897. *_____. "Science and Objectivity." Contemporary
Studies in Philosophical Idealism. Eds. Howie and
Buford. Cape Cod, Mass.: Claude Stark, 1975.
Pp. 81-94. [III, no. 458]

898. _____. "Nature, Man and Science: Their Changing
Relations." International Philosophical Quarterly,
19/1 (March 1979), 1-14.
The conception of nature as evolutionary progress
has now to be abandoned in favor of a model which
exhibits evolutionary change as involving "the environment equally with the living thing. The two constitute
a single organic whole, an open system in dynamic
equilibrium." The distinguishing characteristic of
life is teleonomy, "quasi-purposive determination to
systematic wholeness ... the dominance of constitutive
parts, functions, and processes by the structure of
the total organic system." Nature can be exhibited
as an ascending scale of natural forms, each subsequent, more complex phase both superseding and
preserving the salient elements of the prior. Nature
is thus a single, unified system, "organismic throughout," with each individual element governed in form
and behavior by the pattern of the whole.

899. *Hartshorne, Charles. "Ideal Knowledge Defines Reality:
What Was True in Idealism." Journal of Philosophy,
43/21 (October 10, 1946), 573-582. [III, no. 499]

900. _____. "God as Absolute, Yet Related to All."
Review of Metaphysics, 1 (Summer 1947), 24-51.
Discusses the nature of internal and external relatedness, citing the "violent historical paradox"
which labels deniers of external relations "Absolut-
ists," and defenders of external relations, "plural-
ists." This is the exact inverse of medieval "absolutism," which argues for the exclusive external-
relatedness of God and the world. In this regard,
Bradley's important observation is frequently overlooked or misunderstood: to be Absolute means to
be all-inclusive.

901. *_____. "Royce's Mistake--and Achievement." Journal of Philosophy, 53/3 (February 2, 1956), 123-
130. [III, no. 500]

902. *Hocking, William E. "Some Second Principles." Contemporary American Philosophy, vol. I. Eds. G. P.

Adams and W. P. Montague. New York: Russell
and Russell, Inc., 1930. Pp. 385-400. [V, no.
826]

903. *_____. "Theses Establishing an Idealistic Metaphysics by a New Route." Journal of Philosophy, 38 (December 1941), 688f. [III, no. 461]

904. _____. Science and the Idea of God. Chapel Hill:
University of North Carolina Press, 1944.

905. _____. "On Royce's Empiricism." Journal of
Philosophy, 53/3 (February 2, 1956), 57-63.

906. *Hoernlé, R. F. A. "Idealism and Evolutionary Naturalism." The Monist, 36/3 (October 1926), 561-
576. [III, no. 559]

907. *_____. "The Revival of Idealism." Contemporary
Idealism in America. Ed. Clifford Barrett. New
York: Macmillan, 1932. Pp. 297-326. [III, no. 507]

908. Hooper, Sydney E. "A Reasonable Theory of Morality."
Philosophy, 35 (1950), 54-67.
        A summary of Alexander's moral philosophy and
its relation to Whitehead's notion of order. Morality
is merely one exemplification of that pervasive metaphysical principle, whose task is the enhancement of
the experience of value.

909. *Howie, John, and Buford, Thomas O., eds. Contemporary Studies in Philosophical Idealism. Cape Cod,
Mass.: Claude Stark, 1975. [III, no. 465]

910. Jones, Jack William. Personalistic Tendencies in the
Thought of Josiah Royce. Diss. Boston University,
1968.

911. *Kline, George L. "Some Recent Reinterpretations of
Hegel's Philosophy." The Monist, 48/1 (January
1964), 34-75. [III, no. 511]

912. *_____. "Life as Ontological Category: A White-
headian Note on Hegel." Hegel's Aesthetics and
Logic. Eds. Kenneth L. Schmitz and Warren E.
Steinkraus. New York: Humanities Press, 1980.
Pp. 158-162. [III, no. 513]

913. *Knox, T. M.   "Hegel in English-speaking Countries
     Since 1919." Hegel-Studien, 1 (1961), 315-318.
     [III, no. 514]

914. Krausz, Michael, ed. Critical Essays on the Philos-
     ophy of R. G. Collingwood. Oxford: The Clarendon
     Press, 1972.
     Essays by Alan Donagan, Errol Harris, W. H.
     Walsh, Stephen Toulmin, and others. A bibliography
     of Collingwood's writings reveals that he himself
     may have preferred the term "Absolute Empiricism"
     for his views. The later Collingwood diverges from
     Bergson and Whitehead over the concept of abstrac-
     tion, which, for him, is to think, rather than to
     separate. The book includes a powerful analysis of
     the Hegelian-Collingwoodian reformulation of the on-
     tological argument by Errol Harris, as well as a
     critical evaluation of the Ryle-Collingwood debates.
     Collingwood was a severe critic of Russell's logic
     and metaphysics of logical atomism, pointing up
     severe inconsistencies in that theory. Harris de-
     fends Collingwood's concept of the "scale of forms,"
     arguing that systems of all kinds (especially the
     theoretical constructs of natural science) have this
     scaler character. W. H. Walsh argues that Colling-
     wood's was not so much a modern reformulation as
     a historical critique of Hegel's idealism. Stephen
     Toulmin credits Collingwood with having anticipated
     later observations by Whitehead and Thomas Kuhn
     on the role of paradigm, hypothesis, and a priori
     relativism in contemporary science.

915. *Kroner, Richard. "Mure and Other English Hegelians."
     Review of Metaphysics, 7/1 (September 1953), 64-
     73. [III, no. 469]

916. Loomba, Ram Murti. Bradley and Bergson: A Com-
     parative Study. Lucknow, India : Upper India Pub-
     lishing House, 1937.

917. *Lowe, Victor. "The Influence of Bergson, James, and
     Alexander on Whitehead." Journal of the History of
     Ideas, 10 (1949), 267-296. [I, no. 127]

918. *Macaskill, John. "Intellect and Intuition: A Footnote
     to Bergson and Bradley." Contemporary Review,
     108/7 (July 1915), 91-99. [III, no. 572]

919. *McCarthy, John Willadams. The Naturalism of Samuel
     Alexander. New York: Kings Crown Press, 1948.
     [II, no. 406]

920. McPherson, Mary Patterson. Transcendence and Free-
     dom in the Philosophy of F. H. Bradley. Diss. Bryn
     Mawr College, 1969.
     Morality is a species of self-realization which re-
     quires a transcendence of the finite self as an act
     of freedom.

921. *Mahowald, Mary Briody. An Idealistic Pragmatism:
     The Development of the Pragmatic Element in the
     Philosophy of Josiah Royce. The Hague: Martinus
     Nijhoff, 1972. [IV, no. 776]

922. *Muirhead, John H. The Platonic Tradition in Anglo-
     Saxon Philosophy. London: George Allen and Unwin,
     1931. [I, no. 133]

923. Norman, Ralph Vernon, Jr. Theodicy and the Form
     of Redemption: An Essay in the Christian Under-
     standing of Evil with an Examination of the Notion
     of Redemptive Order in Josiah Royce and A. N.
     Whitehead. Diss. Yale University, 1961.

924. *Perry, Charles M. "A New Herakleiteanism." Jour-
     nal of Philosophy, 25/9 (April 26, 1928), 225-233.
     [IV, no. 630]

925. *_____. "Back to Dialectic." The Monist, 11/3
     (July 1930), 381-393. [IV, no. 631]

926. *Perry, Ralph Barton. "Professor Royce's Refutation
     of Realism and Pluralism." The Monist, 12/3
     (April 1902), 446-458. [IV, no. 779]

927. Rayner, Ernest A. "The Origin and Development of
     Persons." Philosophical Review, 25/6 (November
     1916), 788-800.
     A comparison and critique of Bergson's and Bosan-
     quet's theory of the person.

928. *Reck, Andrew J. Recent American Philosophy. New
     York: Pantheon Books, 1962. [V, no. 846]

929. *_____. "Idealism in American Philosophy Since
     1900." Contemporary Studies in Philosophical Ideal-

ism. Eds. Howie and Buford. Cape Cod, Mass.:
Claude Stark, 1975. Pp. 17-52. [III, no. 480]

930. Royce, Josiah. The Spirit of Modern Philosophy.
New York: Houghton, Mifflin, 1892.

931. _____. The World and the Individual. New York:
Houghton, Mifflin, 1902.
Royce attacks realist doctrines, especially the
idea that the relation between the "idea of an object"
and the "object itself" is wholly external. Objects
are not wholly independent of thoughts about them.
An idea is, rather, a "purpose seeking its object."
Knowledge of truth is attained by degree, since truth
is an interrelated whole, an Absolute. Rejects Bradley's skepticism regarding the possibility of authentic
knowledge of facts constituting the Absolute.

932. _____. The Philosophy of Loyalty. New York:
Houghton, Mifflin, 1908.
In this famous essay, Royce develops the moral
implications of his idealistic metaphysics. If the
Absolute is a timeless community of persons, then
loyalty and the ideal of community and reciprocity
are validated as the principal, unalterable impera-
tives of the moral life.

933. * _____. William James and Other Essays on the
Philosophy of Life. New York: Macmillan, 1911.
[IV, no. 781]

934. * _____. "Peirce as a Philosopher." Journal of
Philosophy, 13/26 (December 21, 1916), 701-709.
[IV, no. 782]

935. _____. Lectures on Modern Idealism. New Haven,
Conn.: Yale University Press, 1919.

936. Rubinoff, Lionel. Collingwood and the Reform of Metaphysics. Toronto: University of Toronto Press,
1970.
Metaphysics, for Collingwood, is the exposure and
critique of abolute presuppositions in other investigations, and the arrangement of these in a coherent hier-
archy, which changes historically. Collingwood's Speculum Mentis (1924) is compared with Hegel's Phenomenology as a "voyage of discovery" and a preface to the author's subsequent metaphysical position. In particu-

lar, Collingwood from this point on builds his case
that philosophy is emergent and systemic, and requires throughout a transcendental critique of forms
of thought and perception--especially of scientific
method. Rubinoff reviews and responds to the criticisms of Collingwood by Russell and Whitehead, and
more recently by Donagan.

937. *Rust, Eric. Evolutionary Philosophies and Contemporary Theology. Philadelphia: Westminster Press,
1969. [II, no. 416]

938. Silkstone, T. W. "Bradley on Relations." Idealistic
Studies, 4 (May 1974), 160-169.
      On the assumption that "monism" is a pejorative
charge, the author attempts to rescue Bradley from
this charge, despite Bradley's own claims to be a
monist. The central problem leading Bradley to embrace monism was his critique of relations--his conviction that relational speech and thought are wholly
indequate to capture and portray the "truth" of reciprocity, organism and holism.

939. *Straton, George Douglas. Theistic Faith for Our Time:
An Introduction to the Process Philosophies of Royce
and Whitehead. Washington, D.C.: University Press
of America, 1979. [III, no. 529]

940. Sturmer, Gerald Douglas. The Early Hegelianism of
R. G. Collingwood. Diss. Tulane University, 1971.
      While his discussion of relations and the overlap
of terms, and the "scale of forms" are advances on
Hegel's philosophy, Collingwood's Hegelianism is explicit in Speculum Mentis and the Essay on Philosophical Method, and pervades his posthumous works
on the philosophies of nature and history. The author lists five major points of continuity between
Hegel and Collingwood: 1) that philosophy consists
in an evaluation of disciplines; 2) that it is systematic; 3) that it consists in thought about "thought";
4) that there is a distinction between "reason" and
mere "understanding;" and 5) that philosophy finally
is its own history.

941. Toulmin, Stephen. "Conceptual Revolutions in Science."
Boston Studies in the Philosophy of Science, vol. III.
Eds. R. S. Cohen and Marx W. Wartofsky. New
York: Humanities Press, 1968. Pp. 331-347.

Despite difficulties and inconsistencies in his position, Collingwood's Essay on Metaphysics (1940)
distinguishes the conceptual logic of science from
the determinate deduction of mathematics (with its
"fixed" first principles).   Since the first principles
of science "evolve," its conceptual structure likewise changes.   Author compares this theory to Kuhn's
suggestion of a "normal" versus a "revolutionary"
change in science.

942. *Whittemore, Robert C.   "Whitehead's Process and
Bradley's Reality."   The Modern Schoolman, 32 (November 1954), 56-74.   [III, no. 534]

PART VI: CONCLUDING COMMENTS

The "Heuristic Fallacy" in Process Metaphysics

I have emphasized throughout the preliminary nature of this study. Any conclusions drawn from it must likewise be seen as provisional. Whereas it does seem possible at this juncture to summarize certain trends and certain inherent difficulties evident in process philosophy, such conclusions deserve and demand further critical study.

First, the very notion of "process" philosophy seems to be more varied--both historically and conceptually--than previously supposed. In particular, the longstanding (but hitherto undocumented) claim of close affinities between idealism and process thought seems to be borne out (again, both historically and conceptually). But this connection in turn requires a more adequate delineation of the different types of idealism than is customary, especially among the critics of idealism. I have suggested that many such critics--especially the British and American realists and empiricists-- seriously confused subjective idealism and Bradley's Absolute idealism with Hegel's thought, thereby interjecting a good deal of needlessly confusing polemic into the evaluation of the idealist tradition generally. [1] I further noted in passing that this practice parallels a similar (and equally unfortunate) tendency toward the critical evaluation of contemporary process philosophies on the basis of what turn out to be ambiguous and often seriously misleading historical (rather than logical) categories.

Secondly, Whiteheadian "process rationalism," together with the contemporary development of evolutionary cosmologies, represents both the culmination and the demise of realism as a distinct philosophical movement. [2] Indeed, one of the more remarkable features of English-language philosophy in the twentieth century is the recurring and persistent con-

210

version of realist critics into process exponents: Whitehead
and Perry early on, followed later by a number of analytic
stalwarts, such as Bertrand Russell and H. H. Price. Thus
it is incorrect to portray process thought, in the manner of
Lovejoy and other critics, as a nineteenth-century anachronism persisting into the twentieth century. Rather, as this
study reveals, many of the schools of process thought are
fully grounded in contemporary interpretations of both natural
science and human experience. [3]

     This feature notwithstanding, the most nagging critical
question from the perspective of historical analysis finally
has to do precisely with the scientific adequacy of a tradition
that claims so strong a basis in science. As a philosophical
interpretation of science and nature, the process tradition as
a whole (but especially the school of evolutionary cosmology)
is often guilty of substituting enthusiasm for precision in
interpreting the significance of scientific data and theories.
The highly speculative and metaphorical approaches of Bergson and Teilhard come readily to mind in this regard, despite
the considerable attempts by several authors cited in this
work to justify them.

     In particular, the critic might detect in all schools
of process philosophy an unwarranted tendency to construe
heuristic explanations (framed within a particular and precise
disciplinary context for the clarification of specific and pre-
cisely-defined problems) as though these were somehow generally applicable cosmological categories. One of the clear-
est examples of this sort of "extrapolative" reasoning occurs
in the school of evolutionary cosmology, with respect to the
category of "purpose." As the bibliographical data in Part
II suggest, the concept of purpose or purposiveness--what
biologist Jacques Monod termed "teleonomy"--continues to
play a heuristic role in biological science, in spite of the
evident hostility of neo-Darwinians and other sorts of radical
reductionists. Past and present evolutionary cosmologists
in the process tradition, however, frequently reason that,
merely on the basis of this creative heuristic function of the
concept of purpose in limited and specific biological contexts,
it is somehow valid also to treat "purpose" as if it were in
fact a generally operant cosmological category.

     I am not now attempting either to disparage or to
answer in the negative the interesting questions pertaining
to the cosmological significance of "purpose," or any other
such category. Rather, the relevant concern here is how
does one proceed to investigate and to "settle" such cosmo-

logical issues? My reply is merely that the successful heuristic use of a concept such as purpose in biology or in quantum mechanics does not itself constitute sufficient warrant for the extrapolation of that model or concept into other areas, nor does it justify the triumphant elevation of that category or model (as is so often done) to the status of some sort of demonstrable and proven cosmological absolute.

As a similar illustration of this dilemma: anthropologists recognize that the idea of God is useful or efficacious in accounting for the organized behavior of some societies or cultures. No one, however, utilizes this observation alone as the basis for a serious proposal to reintroduce the deus ex machina into some other area, such as physics. Nor do we recognize as valid an argument purporting to demonstrate the existence of God in fact merely on the basis of this observation regarding the usefulness of the "God-hypothesis." Yet it seems quite clear that many evolutionary cosmologists make just such moves from the utility of the idea of purpose in a limited domain to its presumed utility in other non-biological contexts, and finally to the far more general and sweeping claim that "purpose" is in fact causally efficacious throughout the whole of the cosmological order.

I shall label as "the heuristic fallacy" this tendency toward unwarranted generalization or extrapolation of specified models and concepts from their limited analogical or heuristic use in the natural sciences to the far more problematic domain of cosmological argument. [4] Ironically, this problem seems to constitute the more general case of what Whitehead himself called "the fallacy of misplaced concreteness," in the sense that Whitehead, too, set limits on the extent to which explanatory models in the sciences could be extrapolated as general description of the real. [5] Whitehead's main point, however, was to criticize the naive realism (or representationism) in Newtonian mechanics, wherein such merely explanatory abstractions were mistaken for literal and comprehensive representations of the real. Indeed, Whitehead's specific concern was that such naive realism ended by attaching more significance to whatever reigning paradigms were in vogue than to the actual events that these abstract models were designed to interpret. This last move, as applied to concepts such as determinism, mechanism, and matter, constituted the "fallacy of misplaced concreteness." [6]

The "heuristic fallacy" merely broadens this insight into a general limitation on cosmological arguments themselves. It calls attention to the inflated ontological signifi-

cance that heuristic models often assume within a discipline
or field of inquiry, as Whitehead's fallacy appears to do.
In addition, the "heuristic fallacy" indicts the unwarranted
extrapolation and application of such models outside their
proven domain of efficacy, and cautions against the corollary
error of citing a model's successful heuristic function within
a precise field of inquiry as somehow of itself constituting
a "proof" or demonstration of its general cosmological significance.

Process philosophers are by no means the only ones
guilty of the "heuristic fallacy." Other examples abound.
Logical rules certainly (to say the least) play a useful role
in the organization of data and in the construction and analysis of arguments. Does this heuristic function of the principles of logic betray some fundamental truth about the con-
stitution of the real--of the "world-in-itself"? Many of the
early logical empiricists--most notably Russell and the early
Wittgenstein--seemed to think so. Such claims, and the
metaphysical excesses to which they led, constitute an illustration of the heuristic fallacy. And, ironically, it was Wittgenstein himself who condemned the error, not only in his
later renunciation of the pre-eminent status of logic in favor
of his pluralistic theory of language (in which logic became
merely one alternative among many possible descriptive,
rule-governed models), but even earlier in the Tractatus,
where his subsequent revisions of the "picture theory" (plac-
ing inherent limitations on logic and the laws of nature as
descriptions of the world-in-itself) suggest in essence both
Whitehead's "fallacy of misplaced concreteness" and what I
have here termed "the heuristic fallacy."[7]

The heuristic fallacy is, then, by no means restricted
in its exercise to the process tradition. This fallacy does
highlight rather plainly (in historical perspective) the chief
defects of all schools within that tradition: either their self-
confident and enthusiastic appropriation and extrapolation of
heuristic models from the natural sciences to cosmology
generally; or their tendency to misconstrue useful heuristic
explanations as if these were proven and established cosmological categories in fact.

In whitehead's philosophy, for example, actual occasions, subjective aims, eternal objects and the two natures
of God function as heuristic categories. That is, these sem-
inal concepts are among the most important of those "general
ideas" that together are intended in Whitehead's philosophy to
frame "a coherent, logical and necessary system ... in terms

of which every element of our experience can be interpreted. "8
The emphasis here, finally, is on the elements of our experience, and on the usefulness of the conceptual scheme to
make some sense of these.   For many contemporary process
philosophers, however, that emphasis has been severely in-
verted, becoming a neo-scholastic focus on the "general
ideas" or conceptual scheme developed by Whitehead initially
only to interpret actual experience.   Whitehead did not intend
the concept of prehension or the doctrine of causal efficacy,
nor do I believe he would have construed his "ontological"
and "reformed subjectivist" principles, as claims that we
have direct and actual experience of his cosmological categories.   We surely do not have, nor can we claim to have,
moreover, the kind of direct and certain experience of these
categories that would permit and verify the elaborate descriptions of them in which some process philosophers put
such confidence. 9   Indeed, I am quite certain that Whitehead
himself meant to caution against the tendency to such metaphysical excesses when he observed:

> There remains in the final reflection, how shallow,
> puny, and imperfect are efforts to sound the depth
> in the nature of things.   In philosophical discussion,
> the merest hint of dogmatic certainty as to finality
> of statement is an exhibition of folly. 10

NOTES

(1) Regardless of one's opinion of the final views expressed
     therein, one should admit that J. E. Turner did a
     superb job in exposing this pervasive fallacy by realist
     critics, especially in the case of R. B. Perry.   Cf.
     A Theory of Direct Realism (New York: Macmillan,
     1925).

(2) This is the final conclusion of Victor Harlow's landmark
     bibliographical study of realism in 1931:   Bibliography
     and Genetic Study of American Realism (Oklahoma
     City, 1931).

(3) Cf. the assessment of the process tradition in this regard
     by Prof. Charles Hartshorne ("Present Prospects for
     Metaphysics," The Monist, 47 [1963], 43-56) and Prof.
     Milic Capek ("The Second scientific Revolution," Dio-
     genes, 63 [1968], 114-133), respectively.

(4) This discussion in fact suggests two distinct but related

definitions of the "heuristic fallacy": HF1 = "a tendency to construe the role of analogical reasoning in
scientific explanations as constituting a valid mode of
metaphysical verification"; HF2 = "an unwarranted
tendency to construe the usefulness of heuristic models
or explanations in any given field as comprising simultaneously a justification for their extension into
other fields, as well as a valid demonstration of their
general cosmological significance. "

(5) Science and the Modern World (1925), pp. 75, 77, 82,
     85. Cf. Process and Reality (1929), pp. 11, 27, 143,
     and 144, all of which simply refer to the earlier 1925
     formulation. This concept does not recur in any sig-
     nificant sense in Whitehead's later writings. Given
     the rather shocking anti-realist implications which
     can be inferred from this fallacy, its later absence
     is not so surprising. It is possible that Whitehead
     came to perceive that the "fallacy of misplaced con-
     creteness" indicated (or at least threatened) much of
     his own later cosmological turn. In a sense, then,
     the "fallacy of misplaced concreteness" is far more
     devastating to process cosmology than is my com-
     paratively benign "heuristic fallacy. "

(6) The struggle against this tendency (to which Whitehead
     first called attention) continues today in contemporary
     physics. Instructors in quantum theory must con-
     stantly caution their students that, while the "Bohr
     model" of the Hydrogen atom or a particular wave
     equation for an "elementary particle" are both useful
     heuristic models, neither model mirrors or portrays
     the "world-as-it-is. " So, for example, it is useful
     to assume that the nucleons in certain atomic nuclei
     behave like tiny harmonic oscillators under certain
     boundary constraints. This permits the physicist to
     utilize a well-known mathematical model to generate
     wave equations for the nucleons, which in turn might
     serve to describe the behavior of those actual entities
     under variations in the initial boundary conditions.
     If such mathematical calculations "fit" actual experi-
     mental results closely enough, the model has proven
     its heuristic value, and may be utilized for other
     similar calculations and descriptions. If no good "fit"
     is obtained, one abandons that model and tries another
     (e. g. , a quantized potential energy "well"). No one
     ever seriously claims that nucleons "are" (or "are
     not") harmonic oscillators, let alone that this or any

other such useful model constitutes some sort of physical or cosmological absolute.

(7)   Cf. Wittgenstein's Tractatus Logico-Philosophicus (London: Routledge and Kegan Paul, 1922), secs. 6. 341,
6. 342, 6. 371.

(8)   Process and Reality, p. 4, emphasis added. So, for
example, actual occasions and their societies and
nexus offer a splendid heuristic model for interpreting
some features of the paradox of personal identity,
including such observed anomalies as fission or fusion
of person-states that leave the body intact but suggest
a "new" or "radically different" personality identity
(cf. Charles Hartshorne, "Beyond Enlightened Self-
Interest: A Metaphysics of Ethics," Ethics, 84/3
[April 1974], 201-216). These models are deficient,
however, in that the concrete immediacy or actuality
of normal experience--Whitehead's own conceptual
"starting point"--are rendered entirely derivative.
The human self, for example, or the ontological status
of any concrete entity is entirely consequent upon the
primary ontological status of Whiteheadian "actual
occasions" in the general conceptual scheme--entities
of which one can have no direct experience.   The
lingering confusion generated by the anomalous status
of "actual occasions" vis-à-vis macroscopic modes of
"actuality" led to a recent interesting (but finally un-
satisfactory) study by F. Bradford Wallack (The Epochal Nature of Process in Whitehead's Metaphysics
[Albany, N. Y. : SUNY Press, 1980]), even as this
problem seemed to necessitate Prof. Ivor Leclerc's
apparent abandonment of a strict Whiteheadian con-
ceptuality in The Nature of Physical Existence (London: George Allen and Unwin, 1972).

(9)   Cf. the lengthy discussion of "genetic versus coordinate
division" of actual occasions as an example, in The
Southern Journal of Philosophy, 7/4 (Winter 1969).
The doctrines and principles I cite simply refute "bifurcation" and subject-object dualism in a real public
world of experience characterized chiefly by an event-
ontology, which the categorial scheme helps us to con-
ceptualize and explain.   This is a critical realist or
"objective relativist" rendering of Whitehead, consistent with his own affirmations and intellectual antecedents, but at odds with the more representationist-
realist slant accorded in the standard interpretations

of his thought. As I read Whitehead, one develops conceptual (cosmological) models so as to yield ever closer correspondence to actual cases, as judged finally by the experiential "fit" obtained between expectations and understanding based upon the conceptual models, and actual experience. It is always the latter, and never the "elegance" (conceptual coherence) of the former, however, that is the test of explanatory adequacy. This distinguishes the "rationalism" of the Whiteheadian school from the traditional pre-Kantian variety. This interpretation is also consistent with the earlier description of the use of the harmonic oscillator and potential energy well models in physics. Based upon fit, one or the other may more closely correspond to an actual situation; neither are understood as pictorial representations of the real; and one refines one's understanding of the model utilized, not for its sake (in the naive realist belief that it is a "picture"), but for the sake of improved experiential correspondence. This finally is the meaning of "degrees of truth" or certitude which is most in keeping with Whitehead's critical realist perspective, as well as with both Wittgenstein's and Whitehead's cautious limitation on the possible extent of metaphysical argument.

(10) Process and Reality, p. x. I am indebted in this discussion to Prof. Julian N. Hartt of the University of Virginia, who once commented on this problem. The present discussion has been usefully clarified in the face of substantial criticism from Professors John B. Cobb, Jr. , David R. Griffin, and their students at the Center for Process Studies (Claremont, CA).

BIBLIOGRAPHY OF BIBLIOGRAPHICAL SOURCES

Baldwin, R. C. , and Lowe, Victor. "Bibliography of the Writings of Alfred North Whitehead to November, 1941." The Philosophy of Alfred North Whitehead. "Library of Living Philosophers, Vol. III." Ed. Paul A. Schilpp. Evanston, Ill. : Northwestern University Press, 1941. Bibliography revised through Whitehead's death in 1947, appearing in the second edition of this work, in 1951.

Bibliography of Philosophy/Bibliographie de la Philosophie. Paris: Librairie Philosophique, Sorbonne. Quarterly: 1953- .

Bredenfeld, Hermann. "Dissertationen über Hegel und seine Philosophie." Hegel-Studien, 2 (1963). A compilation by dates (not subject) from 1842-1960, restricted to German-language dissertations in Germany, Austria and Switzerland.

Comprehensive Dissertation Index, 1861-1972 (w/annual supplement). Ann Arbor, Mich. : Xerox University Microfilms, 1973.

Croce, Hartmann, et al. "Centenaire de la Mort de Hegel." Revue de Metaphysique et de Morale, 38/3 (July-September 1931), 277-510.

Dinkel, Bernhard. Der Junge Hegel und die Aufhebung des Subjektiven Idealismus. Bonn: Bouvier Verlag Herbert Grundmann, 1974.

Dissertation Abstracts International. Monthly. Ann Arbor, Mich. : University Microfilms International.

Flay, Joseph C. "Bibliography". Hegel and the History of

Philosophy. Eds. J. O'Malley, et al. The Hague:
Martinus Nijhoff, 1974. Pp. 194-236.

Ford, Lewis S. , ed. "Special Issue on Whitehead." Southern
Journal of Philosophy, 7/4 (Winter 1969-1970).

Fowler, Dean R. "Bibliography of Dissertations and Theses
on Charles Hartshorne." Process Studies, 3/4 (Winter
1973), 304-307.

Guerry, Herbert. A Bibliography of Philosophical Bibliographies. Westport, Conn.: Greenwood, 1977.

Gunter, P. A. Y. Henri Bergson: A Bibliography. "Bibliographies of Famous Philosophers, Vol. I." Bowling
Green, Ohio. : Philosophy Documentation Center, 1974.

_____, and Sibley, Jack R. Process Philosophy: Basic
Writings. Washington, D. C. : University Press of
America, 1978.
    Each selection concludes with a bibliography of writ-
ings by or about the author of the selection, or pertaining to further analysis of the topic treated.

Harlow, Victor Emmanuel. Bibliography and Genetic Study
of American Realism. Oklahoma City, 1931. Reprinted by Kraus Reprints, New York: 1971.

Hartshorne, Dorothy C. "Charles Hartshorne: A Secondary
Bibliography." Process Studies, 3/3 (Fall 1973), 179-
227.

_____. "Charles Hartshorne: Primary Bibliography."
Process Studies, 6/1 (Spring 1976), 73-93.

_____. "Charles Hartshorne: 1980 Bibliographical Ad-
denda." Process Studies, 11/2 (Summer 1981), 108-
150.

Hegel-Studien. Bonn: H-Bouvier & Co. 1961- .
    Annual publication of the Hegel Commission of the
German Research Association, featuring articles, abstracts, dissertation notices and annual bibliographies.

"Hegel Today." The Monist, 48/1 (January 1964).

Johnson, A. H. "Recent Discussions of Alfred North Whitehead." Review of Metaphysics, 5/2 (December 1951),
293-308.

Contains reviews of a number of important books and articles.

Kline, George L., ed. "Whitehead Centennial Issue." Journal of Philosophy, 58/19 (September 14, 1961), 505-576.

_____. Alfred North Whitehead: Essays on His Philosophy. Englewood Cliffs, N.J.: Prentice-Hall, 1963. A reprint of the Journal of Philosophy special issue.

_____. "Bibliography of Writings By and About Alfred North Whitehead in Languages Other Than English." Process and Divinity. "Festschrift for Charles Hartshorne." Eds. Reese and Freeman. LaSalle, Ill.: Open Court, 1964.

Leclerc, Ivor, ed. The Relevance of Whitehead. London: George Allen and Unwin, 1961.

Leroux, Emmanuel. Le Pragmatism Americain et Anglais. Paris: Library Felix Alcan, 1923. An excellent, but dated bibliography may be found on pp. 333-419.

McCarthy, Joseph M. Pierre Teilhard de Chardin: A Comprehensive Bibliography. New York: Garland, 1981.

MacIntyre, Alasdair, ed. Hegel: A Collection of Critical Essays. Garden City, N.Y.: Doubleday, 1972.

O'Malley, J. J.; Algonzin, K. W.; Kainz, H. P.; Rice, L. C., eds. The Legacy of Hegel. "Proceedings of the Marquette Hegel Symposium, 1970." The Hague: Martinus Nijhoff, 1973. Contains a thorough bibliography by Frederick G. Weiss, arranged chronologically, of books by and about Hegel available in English.

O'Malley, J. J.; Algonzin, K. W.; Weiss, F. G., eds. Hegel and the History of Philosophy. "Proceedings of the 1972 Hegel Society of America Conference." The Hague: Martinus Nijhoff, 1974.

Parker, Franklin. "Alfred North Whitehead (1861-1947): A Partial Bibliography." Bulletin of Bibliography and Magazine Notes, 23/4 (January-April 1961), 90-93.

Parmentier, Alix. La Philosophie de Whitehead et le Prob-

lème de Dieu. Paris: Beauchesne et Fils, 1968.
  Contains an extensive bibliography of writings on Whitehead in French (pp. 587-635).

The Philosopher's Index. Bowling Green, Ohio: Philosophy
  Documentation Center. 1967- .
  Issued quarterly, and also in an annual cumulative
  edition.

The Philosophers Index: Retrospective Index to 1940. Bowling Green, Ohio: Philosophy Documentation Center, 1978.

Record, P. D. , et al. Index to Theses Accepted for Higher
  Degrees in the Universities of Great Britain and Ireland.
  London: ASLIB, 1950-1973.

Reeves, Gene, and Griffin, David. "Bibliography of Secondary Literature on Whitehead." Process Studies, 1/4
  (Winter 1971).
  This material, complete through 1971, is included in
  the Woodbridge bibliography.

Repertoire Bibliographique de la Philosophie. Louvain: Institut Superieur de Philosophie. Quarterly. 1948- .

Riedel, Manfred. Materialen zu Hegels Rechtphilosophie,
  I/II. Frankfurt am Main: Suhrkamp Verlag, 1974.

Schilpp, Paul Arthur, ed. "Library of Living Philosophers."
  Evanston, Ill. : Northwestern University Press.
  Extensive list of articles and bibliographies in several
  volumes devoted to Russell, Moore, Whitehead, Dewey,
  and others. Volumes are now published by Open Court
  Publishers (LaSalle, Ill.), and compiled at Southern Illinois University at Carbondale.

Steinhauer, Kurt. Hegel Bibliography/Bibliographie. Keyword Index by Gitta Hausen. Munich: K. G. Sauer,
  1980.
  Contains complete information regarding all editions
  of Hegel's major works, as well as the kleinere Schriften
  and correspondence. Over 11,000 secondary sources
  are listed, from 1802-1975, in twenty-nine languages,
  with an author/subject keyword index in German.

Steinkraus, Warren E. , ed. New Studies in Hegel's Philosophy. New York: Holt, Rinehart and Winston, 1971.
  Bibliographical section on "science and nature" lists

Bibliography of Bibliographic Sources   223

several publications comparing Hegel with modern science
and scientists, including Einstein, Darwin, and Whitehead.

Stokes, Walter E. "A Select and Annotated Bibliography of
Alfred North Whitehead. " The Modern Schoolman, 39/2
(January 1962), 135-151.

"Studies in Hegel. " Tulane Studies in Philosophy, 9 (1960).

"Studies in Process Philosophy, I/II. " Tulane Studies in
Philosophy, 13/14 (1974/1975).

"Studies in Whitehead's Philosophy. " Tulane Studies in Philosophy, 10 (1961).
The three Studies above, prepared by the philosophy
department of Tulane University, are available through
Martinus Nijhoff (The Hague).

Thayer, H. S. Meaning and Action: A Critical History of
Pragmatism. Indianapolis, Ind. : Bobbs-Merrill, 1968.
Extensive bibliography of pragmatism, pp. 527-545.

Toby, Jeremy L. The History of Ideas: A Bibliographical
Introduction. 2 Vols. Santa Barbara, Cal. : Clio Books,
1977.

Travis, D. C. , ed. A Hegel Symposium. Austin: University of Texas Press, 1962.

Weiss, Frederick G. Beyond Epistemology: New Studies in
the Philosophy of Hegel. The Hague: Martinus Nijhoff,
1974.

Woodbridge, Barry A. , ed. Alfred North Whitehead: A
Primary-Secondary Bibliography. "Bibliographies of Fa-
mous Philosophers, vol. III. " Bowling Green, Ohio:
Philosophy Documentation Center, 1977.

AUTHOR INDEX
[Numbers refer to bibliographic entries, not to pages.]